THE *HEALING* POWER OF "NEGATIVE" THOUGHTS and "UNCOMFORTABLE" SENSATIONS

Stop being afraid of your "negative" thoughts and "uncomfortable" sensations and start using them to heal!

DAVID FRIEDMAN

Author of THE THOUGHT EXCHANGE – Overcoming Our Resistance to Living a SENSATIONAL LIFE

LIBRARY TALES PUBLISHING

PRINTED IN THE UNITED STATES OF AMERICA

Published by:
Library Tales Publishing, Inc.
511 6th Avenue #56
New York, NY 10011
www.LibraryTalesPublishing.com

For general information on our other products and services, please contact our Customer Care Department at 1-800-754-5016, or fax 917-463-0892. For technical support, please visit www.LibraryTalesPublishing.com

Library Tales Publishing also publishes its books in a variety of electronic formats. Every content that appears in print is available in electronic books.

ISBN-13: 978-0692385067
ISBN-10: 0692385061

TABLE OF CONTENTS

INTRODUCTION

Look at any description of New Thought and the word "Positive" will most likely present itself in the first sentence.

Across the board, New Thought wisdom tells us that since our thoughts create our reality, all we have to do to transform our lives is "Think Positive."

Unity often describes itself as "A Spiritual Philosophy for Positive Living."

Books from *The Power of Positive Thinking* to *You Can't Afford to Have a Negative Thought* (which to me has always had an interestingly paradoxical title, since the title itself seems to be a "negative" thought) have sold millions of copies.

Phrases of advice abound, such as, "Cancel, Cancel" (in relation to a "Negative" thought we might have or, God forbid, voice); "Don't be so Negative"; "Release that Negative thought"; Stop spreading Negativity."

So many of us spend hours coming up with "Positive" Affirmations, repeating them over and over and putting them on our refrigerators and desks, thinking that if we say them enough we will banish other thoughts and our Affirmations will "come true."

There are spiritual philosophies that attribute any "Negative" thoughts that might arise to our evil Ego that is out to get us and needs to be ignored or even killed off.

People talk about God being Good, and often interpret that as meaning that only "Positive" thoughts come from God, while "Negative" ones don't. If God is indeed the Creator of Everything, where DO those "other" thoughts come from? The devil? The ego? Us?

(If God created Adam and Eve and EVERYTHING else, then who sent the snake? Must have been God, or God isn't God.)

We frighten ourselves with the notion that any thought we think, will make something happen, so we'd better not be thinking "Negative" ones or we will immediately see upsetting results appear in our world.

And why do so many of us spend so much time trying to be "Positive?" Because we want to feel good. We want to be comfortable. We want to have no pain.

So much of New Thought dangles the carrot that with the right thoughts, the right incantations, the right juggling of our insides, feeling comfortable all the time is not only possible, but is something desirable that we should put all our efforts into achieving.

There are disciplines that tell us that we'll know we're on the right track when we feel good.

There are countless books that say you will experience bliss when you are doing what you're supposed to be doing.

There are methods that teach us how to release, change, let go of, forget about, ignore or avoid any uncomfortable sensations we might experience.

One of the greatest misconceptions in the New Thought, Self-Help world is that when you get what you want, you will Feel Good. In fact, you will feel however you feel, which often, for reasons I will explain in this book, may be extremely uncomfortable. It is, in fact, our ability to "be with" this discomfort that determines how able we are to "be with" success, "be with" fulfillment, and "be with" the manifestation of our dreams.

So many of us have spent years pursuing method after method, workshop after workshop, book after book, to try to get ourselves to not have "Negative" thoughts and "Uncomfortable" sensations.

But try as we might, those "Negative" thoughts and "Uncomfortable" sensations keep popping up. Often, the more we resist them the more they seem to persist.

In my years of developing and teaching The Thought Exchange® I tried every way I could think of to get over, under and around them, to no avail.

So I finally decided to take a different tack. I began wondering if perhaps these "negative" thoughts and "uncomfortable" sensations had a purpose; had a meaning that could be helpful; had a message that we needed to hear.

As I explored these new possibilities, I began to realize that these "Negative" thoughts and "Uncomfortable" sensations were, in fact, a key to healing our childhood, coming to terms with our past, and becoming able to live as true, whole, integrated adults with the ability to make choices freely and lead fulfilled and happy lives in a world of infinite possibility.

So, if you've been struggling with your "Negative" thoughts and "Uncomfortable" sensations (and who hasn't?) read on, and learn how to have them, make friends with them, and actually use them to heal wounds that all the "Positive" thinking in the world has not been able to heal.

This book is about wholeness, completeness, NO part of you left out, NO part of you to censor or fear or suppress. What a concept!

In short, this book is about the Inner Peace that comes from seeing things EXACTLY as they are, without resisting them, trying to change them, trying to release them, or trying to pretend they don't exist.

So join me, as we explore the enlightening, healing, soul-freeing world of "Negative" Thoughts and "Uncomfortable" Sensations.*

*NOTE: Throughout this book I put words like "negative," "positive," "uncomfortable," "protective" and "problem" in quotes. The reason I do this is that these are subjective descriptions, interpretations or opinions rather than absolutes. One person's "negative" thought could be another person's "positive" thought, and so on.

PART I
"NEGATIVE" THOUGHTS AND "UNCOMFORTABLE" SENSATIONS

CHAPTER 1
Where We Live

The first thing we have to understand, if anything in New Thought is to make sense, is that we do not live in the physical world.

Our entire lives take place in the world of Experience. When something "happens" in the "outside" world, the only things we actually experience are thoughts and sensations. The only way we ever register that anything happened is via thoughts and sensations.

Thoughts and sensations are non-physical. Something "happens" and we experience a tingling or a pressure or an emptiness, and we have a thought about what it "means." In our world of Experience, which is where we live, that's ALL that happens. So we experience EVERYTHING in the invisible, non-physical world.

The sensations we experience in any given situation, which seem to come unbidden and over which we don't seem to have any control, are based on whatever thought we're holding based on the past, though often we will be aware of the sensations before we're aware of the thought.

So, for example, we ask someone out on a date and they say "No." This experience in itself does not have any intrinsic meaning. It doesn't in any way predict the future or say anything about who we are. It also doesn't tell us what the other person is thinking or what is motivating them to say no, even if they tell us.

(Often, when we tell people what we're thinking, we're telling them our interpretation of what we think we're thinking, or telling them what we think they might want to hear.)

If, in our earlier life, we were taught, by parents or circumstances, to think that we are worthless, and thus are holding that basic thought about ourselves, we might have a sinking sensation in our stomach and take on a thought like, "Nobody will ever go out with me, I'll be alone for the rest of my life."

If, on the other hand, we had experiences in early life where we lost things or were turned down but were supported and seen, and where things turned out well in the end, we might still have the sinking feeling in our stomach, but the thought we take on might be, "Well, they really missed out on something," or, "I guess they're not the right one," or, "Something better is probably waiting for me."

We also might not even have the sinking feeling in our stomach. There are as many permutations of sensations and thoughts as there are people.

So something happens that is intrinsically meaningless. We experience sensations based on the past (which are also meaningless in the present) and we make up stories about what those sensations mean. And it is within this "meaning" that we hold our thoughts about our past, our present and our future.

ALL of this happens inside us.

CHAPTER 2
We Are The Observer

Contrary to the way it often feels, we are NOT these sensations or thoughts. Who we actually are is a neutral Observer of these sensations and thoughts. This Observer, like sensations and thoughts, is invisible and is not located anywhere in physical space.

So who we are is an invisible Consciousness, aware of and observing our sensations and thoughts. Any meaning attributed to our sensations and thoughts is not attributed by the Observer. It is OBSERVED by the Observer.

(Stop reading for a moment, close your eyes and see if you can experience yourself as a neutral, invisible Observer, located nowhere, experiencing thoughts and sensations rather than being them. Notice how you know you exist. That sense of "I Am" that cannot be seen or located anywhere, but nevertheless is present in your experience.)

Don't worry if it seems difficult to do this. By making this first attempt, you are beginning an awakening that may take some time.

When I am aware that I am the Observer, I become aware that it's not that I have a tightness in my stomach and that that means I can never be a success. I observe a sensation in my stomach, and I observe that I have the thought that I can never be a success.

Although this may seem like a tiny adjustment, it is, in fact, a very powerful and life-changing distinction to make.

CHAPTER 3

There is NO Danger in Noticing ANY Thought or Sensation

If we are unaware that we live only in our internal world of experience, and unaware that who we are is the invisible, neutral Observer of thoughts and sensations, then we may very well be afraid of many thoughts and sensations, thinking that they define who we are, and thinking that they will make things happen that we don't want to have happen.

In fact (and this may be a radical concept to many) IT DOESN'T MATTER WHAT HAPPENS, since the only place we live is in the world of invisible experience.

Many of us live in the illusion that in order to be happy or fulfilled or successful or OK, we have to achieve something or "make something happen." But in fact, what happens has no relationship to our experience, but only reveals, time and time again, what we're already thinking.

That's why someone can be a movie star and want to kill him or her self. Or someone can have almost no money and have a great sense of contentment. Or someone can live in a studio apartment and think it's the most gorgeous place in the world, while someone else living in a mansion complains about it all the time.

In my show business career, I've met people who have numerous hit songs but are constantly worried about the future. I've met people whom I've heard complain that they're overworked and underpaid in jobs in which they're making millions of dollars working only a few hours a week. I've met wildly successful writers who have been distraught that they didn't win this or that award.

And conversely, I've met people who are thrilled to be given any opportunity, no matter how small, people who feel that their families and friends are more important than any achievement, people who decide against big careers because of what they feel will happen to their equilibrium.

Neither of these is better or worse. Often when we hear comparisons like this, we advocate "positive" thinking or "gratitude," but this is not what I'm talking about here.

What I'm saying is that when we can Observe our thoughts and sensations instead of trying to adjust them, run away from them, change them or control them, we get to see what we're thinking and to be with the sensations we're having.

So many of us are only willing to observe sensations we deem comfortable (or try to get comfortable when we're uncomfortable) and only willing to focus on "positive" thoughts and try to change the "negative" ones.

This approach not only proves futile most of the time, (since the more we try to get rid of or overcome these thoughts and sensations, the more they seem to return) but it robs us of information that is essential to our healing and to our ability to be at peace.

It is, in fact, the awareness of these "uncomfortable" sensations and "negative" thoughts that gets us in touch with the information we need to truly make sense of our lives, and experience our selves as whole, full, safe and empowered.

So let's really take a good look at these "negative" thoughts and "uncomfortable" sensations and explore what they are, what they aren't, where they come from, what they have to tell us, and what they do and don't mean.

In order to do this, let's first take a brief look at the nature of the universe in which these "negative" thoughts exist. The invisible, experiential world in which we live.

> "The only place we live is in the world of invisible experience."

CHAPTER 4
We Live in a World of Unlimited Possibilities

As I discussed in previous chapters, we live and experience life ONLY in the invisible world, as Observers of thoughts and sensations.

In this world, ANY sensation can be experienced and ANY thought can be thought at ANY time. Thus, ANYTHING is possible.

No matter what is happening in this moment in time, ANYTHING can happen in the next moment. We can have had a thousand experiences of failure, and those thousand experiences of failure do not in any way diminish the possibility that in the next moment we could have an experience of success. We could toss a coin 5,000 times and it could come up tails 5,000 times in a row, and that in no way makes the odds of the next toss being heads any less than 50/50 .

Interestingly enough, we often forget that this works both ways. No success, no amount of money, no relationship, no achievement in this moment guarantees in any way that the next moment won't bring loss, pain, depression, perceived danger, illness or in fact anything. THIS moment is about THIS moment, and in no way predicts or ensures what the NEXT moment will bring. THIS moment is all there is, and of course when the NEXT moment arrives, that moment will be THIS moment.

Although the information in the previous paragraph may seem like a "downer," when we truly grasp that no moment of "success" ensures in any way what the next moment will be, we begin to understand that there is nowhere to get, nothing to strive for, no mountaintop to reach, no point of safety to cling to. And when we understand this, we are able to really begin to live in the present moment, which is the only moment there is, and thus the only moment in which satisfaction, peace and wholeness can be experienced. But more about that later.

In a recent workshop that I took with a great teacher of mine, Nancy Napier, Nancy put it beautifully when she said something to the effect of, "Each moment is nothing more than a point of unlimited possible outcomes."

So the TRUTH is that possibilities are ALWAYS unlimited. They MUST be.

Yes, there are things that will feel painful, there are things we don't want to think, there are things we may think are not possible, there are things we might prefer, in the moment, over other things. But all this notwithstanding, the TRUTH is, even in all these circumstances, POSSIBILITIES ARE ALWAYS UNLIMITED.

And when we say, "possibilities are always unlimited" I think it's important to clarify that we are not talking about things that could possibly happen in the future. We are talking about the fact that, in the invisible world of non-physical imagination (a world I like to call "The Great Unmanifested") ALL outcomes, ALL circumstances, ALL thoughts exist RIGHT NOW. Not tomorrow, not later, RIGHT NOW. We can go to them and experience them RIGHT NOW.

Only when we are aware of and living in this TRUTH can we take a good, objective look at our "negative" thoughts and "uncomfortable" sensations.

CHAPTER 5
What is a "Negative" Thought?

First of all, let's get something straight. A "negative" thought is not a "bad" thought. It's a thought like any other. The word "negative," of course, comes from the word "negate." And the word negate means "to say "NO" to."

So "negative" thoughts are thoughts that say "No" to something. Here are some of the things "negative" thoughts say "No" to:

"Negative" thoughts can be thoughts we wish we weren't holding. So they say "No" to a particular possibility.

"Negative" thoughts can be thoughts that hold in mind the idea that an outcome that we don't want is either inevitable or at least likely.

"Negative" thoughts say "No" to the limitless possibilities that are and must always be present in the universe by saying that certain things are not possible, when in TRUTH they MUST be possible, no matter what the circumstance.

(An interesting question would be: is a thought like, "This good thing is definitely going to happen" a "negative" thought, because it erroneously limits the possibility of anything going in a way we don't want it to go?)

So perhaps we could boil our definition of a "negative" thought down to the idea of a thought that limits the possibilities in a way that, in our conscious mind, we don't wish to have them limited.

(I say "in our conscious mind" because, as we will see later, we had darned good reasons for taking on these "negative" thoughts in our earlier lives. In fact, had we not taken them on, we might not have survived our childhoods.)

> "A 'negative' thought is not a bad thought. It's a thought like any other."

CHAPTER 6
Why We Take on "Negative" Thoughts

Actually, before we can explore the question of why we <u>take</u> on "negative" thoughts, we have to explore the question of why we <u>took</u> on "negative" thoughts, since the root of our "negative" thoughts lies in the past.

In my previous book, *The Thought Exchange – Overcoming Our Resistance to Living a Sensational Life,* I explored the idea that Thoughts generate Sensations. We have a thought like, "I can go on the stage" and we get sensations like a pounding heart, shaking hands, a sinking feeling in our stomach. Based on this, we might "Exchange" the thought, "I can go on the stage" for the thought, "I can't go on the stage," in order to alleviate the "uncomfortable" sensations. (Of course, if we do this, we won't go on the stage, and thus, won't do the thing we want to do simply because some "uncomfortable" sensations come with doing it.)

It looks like the sensations we get when we try to go on the stage cause us to have the thought that we can't, but in actuality it is some deeply-held, perhaps unconscious, thought that people endanger us, that we will be embarrassed, that we will be hurt, that generates those sensations. Not only does the thought we hold generate the sensations, but the thought generates the way we perceive the sensations.

As I pointed out in Chapter 1, the sensations themselves don't mean anything. It's our history with the sensations that determines the meaning we assign to them. So whereas a regular citizen might have foot pain and run to the doctor, a ballet dancer, who lives with foot pain as part of his or her life, often thinks nothing of it. The ballet dancer may not like it or enjoy it, but it comes with the dream he or she has of dancing.

When, due to things that happened in childhood, a "positive" ("I can") thought has become associated with an uncomfortable sensation, the child, who has no way of solving the situation and cannot tolerate the "uncomfortable" sensation, will take on what I call a "protective" ("I can't") thought to get away from the "uncomfortable" sensation. As we grow older, because of our history, we automatically associate the sensation we feel in conjunction with this particular "positive" thought with danger, so we unconsciously jump to the "protective" thought and think it's true.

When someone tells us to "think positive" or "take on an affirmation," we can't, because that "positive" or affirmative thought is the very thing that brings on the "uncomfortable" sensation, and we immediately jump back into the "protective" thought before we know what hit us.

Obviously, you can see how frustrating and confusing this would be. Every time we move toward holding the thought we wish to hold (the thought that we think will give us what we want, and make us comfortable) we feel "uncomfortable." So we "exchange" that "positive" thought for a "protective" ("negative") thought and feel more comfortable. However, we don't get what we want (since holding a "protective" or "negative" thought produces a result, or to be more accurate, an interior experience of the world, based on that "protective" or "negative" thought), so we go back to our "positive" thought, which immediately causes us to be "uncomfortable," at which point we jump to the "protective" thought...And 'round and 'round we go.

So our "negative" or "protective" thoughts, which seem to do so much damage in our lives in that they thwart us from getting what we want as adults, were actually taken on by us as children as a form of protection.

And to give up that protection is to feel UNCOMFORTABLE. Giving it up may get us what we want, but in order to hold the thoughts we wish to hold, we will have to feel the "uncomfortable" sensations that go with those thoughts.

The following chart, taken from my book *The Thought Exchange,* traces the path of what happens when we take on a "protective" thought, and what happens when we don't take on a "protective" thought, and instead simply feel the "uncomfortable" sensations that arise when we think the thought we want to think.

THE THOUGHT EXCHANGE CHART

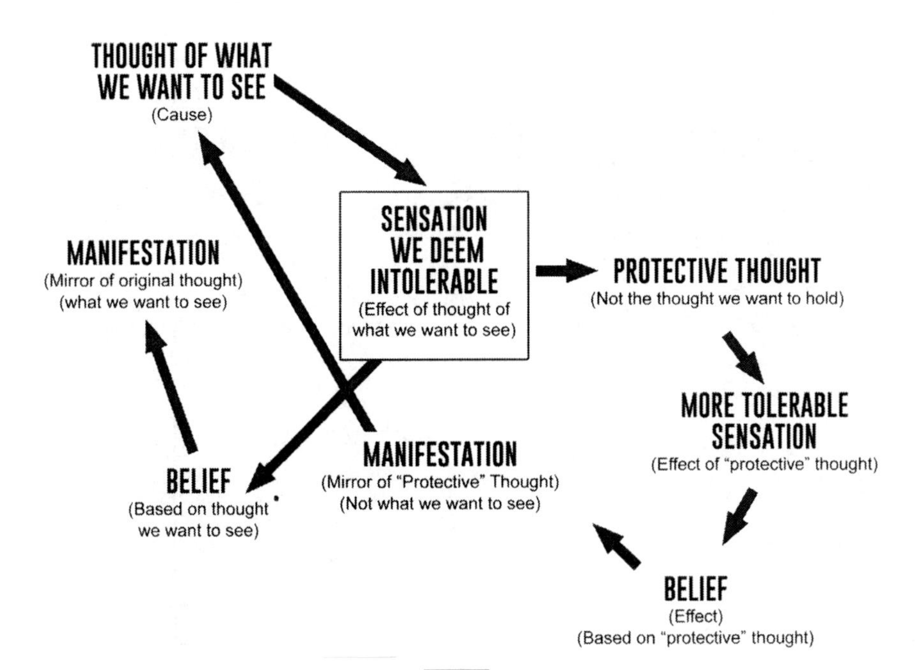

When we think a "positive" thought and feel an "uncomfortable" sensation that comes with it, if we decide we can't tolerate that "uncomfortable" sensation and we take on a "protective" thought to get away from it, we may feel more comfortable, but we will not see the result we want. (To be perfectly accurate, if we're holding the "protective" thought, it doesn't matter what result we see – it will be experienced within the protective "I can't" thought.)

If we can stay with the "uncomfortable" sensation that the "positive" thought produces, we can hold that "positive" thought while experiencing the "uncomfortable" sensation, turn the "positive" thought into a belief (a thought we think is true), and we will experience the thought we wish to experience in the manifestation we see.

Again, the particular manifestation is not as important as the experience we have of it in the invisible world of experience in which we live. We will experience this manifestation within the "positive" thought we are holding.

> "Our 'negative' thoughts were actually taken on by us as children as a form of protection."

CHAPTER 7
"Uncomfortable" Sensations: The Key to Healing and Wholeness

As I said at the beginning of this book, so much of New Thought seems to be about getting away from or getting rid of "uncomfortable" sensations. "Uncomfortable" sensations are often viewed as getting in the way of our prosperity, of our healing and of our happiness. For this reason, not much attention is paid to them except as something to get rid of or get around.

But, as I've pointed out in the last chapter, it's not the "uncomfortable" sensations that prevent us from holding the thoughts we wish to hold. It's the AVOIDANCE of "uncomfortable" sensations. "Uncomfortable" sensations often come with the very thoughts we want to hold. So if we want to hold these thoughts, we have to be able to be with the "uncomfortable" sensations that come with them.

— Why do we have these "uncomfortable" sensations when we take on "positive" thoughts?

—Why do we have "uncomfortable" sensations when nothing dangerous or frightening seems to be going on in the present?

—Why is it essential that we be with these sensations rather than trying to get away from them or suppress them?

—Why is it, in fact, impossible to ever get away from them?

It is because these sensations are part of our history. They are the disowned parts of ourselves, longing, pleading, demanding to be seen, heard and felt. They are, as it were, our Inner Child.

What happened, in the past, happened. It will never not have happened. And the parts of us from that past that were unseen by a competent adult are still back there (and ALWAYS will be). The past cannot be changed. It cannot be forgotten. It can only be incorporated, held and lived with. It is only when we can do this that we have freedom, in the present, to think and do whatever we wish.

It's time to go back and get our Inner Child.

> "It's not the uncomfortable sensations that prevent us from holding the thoughts we wish to hold. It's the AVOIDANCE of 'uncomfortable' sensations."

PART II
OUR "INNER CHILD"

CHAPTER 8
The Unheard, Unseen Child Inside Us

If we follow the information in the previous chapters to its logical conclusion, we can see that the taking on of "negative" or "protective" thoughts to avoid sensations that we perceive as dangerous is a technique we created as children to cope with sensations that were too hard for a child to cope with. These sensations CAN be coped with by an adult, but we have associations to them from our history that say that we can't cope with them, and that we have to run from them.

So in some way, our original "technique" of trying to get away from "uncomfortable" sensations by taking on "protective" thoughts ("negative" thoughts, dating back to when we were children) is still in play in our adult lives.

Most of us spend most of our adult lives trying to get rid of this thinking, to overcome it, to become more secure by finding the right job, the right amount of money, the right amount of success, etc. always to no avail. The more we try to push the sensations of the child down by taking on "positive" thoughts, the more the sensations arise, since it's the "positive" thoughts that are generating them. The more we try to ignore our "uncomfortable" sensations and our "negative" thoughts, the more they seem to persist.

If you think of them as the thoughts and sensations of an unheard, unseen child, this makes sense.

If you had a child in front of you who was very upset, what would you do? Would you say, "I'm not paying attention to you because you're getting in the way of my career?" Would you say, "I release you now?" Would you say, "I am affirming that your 'problem' doesn't exist?" Of course not.

You would listen to what the child has to say, feel what the child is feeling and be with the child. And when you were with what the child was feeling and hearing what the child was thinking, you wouldn't feel swamped in the same way the child feels swamped, because you are not a child.

The reason the child has the thoughts and sensations he or she has is because something happened, but the reason the child can't feel better is because the child has not been seen and heard with his or her "problem." The child has had no adult who has empathized with him or her. The child has had no mirror in which to see him or her self, no other adult to verify that what the child is feeling is human, is feelable, is seeable, is bearable. So the child remains stuck in crying, complaining, shutting down or any number of tactics to try to get an adult to see and feel its pain.

There is a child stuck in each of us, in varying degrees of course, depending on our history. That child had disturbing things happen to it, but the interesting thing is, it's not the disturbing things that happened that are causing the pain and stuckness. It's that they were never fully seen and mirrored by a competent adult.

We often spend years in therapy blaming our parents for not having been able to empathize with us as children. But the fact is that if we still have an Inner Child in us who is lost, who is holding "protective" thoughts and has not been seen or heard, it's because WE have been treating our Inner Child in EXACTLY the way our parents treated our Inner Child. We've been afraid of it, ignoring it, not wanting to feel what it feels or think what it thinks, trying to overcome it, treating it as though it's ruining our life and killing our dreams.

So it is WE and nobody else who are keeping our Inner Child firmly in a place where he or she cannot be seen or heard. And WE are the ONLY ones who can give our own Inner Child what he or she needs.

> "If you had a child in front of you who was very upset, you would listen to what the child has to say, feel what the child is feeling and be with the child."

CHAPTER 9
The Child Living in the Adult's Body

So we have a historical (and often hysterical) Inner Child living inside us. This child has "uncomfortable" sensations when we take on certain "positive" thoughts. This child sees danger in moving forward. This child is panicked about certain things that we, as adults, need to do to move forward in life, to have a livelihood and to get the most out of our adult lives. Although there is nothing to panic about in the present, (there might be things to cope with or things that are upsetting, but an adult can deal with those) the child has GOOD REASON for feeling the way he or she does, based on what happened in the past.

While we, as adults, are focused on getting ahead, on expressing ourselves, on moving forward in the world, the child is focused on one thing and one thing only: being seen and heard in its pain. Having a competent adult feel what it feels and think what it thinks.

But the child is living in the body of an adult who is ignoring its thoughts and trying to ignore its sensations. And when a child is upset and gets ignored, what does it do? That's right. It screams. It acts out. It acts up. It tries to get attention.

And what did our parents do in those times when, shall we say, their parenting skills weren't at their best? Yup.

They told us to shut up. They punished us. They didn't hear us. In extreme cases they hurt us or injured us, or let us know in no uncertain terms that we were wrong, foolish, off base, etc.

And if we're having "negative" thoughts that we're trying to push away or overcome, or "uncomfortable" sensations that we're trying to ignore or release or get rid of, what we are doing is the same thing our parents did to us. Ignoring, refuting, punishing or disbelieving our Inner Child.

But since our Inner Child can't live without getting the mirroring and empathy it needs, the Inner Child will try in any way it can to get that attention.*

> **"What we are doing is the same thing our parents did to us. Ignoring, refuting, punishing or disbelieving our Inner Child."**

*Although, of course, I am aware that our Inner Child is perceived by each of us as a person with a gender, I will often, for grammatical expediency and universality, refer to the Inner Child as "it" throughout this book. Please feel free to substitute the gender of YOUR own Inner Child.

CHAPTER 10
The Inner Child's Quest For Attention

So we have an Inner Child who is feeling "uncomfortable" sensations and holding "protective" thoughts, living inside an adult who is ignoring it and moving through the world doing things that are frightening and activating to the Inner Child without noticing what's going on in the Inner Child. What is the Inner Child to do?

The first tactic the Inner Child usually tries (and this tactic can go on for decades) is to try and get what it needs from someone else. There are a number of reasons why this doesn't work.

First of all, the way the child does this is to try to demonstrate its childish thoughts and feelings to another adult in hopes that the adult will see them and take care of them. The trouble is, this Inner Child is appearing in adult situations in an adult body, so other adults are seeing before them another adult who is acting like a child. And who wants that? So other adults will shy away from our Inner Child in the same way our own adult is shying away from it.

In addition, the Inner Child is talking about and acting upon things that happened in the distant past as though they were happening in the present, attributing meanings to what others do or say that have nothing to do with the present, and trying, as it were, to get something in the present which will make the past "have been different," which of course is impossible. What the Inner Child wants "in the past" cannot possibly be gotten from someone in the present, so all attempts to get it become futile.

Thirdly, (and this is explored at great length in my book *The Thought Exchange – Overcoming Our Resistance to Living a Sensational Life)* when we look at the world, all we are really seeing there is our own thoughts. It's not that we're causing things to happen, but as I said in Chapter 1 of this book, we can only see what we're thinking in anything that happens. So the child will only see its own thoughts of fear and lack and being ignored should it look into the world to try to get something other than those thoughts.

It's amazing how this works. I have had Thought Exchange clients who have fought tooth and nail to get me to be the parent they never had. They would try every tactic to get me to give them EXACTLY what they wanted in EXACTLY the way they wanted it, all the while holding the thought that they could not be understood. And that thought ALWAYS played. I've actually had experiences where a client would say something like, "The sky is blue," and I would say, "So I see that you're saying that the sky is blue," and they would say, "NO! You don't understand me. That's NOT what I'm saying."

So going out into the world to try to find another adult to heal past wounds is a dead end. The only chance the Inner Child has is to get the Adult within which it lives to feel and think what it (the Inner Child) feels and thinks. If it can do that, it can finally be recognized.

CHAPTER 11
Getting Our Own Adult's Attention

So how does our Inner Child get our attention? The first way is by feeling its "uncomfortable" sensations and thinking the "protective" ("negative") thoughts it thinks. When these "uncomfortable" sensations happened long ago, and the child took on "protective" thoughts, what it needed was for a competent adult to recognize that the child was experiencing this and be with the child, not by feeling the "uncomfortable" sensations and thinking the "protective" thoughts FOR the child, not by feeling the "uncomfortable" sensations and thinking the "protective" thoughts AS the child, but by feeling the "uncomfortable" sensations and thinking the "protective" thoughts WITH the child.

The child still needs this, as this is what it never got. It has tried to get this from the outside world, only to find that all it got back was the same ignoring and rejection it got originally. So now its only chance is that the adult within which the Inner Child lives will experience the Inner Child's sensations and notice its thoughts (by the adult thinking them him or herself). Remember, even though we're using the construct of Adult and Inner Child, there's really only one person here – Us with all our history.

But most of us have been trained or have trained ourselves as adults to ignore, try to get rid of, or try to overcome or affirm away these thoughts and sensations.

So the next thing the Inner Child tries to do is get our attention by putting us in circumstances where we will feel the same level of pain and have the same thoughts as the child had back then. Unconsciously, the Inner Child draws us to circumstances that will be as upsetting to our adult self as the child's circumstances were to the child.

Now, it's important to realize that the original circumstance the child was in would most likely not have the same effect on the adult that it had on the child. If it was devastating, at the time, that you didn't get a lollipop, it's not going to be devastating to you as an adult to not get a lollipop. That would not get the adult's attention and cause it to feel what the child felt. But a big rejection would. Losing a job would. Having a serious illness would. Having someone near you die would. (Again, remember, the Inner Child isn't causing this, just bringing our attention to its sensations every time something happens that brings them on, in hopes that we will feel them too.)

But again, we have been trained to fight things off in the "outside" world, to reject our own thoughts and sensations and try to "solve" the "problem" in front of us. This can be EXTREMELY frustrating to the Inner Child. The Inner Child is gravitating toward all these incidents to try to get you to notice how it feels and be with it, and you keep turning outward trying to get rid of the very situation the Inner Child drew you to so that you could feel what the Inner Child is feeling.

It would be as if a child came to you and said, "My mother is abusing me," and you went and killed its mother. Yes, the abuse would stop, but the "problem" wouldn't, because now not only do you have a child who experienced abuse (and whose thoughts and sensations are still un-mirrored by anyone), but now you have a child who doesn't have a mother, and who thinks the reason it doesn't is because it said something about its pain.

So, the Inner Child has been drawing us to circumstances that it hopes will cause us to feel and think what it thought and felt, and we keep turning outward to fend off the circumstances. The Inner Child has no choice but to escalate.

This is when we begin to have failure after failure. Loss after loss. Health challenge after health challenge. At a certain point we can't take it anymore, and we give in to the painful sensations and the "negative" thoughts and just experience them. It feels hopeless. It feels like we're in an impossible double bind. It feels like there's no way out and never will be.

At last, we feel EXACTLY as the child did when it went through whatever traumas it went through.

At last, the level of the adult's trauma equals, for an adult, what the trauma was for the child.

At last, we can no longer run from the "uncomfortable" sensations and "negative" thoughts we've held since childhood.

At last...THE HEALING HAS BEGUN.

PART III

THE BASIC SKILL

(Being With "Problems," "Negative" Thoughts and "Uncomfortable" Sensations)

CHAPTER 12
"Problems" - the Key to Healing

When we understand that who we REALLY are is an Invisible Observing Consciousness, and that our lives are ONLY lived on the Inside, in the Invisible world of Experience, EVERYTHING that "goes wrong" or "upsets us" becomes not about solving some "external" problem, but about reconnecting to our Whole Experiential Self.

In fact, "problems" become the key to healing because they bring up the "negative" thoughts and "uncomfortable" sensations we need to experience in order to reconnect with our Inner Child. It is only in making this connection that we can stop running from our past (and thus stop being run by it) and embrace our Inner Child, with all its "uncomfortable" sensations and "negative" thoughts, as part of ourselves, so that we are free to move forward in the present WITH our past.

It is important to remember that no matter what is going on, it is ONLY experienced as thoughts and sensations. These thoughts and sensations would ONLY have meaning if we lived in the physical world. BUT WE DON'T. We are LOOKING AT the physical world and experiencing it as thoughts and sensations that are experienced inside our Observer. (Substitute Noticer or Experiencer if those images work better for you.) So the thoughts and sensations we're having are intrinsically meaningless, and are therefore harmless.

The ONLY thing ANY event does is refer us back to what WE are thinking. And what WE are thinking, if it's a "negative" thought, (which we will recognize if we see something in the "mirror of the world" that we don't want) is only there because we are "protecting" ourselves from a sensation that we found intolerable when we were younger, by taking on a thought that we think won't produce that sensation.

When we can feel and be with this sensation, and be with the "negative" thought that the child came up with to protect itself from the "uncomfortable" and, to the child, intolerable sensation, we are being with the child in a way that the child was not "been-with" in childhood. This is ALL the child ever wanted and needed, and the child now becomes safe, stops acting out, stops "screaming" for what it's not getting. The child may still feel the way the child felt (because whatever happened to the child still happened), but the child's sensations and thoughts are being not only recognized, but perfectly mirrored in that they're actually being felt and thought by our own Inner Adult self.

When we do this (simply experience the sensations and think the thoughts with the child as opposed to suppressing the child, running away from the child, "releasing" the child or trying to "overcome" the child), ALL the parts of our lives, ALL the history, The Inner Child, Our Present Adult, come into our awareness, and each part is able to be a Whole part of the Whole.

Our Inner Child finally gets, from us, what it didn't get from our parents and cannot get from the outside world. It gets seen, heard and incorporated into the whole.

Our Adult is now able to function as an adult, not as a child trying to get things from the world that can't be gotten.

And our lives, no matter WHAT happens, feel centered, real and ALWAYS filled with endless possibilities.

In these next chapters, I will take you through the process by which we take care of our Inner Child and reclaim our lives. It involves being with and experiencing the child's sensations and thoughts and thus giving the child what it never had and what it cannot get from anyone else but ourselves.

What we will be working with here is what I call the BASIC SKILL that underlies our ability to heal the Inner Child, to experience ourselves as a whole, to hold and act upon our dreams and to solve "problems" in our lives.

So much of New Thought has told us that in order to be successful and happy we have to "overcome," "release," "get rid of" or "transform" our "negative" thoughts and "uncomfortable" sensations.

After year after futile year of trying to do that, I have come to the conclusion that the opposite is true.

The key to being successful and whole and at peace is our ability to "experience" any "problem" we're having, to "feel" the uncomfortable sensations that come with it, and to "think" the "negative" thoughts that arise. Only by "being with" these things can we reconnect with our Inner Child and become whole.

We are all so busy trying to get away from and solve our "problems" that we miss the very reason they're there; to help us develop the capacity to be with the pain from our past from which we've been running all our lives.

No matter how hard you try, you can't run out of your own body, and you can't run away from your own past. It comes with you.

When people tell me they want to be successful, I often ask them, "Are you willing to be that uncomfortable?"

So here we go. We're going right into what we've been avoiding all our lives. We're not solving it. We're not running from it. We're not fixing it. We're simply experiencing it.

In the next chapters, I will take you through the process that will bring you to the point where you are able to "solve" ANY "problem," hold onto ANY dream and work toward ANY goal, without being stopped by your past.

Hang on. There will most likely be "uncomfortable" sensations to experience, challenging thoughts arising, painful memories brought up. But remember, although these may have been unbearable to the child you were, they are not anywhere near unbearable to the Adult that you are now.

So, as my partner, Rev. Shawn Moninger, likes to say, "Put on your hard hats. We're goin' in!"

> **"No matter what is going on, it is ONLY experienced as thoughts and sensations."**

CHAPTER 13
Step 1
Meditation

We begin with a meditation designed to put you in a position to do this work. In this meditation, you will move from the Illusion that things are "happening" in the "outside" world to the Experience that EVERYTHING is actually happening in the Invisible World of Experience.

This meditation will shift you from focusing on "solving" the "problem" in the outside world, to being positioned to use ANY "problem" you see as a gift which reflects back to you what you need to see and experience within yourself.

If you've read my first book, *The Thought Exchange – Overcoming Our Resistance to Living a Sensational Life,* you may remember some of this meditation, but this one takes you further, so stick with it. The whole meditation should take about 15 minutes.

If you have a recording device, you might want to record the meditation so you can listen to it in your own voice.

If you don't have a recorder handy, you might have someone read the meditation to you, or if you just want to continue reading the book, read it to yourself and stop and close your eyes when it says "PAUSE."*

*A CD entitled *Thought Exchange Meditations,* containing this Meditation as well as other thought exchange meditations, read by the author, can be purchased or downloaded by going to TheThoughtExchange.com.

MEDITATION on "Who You Really Are"

Close your eyes and get comfortable.

With your eyes closed, notice the bodily sensations you're experiencing. By sensations, we mean things like tightness, hotness, coldness, pressure, a "sinking feeling," pounding, rushing, tingling, numbness, pain.

Sensations are not the same as thoughts about sensations.

Thoughts like, "I'll never have anything, I feel like my head is going to explode; I'm ashamed; I'm guilty; I'm frustrated," are not sensations, but rather are our interpretations of what we think sensations mean, what we think they portend for the future, what we think they say about our past or say about us.

Feelings are also not sensations. They are, in fact, also thoughts about sensations, interpretations of what we think sensations mean. What we typically call feelings, such as, "I'm happy; I'm sad; I'm angry; I'm in love," are actually thoughts that are interpretations of what we think our sensations mean.

What we are looking for here are just the pure sensations. The experience of what's going on in your body, not your thoughts about it.

Sit for a moment and just move your focus around your body, experiencing WHATEVER sensations you're having. Although one sensation may first capture your attention, notice if different parts of your body are experiencing different sensations. You could be tight in one place and relaxed in another.

You could be experiencing a pain somewhere and no pain somewhere else. There's no right way to do this, there's nothing you're "supposed" to be feeling, nothing you need to change or that needs to be different from what it is. Just NOTICE your sensations.

We're going to pause for a minute to allow you to do that.

PAUSE FOR A MINUTE

Now, notice your thoughts. Notice what you're thinking. They could be thoughts about your sensations. They could seem to have nothing to do with them. They could be thoughts about the future, or thoughts about the past. You could be thinking how bored you are with this meditation, or how happy you are, or about what you're going to have for lunch tomorrow. It doesn't matter what they are, just notice your thoughts. Notice if you're having trouble noticing your thoughts, or if they keep changing, or if one or more keeps coming back. Again, there are no right answers here, nothing to change or release or suppress. Just notice whatever thoughts you're having. We're going to pause for a minute to allow you to do that.

PAUSE

Now, NOTICE WHO'S NOTICING ALL THIS. Notice that there is someone (or something) looking at these thoughts and sensations, seeing these thoughts and sensations, experiencing these thoughts and sensations. See if you can become aware of yourself not as these thoughts and sensations, but as an invisible consciousness, located nowhere in the physical world, noticing thoughts and sensations.

This invisible consciousness is who you REALLY are. You are nothing (no-thing) located nowhere. You are an invisible Noticer with no opinion (you may notice opinions, but those opinions are not the opinions of the Noticer, they are thoughts that the Noticer is noticing.)

See if you can experience yourself as this invisible Noticer noticing thoughts and sensations, rather than as the thoughts and sensations themselves. We'll pause for a moment to allow you to do that.

PAUSE

So, you are an Invisible Noticer, located nowhere. And as the Invisible Noticer, you have the capacity to notice anything, to experience ANY sensation and to think ANY thought. Having one sensation does not in any way limit your infinite possibilities of experiencing any other sensation. Having one thought does not in any way limit your capacity to have any other thought. You are essentially an unlimited empty space in which ANYTHING and EVERYTHING can be experienced.

Take a minute to be aware of this.

PAUSE

So, now that you're aware that you are an Infinite, Invisible Consciousness within which any and all sensations and thoughts can be experienced, let's take a fresh look at those sensations and thoughts and see how this knowledge of who we actually are changes how we experience them.

Go back to noticing your sensations. Just notice the one that first captures your attention, and then look around your body and notice all the different sensations you may or may not be having. Again, I remind you, there's no right way to do this. You're just noticing.

As you're noticing your sensations, you may also notice that thoughts keep arising. Thoughts about what these sensations mean, about the past, about the future, about what these sensations will prevent you from doing or cause to happen. This is natural. When you become aware that a thought has arisen, don't fight it, don't try to change it, don't explore it. Simply notice the thought, and then return your attention to your sensations. The object is not to get rid of those thoughts or prevent them from happening, just to notice them whenever they arise, and turn our attention back to our sensations.

We're going to take a minute for you to practice doing this. Just focus your attention on your sensations, and no matter how many times thoughts arise, simply notice them and return to focusing on your sensations until the next thought spontaneously arises.

PAUSE FOR A MINUTE

Now, remembering that who you are is the Invisible Noticer noticing these sensations, see if you can experience them as intrinsically meaningless. If you are just the observer of these sensations, they have no ability whatsoever to touch you where you actually live. Experiencing a sensation does not in any way expand or diminish your ability to experience sensations. Experiencing a sensation does not in any way change who you are. You don't lose or gain anything in the place where you live, as the Invisible Observer, Noticer, Experiencer when you experience a sensation. It's just a sensation, being experienced as a sensation. Meaningless.

Take a minute and see if you can be with your sensations and experience them as intrinsically meaningless.

PAUSE

Now, if you're like every other human being on the planet, you probably noticed that as you were experiencing your sensations, thoughts were arising. And these thoughts may have attributed meaning to the sensations.

Focus on one sensation. Perhaps on the one that first grabbed your attention. Perhaps on the one that seems strongest at the moment. Just pick one and focus on it.

Notice the thoughts that arise as you focus on the sensation. See if you can experience each thought as just a thought. No meaning. Just one out of an infinite number of possible thoughts that you could be thinking at this moment. Or to put it more accurately, just one of an infinite number of possible thoughts that you could be noticing, observing, or experiencing at this moment.

I like to think of these thoughts as blades of grass that are part of a huge, infinite lawn. When you are thinking a thought, it is one blade of grass. Five thoughts are five blades of grass. But the whole, vast lawn is always there and all the other thoughts exist, right alongside the ones you're having.

Take a moment, be with your sensations as simply sensations with no intrinsic meaning, and when thoughts arise, see if you can experience them simply as thoughts which, although they seem to ascribe meaning to your sensations, in fact also have no intrinsic meaning. They are just thoughts. Take a minute to be with your meaningless thoughts and sensations.

PAUSE

So, who we are is an infinite, invisible space, located nowhere, experiencing meaningless sensations and thoughts.

Now, add the "outside" world to this.

Think of something that has happened or that is happening that is bothering you, that you're struggling with, that you'd like to change.

BRIEF PAUSE

Notice the sensations you have when you think about it.

BRIEF PAUSE

Notice the thoughts you have when you think about it.

BRIEF PAUSE

See if you can be aware that the ONLY way you are experiencing this thing that seems to be happening in the "outside" world is that you are having sensations and thoughts INSIDE YOURSELF. There is NO experience that takes place outside of you.

So the only way we EVER experience anything is by having meaningless sensations and meaningless thoughts that are experienced by our infinite, invisible Observer, Noticer, Experiencer.

Now, see if you can reconnect with the fact that who you are is the Invisible Observer, Noticer, Experiencer, experiencing these sensations and thoughts. They have absolutely no effect on you. You are constant.

You are infinite. Your capacity to experience can neither be expanded nor diminished by thoughts and sensations. You are just here, unchanging, infinite, invisible, empty, located nowhere.

Now remember the "problem" you picked. State it to yourself.

BRIEF PAUSE

Notice your sensations and thoughts.

BRIEF PAUSE

Experience yourself as the Observer to whom those sensations and thoughts are meaningless.

BRIEF PAUSE

So, knowing that who you are is an invisible Observer, Noticer, Experiencer, located nowhere, experiencing invisible, meaningless sensations and thoughts, which are the ONLY way you ever experience ANYTHING, even things that seem to be in the physical world, open your eyes.

> "In this meditation you will move from the illusion that things are 'happening' in the 'outside' world to the Experience that EVERYTHING is actually happening in the Invisible."

CHAPTER 14
You're Ready to Do the Work In the Present to Connect With Your Past

Having done this meditation, you are now in a position to do the work of connecting with your past and liberating your present to unlimited possibilities. This has become possible because you are now able to look right at and experience the sensations you've been avoiding, as well as the "protective" thoughts you've been holding to help you avoid those sensations. You can do this because you now have the experience that you are not, in fact, those sensations and thoughts, and that they cannot, in fact, harm or alter you, add or take anything away from you, or limit your possibilities in any way.

This does not mean that you will not experience pain and discomfort and that you will not have thoughts of fear, hopelessness, lack, impossibility, etc.

In fact, the point IS to experience these sensations and think these thoughts. This is the only way you can go back and get the child that is lost in the past. By BEING with it. Not by fixing it. Not by making it "all better." Not by changing what happened. Not by changing the child's perception of what happened. The child will still be in the past, but he or she will no longer be lost, no longer be trying to get your attention, and no longer be fighting to get his or her needs met in the "outside" world that cannot be met in the "outside" world and that cannot be filled by anyone or anything in the "outside" world.

A lot of what I ask you to do will seem counter-intuitive, perhaps dangerous, because I am asking you to walk right into the places you've avoided your whole life. Right into the impossible, unfixable double binds that the child experienced; right into the thoughts of hopelessness and no future; right into that awful sinking feeling you've always dreaded.

But rest assured, these things that were impossible to be with for a child are far from impossible to be with for an adult.

So just do your best to take the instructions and carry them out, no matter how challenging, uncomfortable or against what you want to do they may seem.

Let's begin.

> "Things that were impossible to be with for a child are far from impossible to be with for an adult."

CHAPTER 15

Step 2
Pick A "Problem," Any "Problem"

Look at your life IN THE PRESENT and see if you can find a "problem." (This is usually the EASY part..)

It can be anything that's making you uncomfortable, anything that you wish were different. It can be someone who doesn't treat you in the way you want to be treated. It can be that your career is not going where you want it to go. It can be that you don't have enough money. It can be that you can't seem to get into a relationship even though you want to be in one. It can be an immediate crisis. Your house just got robbed. Or you were accused of something at work that you didn't do. Or it can be something ongoing, like you feel uncomfortable talking to people, or you always make the wrong choices in the stock market. Pick "any" "problem." It doesn't have to be your biggest one. It doesn't have to be the most important. ANY "problem" will do.

CHAPTER 16
Why We Work in the Present

So often, when people undergo therapy, they try to go back to the past. They remember what their mother or father "did to them." They "express" their anger or their sadness while going over and over all the details of what happened. It's like they're trying to let their parents know, IN THE PAST, what they did and how awful it was.

Why?

So that their parents will "get it?"

(What good would that do, even if it were possible, which it isn't. Their parents might get it in the present, but that doesn't change the fact that they didn't get it in the past, and that experience still lives in the mind and body.)

So that their parents will change?

(IN THE PAST? Impossible!)

So the past will not have happened?

(Obviously that's not possible. It happened. But most of us spend our lives trying to have had a different childhood.)

So that they can show the child that it's OK?

(It may be OK now but it WASN'T OK in the past. Trying to tell the child any different is like telling someone who was in a concentration camp that it didn't happen or that it wasn't so bad, or to forget about it because they're not in the concentration camp now. No matter what the present is, the memory still remains in the mind and in the body.)

So that they can feel what the child felt?

Now we're getting closer. But the "problem" is we cannot feel what the child felt by going to the past, because as adults we cannot possibly feel the same way the child felt about the incidents the child went through.

If, as a child, it was devastating that you didn't get a toy you wanted, an adult can look at the child and understand that the child was upset, but an adult would not be upset in the same way about not getting a toy.

Even if we're talking about something very serious that happened to a child, like molestation or physical or emotional abuse, an adult could not possibly feel exactly the same way as the child because an adult has choices and power that the child never had. An adult can leave, support him or herself, physically fight back and verbally defend him or herself in ways the child couldn't possibly. An adult is not dependent in the same way a child is.

So no matter how empathetic we are, we CANNOT, as adults, feel the same way the child felt about the same incidents.

However, there ARE things that will make an adult, in the present, feel the same way the child felt in the past. And you can bet your bottom dollar the child, in its effort to reach and be seen by an adult, is going to find them!

More about that later, but now, on to step 3.

CHAPTER 17
Step 3
Don't Fix It. Feel It!

Look at the "problem" you've chosen.

Now, our natural inclination, when we have a "problem," is to try to figure out how to get out of it. As adults, that's what we do. But this time, I'm going to ask you to do something different.

INSTEAD OF TRYING TO FIX YOUR "PROBLEM," SIMPLY GO TO THE SENSATIONS YOU'RE EXPERIENCING.

Think about the "problem" and just notice what's going on in your body. Remember, by sensations I mean tightness, pounding, hotness, coldness, emptiness, rushing, pain. Not fear, anxiety, guilt, shame, love, hate, "my head is going to explode" or "I'll never have what I want." Those are thoughts. We want SENSATIONS. Just notice your SENSATIONS.

Try not to interpret the sensations. Simply experience them.

They don't have to be big. They don't have to be what you expect. You may find that what you're experiencing is resistance to sensations; a feeling of numbness, the experience of an absence of sensations, or the sense that your insides are trying to move away from sensations. If the resistance to sensations (in the form of moving away, of not noticing them, or any other form) is what you come across, just be with that. Don't try to push past the resistance or force yourself to go deeper. JUST BE WITH WHATEVER YOU FIND WHEN YOU GO TO YOUR BODY TO BE WITH YOUR SENSATIONS.

If you begin to feel overwhelmed, remember that YOU are the invisible Observer, Noticer, Experiencer, and the sensations cannot harm you or change you in any way. You're just noticing them and being with them. Like sitting next to someone who is in pain. You can be with their pain but you are not their pain.

Pause for a minute, and just experience whatever sensations you experience.

Now, you are probably noticing that thoughts keep arising as you experience your sensations.

You're right on track. This brings us to the next step.

> "Instead of trying to fix your 'problem,' simply go to the sensation you're experiencing."

CHAPTER 18
"Protective" Thoughts

When you are simply experiencing and just being with the sensations that go with a "problem," you are not only experiencing the discomfort you may have as an adult. You are experiencing the sensations the child experienced.

Another way of saying this is that the sensations you are having difficulty staying with are the sensations the child experienced that you have suppressed, run from, avoided or tried to escape.

If you look back at the Thought Exchange chart on page 25, you will remember that sensations are generated by thoughts. One of the great paradoxes, and thus the cause of confusion, is that it was originally the child's "positive" thoughts that generated the "uncomfortable" sensations.

The child may have said, "I'm beautiful!" to which the parent responded, "Don't be so full of yourself!" Or to which some relative responded by taking sexual advantage of the child. At any rate, some "negative" experience became associated with the "positive" thought.

If the child had no competent adult handy to be with the child, recognize what the child was feeling, and come to the defense of the child, the child would have had to use its own devices to get away from the intolerable sensations it was feeling.

In cases of extreme abuse, the child may resort to forgetting or blacking out the incident entirely. In even more extreme cases, the child may split off into multiple personalities so that any time the pain comes up it can jump away from it by being in a different personality that is not aware of the pain of the other personalities.

But the most common way in which the child will try to get away from "uncomfortable" sensations associated with a certain thought is to make sure it NEVER thinks that "positive" thought again. So every time that "positive" thought comes up, the thought that the child can do something, the thought that the child is capable, the thought that the child can be happy (whatever the thought was that became associated with the "intolerable" sensation), the child will EXCHANGE that "positive" thought for a thought that will not produce that "uncomfortable" sensation.

We call these thoughts "Protective" thoughts because they "protect" the child from the "uncomfortable" sensations that it couldn't tolerate. They do this by generating sensations that are less uncomfortable to the child (even though, of course, these "protective" thoughts generate "results" that the child, and thus the adult within whom the child lives, ultimately doesn't want).

If the thoughts that generated these sensations were positive ones, like "I CAN do it; I am GOOD; Something GOOD will happen," then the "protective" thoughts must be "I CAN'T do it; I am BAD; Something BAD will happen." These thoughts are often called "negative" or "sabotaging" thoughts, and most New Thought and Self-Help books tell you to try not to have them. To banish them with affirmations. To exchange them immediately for positive thoughts. To try not to think them. To say "NO" to them.

BUT WE ARE GOING TO DO THE OPPOSITE.

"It was originally the child's 'positive' thoughts that generated the "uncomfortable" sensations."

CHAPTER 19

Step 4
When You Come Across The Child's Protective Thoughts, Think Them!

When we left off at the end of Step 3, you were being with the sensations that arose when you thought about your "problem," and noticing that thoughts were beginning to arise.

When "protective" or "negative" thoughts arise, THINK THEM.

Don't try to change them. Don't try to correct them. Don't push them away. THINK THEM.

So if, for example, you just asked someone out on a date and they rejected you, notice the sinking feeling all over the front of your body (or whatever sensation you happen to be having) and notice that you're thinking, "It's impossible for me to meet anyone ever" (or whatever "protective" thought you happen to be having).

And just SIT with the SENSATIONS and the THOUGHTS. Have them. Be with them. Allow them.

Be with them for as long as you need to. Go about your day, but every time you notice them, BE WITH THEM.

There's a very important subtlety to "being with" the Inner Child's Thoughts and Sensations. You have to actually feel the sensations and think the thoughts in your own body and mind. Since your Inner Child lives in YOU, your Inner Child feels its sensations and thinks its thoughts in the same body and mind as you, the Adult. This unique "sharing" of one body and mind is the reason that your Inner Adult is the only one who can know 100% EXACTLY what the Inner Child's experience is like. Thus, experiencing the Inner Child's sensations and thinking the Inner Child's thoughts in the same body and mind as the Inner Child is the only way your Inner Adult can connect fully with your Inner Child. It is also the only way your Inner Child can be seen, heard and felt in a way that it never was when whatever happened originally occurred.

So you have to feel the sensations fully and actually think the thoughts. But at the same time, you MUST be aware that you are feeling the Inner Child's sensations and thinking the Inner Child's thoughts FROM THE PAST.

If you think about it, where is the past right now? It doesn't exist. It only exists as thoughts and sensations in the present. So the way you connect to the Inner Child is by experiencing its sensations and thoughts in the present, in your own body. But you must always maintain the sense that you are OBSERVING the child's sensations and thoughts so you don't "believe" that these sensations and thoughts are about the present.

They are the past being experienced in the present, and as such they must not be acted upon in the present or thought to be true in the present, because they are actually not about the present. The present is simply stimulating a memory which allows the Inner Child to feel the way it felt in the past. But unlike in the past, when the Inner Child felt these sensations and thought these thoughts all alone, had nobody to be with, run to or experience empathy with, and thus had no choice but to run to "protective," limiting thoughts, this time YOU are there with it.

I like to think of it as someone else telling me about something very upsetting that happened to them. I can feel what they felt and be very empathetic, but it's not happening to me in the present. In fact, it's not happening to me at all.

> "This unique 'sharing' of one body and mind is the reason that your Inner Adult is the only one who can know 100% EXACTLY what the Inner Child's experience is like."

CHAPTER 20

The Healing Power of "Negative" Thoughts and "Uncomfortable" Sensations

When you are feeling the Inner Child's "uncomfortable" sensations and thinking the Inner Child's "protective" thoughts, you are now, as an adult, right where the child was when the "intolerable" sensations occurred and the child took on "protective" thoughts to get away from them.

You are an adult, "merged" with the child, in the same body, with the same exact sensations and the same exact thoughts as the child.

The child finally has an adult who completely "gets" what happened, and COMPLETELY empathizes with the child in that the adult is actually feeling the sensations and thinking the thoughts, both as the adult and as the child, at the exact same time.

This is a condition most of us have avoided for our entire lives because we thought that it would swamp us the way the child was swamped. But now, since we did step 1 of this process, we know that we ARE NOT these thoughts and sensations, but rather an indestructible, infinite, located-nowhere-in-the-physical-world Observer, Noticer,

Experiencer. So these sensations and thoughts cannot swamp us. We can fully FEEL these sensations and fully THINK these thoughts while knowing that what we're actually doing is observing them from the safety of our unlocatable, nothing-but-empty-space, filled-with-infinite-possibility, unchangeable, unhurtable REAL selves.

So when we go to the child's sensations and thoughts, we are maintaining a delicate balance. We are fully feeling the child's sensations (not looking at them from outside the child, not talking to the child, not trying to comfort or teach the child.) We are fully thinking the child's thoughts (not saying "I see your thoughts" or "I know" or "That's OK.") It's very important that we REALLY do this. That we REALLY "go there." Notice and experience the total hopelessness, notice and experience the pain, notice and think the thoughts that nothing good will ever happen or that we're doomed. REALLY be with them.

And yet, as I said above, we MUST, at the same time, be aware that we are Observing all this, Experiencing all this within our Observer. In this way we can feel the full force of the sensations just as the child felt them, think the exact thoughts the child thought, and not fall apart or succumb to them by acting out as though they were true.

We have now completed the process of reconnecting our child to a completely empathetic adult who sees what happened, feels what happened and thinks the same thoughts the child thought.

THIS IS THE BASIC PLACE FROM WHICH ALL HEALING AND ALL CHANGE CAN OCCUR.

You now have the BASIC SKILL in that you have developed the ability to be with a "problem," and by being with it, be with the sensations and thoughts of the Inner Child.

Now, WHENEVER there is a "problem" that triggers the child's "uncomfortable" sensations and "protective" thoughts, the adult is right there with it, feeling the sensations and thinking the thoughts. The child does not have to act out to get the adult's attention. The child does not have to create and gravitate to challenging, uncomfortable circumstances in the world to make the adult "see" what it went through.

Now the adult is free to act in the world as an adult, to meet "problems" with adult solutions, to pursue dreams at face value, rather than with the secret agenda of trying to get something from the world that cannot be gotten.

"The child finally has an adult who completely 'gets' what happened, and completely empathizes with the child."

CHAPTER 21
If You're Having Trouble Doing This

If you do the above steps, they WILL work. You will experience the freedom to live your life as an adult while being able, at the same time, to be with your childhood wounds without being stopped or held back by them.

That being said, many of us may find it extremely challenging to simply sit with our "problems," think our thoughts and experience our sensations, because in doing so we are moving directly toward things that we've been afraid of, run from, and been told are dangerous.

Finding ourselves feeling and thinking things we've fought tooth and nail not to feel and think can be overwhelming. And for many of us, everything we've been taught has told us that "negative" thoughts are DANGEROUS, "uncomfortable" sensations MUST be gotten away from, and "problems" MUST be solved.

During the course of doing the work of simply being with our "problems," thoughts and sensations, I realized that many of us need "help" with the challenges, fears and resistance that come up as we do this work.

So here are some hopefully helpful hints as to how to be with "problems" and concerns that may come up as you do this work, and how to frame the work so that you have a sense of safety and possibility.

<u>We have an Inner Adult that can help our Inner Child be with the fear.</u>

When we begin to allow ourselves to simply be with our "problems" and the sensations and thoughts that go with them, with nowhere to get, nothing to achieve, nothing to fix, we may quickly find ourselves re-experiencing the deepest pain of our Inner Child.

If this pain, when it originally occurred in the past, was unseen and unrecognized by a competent adult, the Inner Child will often be terrified.

So the first thing we must give the Inner Child is the support of an adult who can feel exactly what the Inner Child feels and think exactly what the Inner Child thinks. There's only one adult who can do that: Our own Inner Adult.

Our Inner Adult is the part of us that lives in the present and is capable of experiencing the sensations and thoughts that the Inner Child is not capable of experiencing alone.

The job of the Inner Adult is twofold.

First, to "witness" the Inner Child by experiencing exactly what the Inner Child is experiencing.

Second, to advocate internally for the Inner Child by COMPLETELY understanding EVERYTHING the Inner Child is experiencing, from the Inner Child's point of view. Nothing to fix. Nothing to teach. Nothing to navigate with the outside world. Just being with the child with an implied, "I know exactly what it feels like to be you because I'm feeling it myself."

This is what the Inner Child has always wanted, and never got. And it's ALL the Inner Child needs. Anything the

Inner Child has been trying to get from the outside world (unsuccessfully) it can immediately get from our Inner Adult. The Inner Child doesn't care where it gets it. It just has to get it. And by connecting with our Inner Adult, the Inner Child is connecting with a constant, consistent source of what the Inner Child needs whenever the Inner Child needs it. And what the Inner Child needs is to be seen, felt, heard and held as is.

<u>The Inner Adult is feeling exactly what the Inner Child is feeling, but AS an Adult.</u>

The challenge here is that when we, as an Inner Adult, begin to experience the Inner Child's "uncomfortable" sensations and "protective" thoughts, we, as adults, can be thrown by this. Sometimes people think they don't have an Inner Adult because the Inner Adult feels so much like the Inner Child.

So first, we must remember that although our Inner Adult is feeling as upset as the Inner Child feels, and thinking the thoughts the Inner Child thinks, the Inner Adult is feeling and thinking these things AS an adult, WITH the Inner Child, not AS the Inner Child.

<u>There is NO action to be taken in the present.</u>

Being with the Inner Child is not about the present, not about solving anything, not about getting anywhere. It's not about the Inner Adult having to do anything in the world or having to help the Inner Child. It's simply about the Inner Adult taking care of the Inner Child by being with the Inner Child.

Only when we do this in this way can the Inner Child be assured that there are no "consequences" to its feeling and thinking whatever it's feeling and thinking. This 100% focus on the Inner Child also ensures that we will not act out the Inner Child's thoughts and sensations in the present.

So often, people try to "use" the Inner Child to get somewhere in the present. This is tantamount to trying to fix, change, soothe, teach or silence the Inner Child's thoughts and sensations, and it NEVER WORKS. The Inner Child, sensing that we are trying to get away from it, pass over it or change it, will immediately reassert itself by sending us more "uncomfortable" sensations, more "protective" thoughts and more of its interpretations of circumstances, in hopes that we will see, feel, hear and experience its plight.

So the object is to just BE with the Inner Child. Period!

<u>The thoughts and sensations of the Inner Child are just thoughts and sensations, and as such have no intrinsic meaning or power to affect the present</u>

When we are simply sitting with the Inner Child's fears and limitations, with 100% focus on the Inner Child, the next concern that often comes up is that we're going to be stuck there. There is so much superstition about, "If you think a 'negative' thought then 'negative' things will happen," that we're often afraid to just sit in the "negative" place with the child, allowing the child's fears, sensations and thoughts to be recognized and validated.

The Inner Adult "knows better." The Inner Adult knows that there is not the same danger now, in the present, as there was for the Inner Child then. The Inner Adult knows that there are options of which the Inner Child is unaware. But still, when the Inner Adult really begins to experience what the Inner Child is experiencing, it sometimes becomes hard for the Inner Adult to remember what it knows and stay with the Inner Child's experience.

What can help us to allow ourselves to be where the Inner Child is, is to remember that what the Inner Child is thinking are just thoughts. The Inner Child must totally be allowed to experience what it's experiencing (with the support of our Inner Adult) even though those thoughts are not true in the present and the Inner Child's sensations don't "mean" what the Inner Child might think they mean. If the Inner Child is feeling "uncomfortable" sensations and thinking, "It's all hopeless, I'll never have anything," that's not true now, for us as adults in the present, but it IS what the Inner Child thought in its original situation, so we must allow the Inner Child to think it.

Just because it's not true doesn't mean the Inner Child shouldn't be allowed to experience it. Conversely, the fact that the Inner Child is experiencing it doesn't mean it's true.

As part of our function of being the Inner Adult holding the Inner Child, we can know this, but this is not a lesson we have to teach the Inner Child. In fact, even if we wanted to, we couldn't teach it to the Inner Child, because we cannot change what happened to the Inner Child in the past or how the Inner Child felt at that time. Our sole function now is to simply be with the Inner Child's experience, whatever it is.

The Inner Adult can be with the Inner Child's thoughts of limitation while, at the same time, holding the knowledge that infinite possibilities ALWAYS exist.

What really enables us to simply be with the Inner Child exactly as it is, is that our Inner Adult, while being right where the Inner Child is, (feeling the Inner Child's Sensations, thinking the Inner Child's thoughts and validating and mirroring the Inner Child's experience) can gently hold, for the child, without the child having to hold it, the knowledge that no matter what limitations the Inner Child is seeing, no matter what the Inner Child thinks, the Truth is that there are ALWAYS unlimited possibilities in every situation. Even if the Inner Adult can't see those possibilities.

I like to hold the image in my mind of the Inner Adult sitting and holding the Inner Child in a tent, the borders of which are the limits of what the Inner Child can see as possible. And while the Inner Adult is sitting there absolutely reflecting and being with what the Inner Child is experiencing, the Inner Adult is also aware that there are infinite possibilities all around, just outside the tent. Even if the Inner Adult doesn't know what those possibilities are, the Inner Adult KNOWS that they MUST be there.

The image might look something like this:

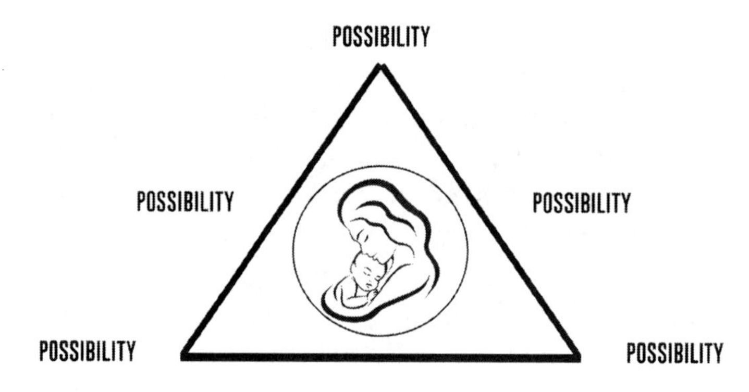

The point of this is that the Inner Adult can be with and reflect back the limitations of the Inner Child without losing the knowing that the possibilities are always unlimited.

<u>At any moment, we can remember that all this is "going on" inside the infinite Observer that we truly are, and that there is no way any of this can harm us.</u>

Another thing that can ultimately be extremely helpful is that while we are being with the Inner Child, feeling what the Inner Child feels, thinking what the Inner Child thinks, and holding the knowing that infinite possibilities exist, we must remember that all of this is going on within the "holding" of the Observer/Noticer/Experiencer that we REALLY are. In this way we remember that the whole experience cannot harm or injure us in any way, since who we REALLY are has nothing to do with any of this. We're just observing it.

So, as you go through the four steps, remember:

As you notice a "problem" you're experiencing, your Inner Child is allowed (actually encouraged) to feel any "uncomfortable" sensations and have any "negative" thoughts it has.

Your Inner Adult is there to feel with, think with, be with, validate and mirror the Inner Child exactly as it is. No criticism, no advice, just presence.

Your Inner Adult, while doing this, can maintain the knowledge that all around the perceived "problem" are infinite possibilities of solution, whether we know what they are or not.

All of this is being held within who you REALLY are, an invisible, infinite, unassailable, safe Observer, Noticer, Experiencer whose infinite-ness is unaffected and unchanged by any of this.

So with this in mind, you're ready to live life in the present, as an adult caring for an Inner Child who you love and are perfectly capable of caring for.

> "The object is to just BE with the Inner Child. Period!"

CHAPTER 22
Welcome to Your New, Adult Life

Having done the four steps, and the steps in Chapter 21, and being willing to do them whenever they arise (which will now be easier because you know you can), you are now a whole person, capable of being with sensations and thoughts from which your Inner Child had to run.

You are now capable of being with these sensations and thoughts WHENEVER they arise. Whenever a "problem" comes up, you can experience being in it, rather than having to run away from it and solve it. You actually want to stop and be in the "problem," because you know that the reason it's there is to point you toward your Inner Child's sensations and thoughts. Whenever an "uncomfortable" sensation arises, you can have it. Whenever a "negative" or "protective" thought arises, you can think it, while always remembering who you REALLY are.

It's not that you've done the process and are now finished with it forever. It's that you can do the process constantly, whenever a "problem" arises, so you are ALWAYS with your Inner Child. The Inner Child is still living "back there" and always will be, but you are always with it, so it is seen, heard and felt and is not living your life in the present for you. YOU are living your life while being with the Inner Child at all times.

When you do this, you are living life as an adult, not as a panicked, screaming unseen child. Your motives are pure. You want things because you want things, not because you hope that they will heal something from the outside that you "know" cannot be healed from the outside. You are not puzzled or thrown by your sensations and thoughts. You don't need to get rid of them.

It's not that you will never feel "uncomfortable" or thrown again. It's not that you'll never have challenges. It's that you've regained your ability to feel "uncomfortable," be thrown, be upset, be worried, have challenges or feel or think ANYTHING, as an ADULT. And thus you've regained your ability to act in the world as an Adult, without the Inner Child being left behind or feeling unseen and unheard.

Now all you have to do is live your life. When you can be with the Inner Child's sensations and thoughts, you will notice that adult thoughts arise spontaneously. When we can feel and be with the sensations that generated our "protective" thoughts, we are not stuck in those protective thoughts, and other possibilities immediately become apparent. When we think these new thoughts, we will notice that our "uncomfortable" sensations and our "protective" thoughts are still there, but they are not running the show. We're thinking the thought we want to think, having whatever sensations we're having, noticing whatever "protective" thoughts come up, and we're able to act on the thoughts we wish to act on.

We are free. We are unlimited. We are, AT LAST, grown up. Albeit, we will always be grownups with a child in our care, but it's a child we are perfectly capable of taking care of and even happy to be taking care of. Ultimately, we understand that this is a child we LOVE. We are WHOLE. We are ONE. We are free to once again live in all the riches life has to offer, with our Inner Child, our history and our present intact.

CHAPTER 23
The Four BASIC Steps in Review

1. DO THE MEDITATION TO EXPERIENCE THAT WHO YOU ARE IS AN INVISIBLE UNLIMITED NOTICER, OBSERVER, EXPERIENCER.

2. PICK A "PROBLEM," ANY "PROBLEM."

3. EXPERIENCE THE SENSATIONS YOU EXPERIENCE WHEN YOU THINK ABOUT THE "PROBLEM."

4. THINK THE THOUGHTS THAT ARISE, WHILE REMEMBERING THAT WHO YOU REALLY ARE IS AN INVISIBLE, UNLIMITED NOTICER, OBSERVER, EXPERIENCER.

And if you run into any difficulty doing this, remember that who you REALLY are is an Invisible Observer, unaffected by any of this, holding Unlimited Possibilities which surround an Inner Adult who is being with whatever "uncomfortable" sensations and "negative" thoughts the Inner Child is having due to experiences that happened in the past.

Every time you do this you put yourself in a position where the world of Infinite Possibilities is open to you.

You can think any thought because you can experience any sensation.

You can experience any "problem" and know that what's really happening is that you are reconnecting with the sensations and thoughts of your Inner Child.

You can "solve" problems without leaving the Inner Child behind.

You can dream dreams and stay with those dreams, because you are able to stay with the "uncomfortable" sensations and "negative" thoughts that might come up when you dare to dream your dreams.

You can take action toward your dreams because you are able to be with the "uncomfortable" sensations and "negative" thoughts that might arise when you take the actions you need to take.

Now that you have the ability to be with "problems," experience "uncomfortable" sensations and notice "negative" thoughts, you have the ability to experience whatever you want to experience in the REAL world.

There are specific, practical techniques that I will share with you that will allow you to do all this, but before I share them, I think it's important that we talk about what the REAL world is, and what it is you REALLY want. Only in this way will you be able to know what you're going for and be satisfied and fulfilled when you experience it.

So let's spend some time in the REAL world, and then, I promise you, I will share with you the "secrets" in practical, concrete, doable terms of "being" whatever you want to be, "doing" whatever you want to do, and "having" whatever you REALLY want to have.

PART IV
LIVING IN THE REAL WORLD
(The Invisible World of Experience)

CHAPTER 24
What's the Point?

If you've been following this book so far, you should have a pretty clear idea that we do not live in the physical world, and that ALL we REALLY are is invisible, infinite, unassailable, unchangeable consciousness experiencing intrinsically meaningless (albeit often "uncomfortable") thoughts and sensations.

This realization can be very disconcerting, and this is often the point at which I lose people. Since most of us have been living our whole lives thinking that the physical world is the real world, that the object of life is to manifest things, to have things, to achieve things, to "make a difference," to "accomplish" something, to be comfortable, to "win," to be "happy," it usually throws us for a loop to even contemplate the idea that these things, in and of themselves, might not matter.

The question that usually rings in our mind is, "If nothing in the physical world matters, what's the point? Why do we do anything? Why do we strive for anything? Why do we want anything?" And perhaps, most importantly, "Why do we have to go through all these "negative" thoughts and "uncomfortable" sensations?"

The question boils down to, "If interior, invisible experience is the whole ball of wax, of what use is the physical world? Why do we have it?"

Well here's the thing. In Truth, the physical world is an essential part of our experience, just not in the way many of us have traditionally thought it to be. In Truth, the relationship between the physical and invisible world is exactly the opposite of what it appears to be. What seems to be "cause" is actually "effect," and what seems to be "effect" is actually "cause."

The common "wisdom" with which most of us were brought up is that the object of life is to manifest things in the physical world, and that when we can do that, the result will be that we will be fulfilled and happy. In this context, spiritual pursuits such as positive thinking, meditation, tithing, are thought of as "tools" that can help us achieve the goal of manifestation.

This is exactly the opposite of what is True.

Rather than spirituality (the invisible world) being a tool to get things in the physical (visible) world, it's actually the other way around. The physical world is a tool that we can utilize to experience what we REALLY want, which can only be found in the invisible world of experience. It's an important tool, and when we learn how to use it, our "relationship" with the physical world is the gateway to what we're REALLY after.

So, in order to experience the life we're truly after, in the place where life is truly lived, we must make the transition from thinking that we're doing all this "spiritual stuff" so that we can have something in the REAL, physical world, to understanding that the "spiritual stuff" IS the REAL world. The "spiritual stuff" is the point. The WHOLE point. It's the ONLY world that exists, or at least the ONLY world we can experience.

If you find this disappointing or disconcerting, have no fear. (Or have fear if you have it, but know that it's just fear.)

You still get to go after the things you want. You still get to manifest. You still get to "win" and "lose" and "triumph" and fall in love and own things. The context in which these things occur, though, will be different. And I promise you, it will be MUCH more safe, much more fulfilling and much more satisfying.

So stay with me.

> "What seems to be 'cause' is actually "effect," and what seems to be "effect" is actually 'cause.'"

CHAPTER 25
The PHYSICAL World is a Mirror

In the last section, we cultivated the BASIC SKILL of being able to be with "problems," "negative" thoughts and "uncomfortable" sensations.

Once we are able to do this, we are able to use the world for what it really is.

What the world REALLY is is a mirror that we can use to see ourselves and see where our consciousness is. When we look at ourselves in a mirror, what we see in the mirror is not real. If we are standing five feet in front of a mirror, it will look like there's someone standing five feet behind the mirror. But there isn't. There's no person in the mirror. There's only a person in front of the mirror being reflected EXACTLY in his or her EVERY detail and every move. If we move toward the mirror, the reflection in the mirror appears to move toward us. If we make even the tiniest move, the reflection in the mirror will make the exact same move at the exact same time we make it. If we think there's actually something in the mirror and try to walk toward what we see there, we will hit the glass, because there's NOTHING IN THERE! Nothing to be changed. Nothing to be fixed. NOTHING!

But, as we know, this doesn't mean that the mirror is useless. We use a mirror to see ourselves. (I've always found it kind of disconcerting to realize that if I didn't have a mirror I would NEVER know what my face looked like.)

So, when we look at ourselves in the mirror, we can use the reflection we see there to fix and correct a lot of things on ourselves. When we look in the mirror and see that our hair is not combed or our makeup is a mess, things we would not be aware of if we didn't look in the mirror, we can then pick up a brush and comb our hair, or pull out the powder and fix our makeup. We would never look in a mirror, see that the makeup we see in the mirror doesn't look good, and put makeup on the mirror. That would be ridiculous! Imagine if we got up in the morning, looked at ourselves in the mirror, said "Ooh, you look awful," put makeup all over the mirror so that what we would see in the mirror was a face with makeup on it, and went out of the house. NOTHING would have changed about us because we put makeup on the MIRROR. WE would still "look" exactly the same.

Dancers work in front of mirrors because that's the only way they can see what their bodies are doing. They see the dance in the mirror, but there is no dancing going on in the mirror. If they see something they want to change, they can only change it on their own bodies. They can't go to the mirror to do it, because all the mirror can do is reflect what's in front of it. When the dancer changes, on him or herself, what he or she sees in the mirror, the mirror will automatically change to reflect the change the dancer has made. It has to. But there's still nothing happening in the mirror. It's just reflecting what's in front of it.

So, just as we work with a mirror to see ourselves, we are working with the physical world. We are not in it. We are not of it. There's nothing we need in the physical world, just as there's nothing we need in a mirror. The event, the money, the success, the relationship are not at all important in and of themselves. But they are useful in several ways.

First of all, they're useful in that they bring up, or shed light on, different sensations and thoughts that we have in the REAL world (which remember is the invisible world inside of us.) So we get to not only see what's inside of us, but to practice being with it. They're just sensations and thoughts. They have no intrinsic meaning. They can't hurt, change, expand or contract the invisible consciousness of infinite possibilities that we are. And by practicing being with those sensations and thoughts, we get closer and closer to an experience of peace. An experience of love. An experience of forgiveness.

In my study of New Thought and in my work in Thought Exchange, I have come to the conclusion that peace, love and forgiveness are ALL the same thing: Allowing things to be as they are. And allowing ourselves to experience things as they are. And we can ONLY allow things to be as they are when we KNOW that we can't be hurt by them. So by going through events in the world, knowing they can't hurt us or diminish who we really are in any way, we get to practice and experience our infiniteness and the fact that at ALL times we can have peace, love and forgiveness by simply being with whatever is going on inside us. Exactly as it is.

So all these events that happen, especially the repeated upsets, have been designed by us (again, albeit unconsciously) to give us practice in being with thoughts and sensations that we have run from as children, because as children we had nobody to be with us when we were having them. The harder the incident, the more practice and growth we get, if we know how to use it for that instead of trying to "solve" our "problems."

It's like being in the marines. The drill sergeant makes you do hundreds of push-ups. They're very unpleasant.

But a marine doesn't spend his efforts trying to figure out how to get the drill sergeant to stop, because the marine knows that the more push-ups he does, the more prepared he is for what he has to do, the more strength and stamina he has at his disposal.

So we create these incidents, these challenges, these "problems.," apparent lack of money, breakups of relationships, career challenges, health issues, and by our being with them, our Inner Child finally has someone to be with it through these thoughts and sensations, and we are able to reclaim the thoughts we have rejected and widen our ability to know that who we are is infinite invisible consciousness with infinite, immediate possibilities for experience. NO MATTER WHAT'S GOING ON.

We generate these situations to give ourselves that opportunity, but so often we fall into the illusion of thinking that the situations are the point, or that they're even real, and we try to change them or get rid of them, rather than turning inward and experiencing them for the sake of reclaiming and expanding our ability to experience.

The situations, the incidents, the "problems," are not the point, just as the reflection in the mirror is not the point. To try to solve the "problems" or change the situations would be like looking in a mirror, seeing our reflection, and trying to get it to change without our doing anything. A mirror cannot change without what's in front of it changing. And when what's in front of it changes, what you see in the mirror is still not real or the point, it's just a reflection.

So everything we want, everything we do, everything that happens, only "happens" in the invisible world inside of us, in the form of sensations and thoughts observed by who we REALLY are, the invisible, infinite Observer, Noticer, Experiencer.

This being so, the dreams, the physical world, the goals, the challenges, are not where life is really happening. They are tools to work with that are meaningless in and of themselves, but that help us to achieve experience, mastery and freedom in the place where life is really happening.

In a certain way, they are like games.

Knowing this TRUTH, we can now look at what we want and why we do things, with a fresh eye.

> "What the world REALLY is a mirror that we can use to see ourselves and see where our consciousness is."

CHAPTER 26
The "Game" of Life and Why We Play It

Lately, I like to liken life to playing a game of *Monopoly*. Remember *Monopoly*?

Going through our life in the physical world is like playing *Monopoly*. Why do we play *Monopoly*? You lose a house, you get very upset. Someone lands on your hotel. You get a lot of money. You're thrilled. You didn't lose a house. The money you won isn't real. You know that at any moment you can step away from the game and nothing has been lost. Or gained.

And yet, *Monopoly* and other games are so popular. Why? Because when we play games, we get to safely have interior experiences and practice being with them.

When we play *Monopoly*, we get to work with our ambitions, our dreams, our passion, our fear, our ability to tolerate winning and losing and know that neither one matters. One of my favorite quotes is from the Kipling poem "If", in which he says;

> "When you can meet with Triumph and Disaster
> And treat those two imposters just the same"

And when the game is over, we get to walk away completely in tact. Not a shred of infinite possibility has been lost. In fact, where we REALLY live, in the invisible world of infinite possible thoughts and sensations, NOTHING has happened except we've gotten a little more practice at expanding our ability to be with the complete panorama of our thoughts and sensations. And it's this ability that allows us to take on ANY of the infinite thoughts available to us at all times, no matter what's happening, because we can be with any "uncomfortable" sensations and "negative" thoughts that might come with them.

What if life is actually the biggest game of all? "Oh, my God, this disaster happened! Yay, I fixed it! I'm winning! I'm losing! Yippee, I'm right! Oh, no, I'm wrong!" Like the weather report. "Bad news, it's going to rain tomorrow. But thank God, it's going to be sunny the day after tomorrow."

The truth is, we have just as much ability to be joyful on a rainy day as we do on a sunny day, and visa versa. Why? Because we know that we are not that rainy or that sunny day. (Of course, the ability to enjoy a rainy day depends on our ability to be with any "uncomfortable" sensations that might come with a rainy day, and regard them as intrinsically meaningless.)

We have just as much ability to be joyful if our team has won the Super Bowl as when they have lost. Why? Because nothing was won or lost where we really live. Most of the country is incredibly committed to one team or another winning the Super Bowl, because it gives us the chance to safely explore thoughts of passion, commitment, preference, excitement and deal with the EXPERIENCE of winning and losing. That's why we are sports fans. That's why we play *Monopoly*. That, in fact, is why we pursue careers and goals and romances. That's why we play any game. The winning and losing means nothing in itself. When it's over, who we are is the same infinite invisible consciousness no matter what.

Notice, at next year's Super Bowl, the tremendous build-up before it, the excitement, the strong opinions, the loyalties, the arguments. And then notice, when it's over, we hold on to celebrating or bemoaning for a few minutes, a few hours, a few days, and then it's done. And we start the cycle again.

I'm reminded of a game we used to play at parties as teenagers called "Sardine." To play this game, we turned out all the lights and crawled around on the floor. One person was designated as "The Sardine." When you bumped into somebody while crawling around on the floor, you very quietly asked, "Are you the Sardine?" If they were "The Sardine" then you became "The Sardine" and moved on. If they weren't "The Sardine" then you both just moved on.

The interesting thing about this game was that everybody had a different opinion about being "The Sardine." Some people would think, "Oh, no, I don't want to be the Sardine." Some people would think, "Yay, I'm the Sardine." Some people would really try to rush around in hope of bumping into "The Sardine" so they could become it, while others would slink off into a corner to avoid the possibility of bumping into someone and becoming "The Sardine." Some people, once they became "The Sardine," would slink off into a corner or even leave the room so nobody could take the title of "Sardine" away from them.

The game was totally ridiculous, but we loved playing it. Why? Because we were all together, experiencing whatever our interior thoughts and sensations were, in a game that didn't mean anything and that had no outcome. The only "outcome" was the experience we had playing it, and although we were experiencing all sorts of fears and ambitions and judgments and worries, what we actually did was laugh and laugh and laugh. Because it was all meaningless. It was just FUN, for no reason.

Theater is a game. When actors do a play, they come to the theater as themselves, put on their makeup, their costumes and their "characters," step out on stage and spend two hours falling in love, killing people, having disasters and triumphs happen. Then, they take a bow, go back to their dressing rooms, take off their makeup and their costumes, and go back out into the world as themselves. They experienced the play, but the play didn't REALLY happen in the world in which they live. It was a play. Nobody REALLY got killed, nobody REALLY fell in love, nothing happened in the REAL world. The audience experienced the play too. Nothing REALLY happened in their lives either, but they got to be with THEIR OWN sensations and thoughts and interior, invisible experience. The audience is not in the play. The play isn't happening to them. They're looking at the play and experiencing THEMSELVES.

If who we are is really invisible consciousness, then our whole lives could be thought of as the exact same thing as the "game" of theater. We are invisible souls (ourselves). We put on our costumes and makeup (our bodies), go out on the stage and have all sorts of experiences, and then when it's over (when we "die"), we simply take off the costume and continue to be ourselves. Nothing lost, nothing gained except experience.

There are three things that EVERY game has:

Rules, an Object and a Purpose.

Rules are the parameters of how the game is played. They certainly are arbitrary and made up and can be broken, but if you break them you're not playing the game. And if you don't play the game by the Rules, you may get to achieve the Object of the game, but you will not benefit from the Purpose of the game.

The Object is why, in the physical world, you are playing the game. In order to play any game, once you know what the Rules are, you have to know what you're going for, what constitutes winning and what constitutes losing. In *Monopoly*, the Object is to get all the money. In the Superbowl the Object is for your team to score the most points. In Sardine, the Object is made up by each player. It is either to be "The Sardine" or to not be "The Sardine," depending on what the individual player makes up.

Knowing the Rules and the Object, you can now play the game. But since, as we discussed above, nothing REAL is happening when we play a game, whether we win or lose the game, there must be a reason why we play it.

This reason is what I call the Purpose of the game. Since anything in the physical world is nothing more than a mirror reflecting the thoughts we're having and the sensations we're experiencing, the Purpose of any game is to have an interior experience.

In baseball, the Rules of the game are that you hit the ball and run around the bases. The Object of the game is to run around the bases more times than your opponent and thus score more runs. The Purpose of the game is to experience your passion, your desire, your determination, your physical skills, your ability to hold a thought (of victory) even if you are experiencing "uncomfortable" sensations, to notice your thoughts of self-worth or lack of self-worth, of competitiveness and many other things, and to be able to be with the thoughts and sensations you have when you win and when you lose. All inside!

In the theater, the Rules are that the actors get on the stage, say the lines and enact the play. The Object is to present audiences with a slice of life that they recognize and is in some way meaningful and moving to them. The Purpose is to safely give the audience an interior experience of their own desires, longings, passions, thoughts and sensations.

In theater, you could stop the show in the middle, step out of character and talk to the audience, but that would be breaking the Rules and restrictions of the "game" of theater. In Baseball, you could run from 1st base directly to 3rd base, but you wouldn't be playing by the Rules and restrictions of the game of baseball.

We create these Rules and restrictions because they give us the best chance of learning the internal lessons, which are the reasons we play the game, by safely setting up the conditions with which we wrestle in life so we can experience them, inside, and master them. The game itself doesn't matter. The show itself doesn't matter. But playing the games by the Rules gives us the opportunity to move closer to the only thing we really want. Complete access, at every moment, to the infiniteness that we are.

We all know the song "Row, Row, Row Your Boat." Funny that it should be so universally popular, and yet most of us have never really listened to the words.

Row, row, row your boat

Gently down the stream

Merrily, merrily, merrily, merrily

Life is but a dream

What if life is just a dream? Think about a dream. All sorts of things happen, some of them upsetting, some of them lovely, but nothing is really happening. Nothing physical that is, even though it seems like it at the time. The effect of a dream is that we have the experience, we learn things about what we're thinking and feeling, we experience being with sensations. But then we "wake up" and nothing is left of the dream except the experience, which we carry in the invisible world inside of us. And these experiences lead us closer and closer to the Truth that who we REALLY are is Unlimited Invisible Consciousness, and nothing can diminish that or hurt us.

(I've often thought, "If there's life after death, why don't people who have died come back and tell us?" But if life is truly a dream, would you go back to a dream to explain, to the dreamer, where you are now?)

Like all the other games I've described, life also has its Rules, its Object and its Purpose. The Rules vary widely and are basically made up by us (just as games are made up by us). The Object is also whatever we, or a group of us, say it is. And the Purpose of life, like all games, is to have experiences in the place we REALLY live. In the invisible world of consciousness.

So, knowing this, knowing that anything that appears to be "happening" in the physical world is just a part of a game that is designed to give us experience on the "inside," let's take a look at the "games" we play in life, what it LOOKS LIKE we want, and what we REALLY want.

> "What is life is actually the biggest game of all?"

PART V

WHAT DO WE WANT AND WHY DO WE WANT IT?

OK. So we get it. Life is a game. We make up the Rules, we make up the Object of the game, but no matter which game we're playing, the purpose is to give us an experience inside. The only place that game is happening is inside ourselves, in the invisible world of our thoughts and sensations. When we look at the physical world, all we are seeing is our own thoughts and sensations. The physical world is a mirror. There's nothing really happening out there, no matter how real it looks and no matter how real it feels.

But if life is a game designed to give us something on the inside, and we have to play that game in order to get what the game has to offer, we have to play the game as if it's real, almost forgetting while we're playing that it's not real, while at the same time, way in the back of our consciousness, not forgetting who we really are, knowing that the game is, in fact, not real.

It's tricky.

We are invisible, spiritual beings having a human experience. And with that human experience comes desire, longing, ambition and the thought that there is something to get that we don't already have. Deep down (and in many cases not so deep down) we think that things and outcomes and achievements and circumstances are the point. Many of us began to study all this "spiritual stuff," or at least first became interested in Spirituality, because we thought it was a way to get stuff in the physical world. All of us, being human, are in some form, playing the game. Most of us, with the possible exception of a few transcendent souls living atop the Himalayas, are playing the game as if it's real.

So first, let's take a look at how most of us play the game, by looking at what most of us think we want.

CHAPTER 27
What We *Think* We Want

As I began to write this chapter, for some reason I flashed on the Miss America pageants that I used to watch every year as a kid. At some point in the pageant, the Master of Ceremonies would question the contestants and ask them things like, "What do you want most?" Or, "What is your goal in life?" And invariably they would answer, "I want world peace. I want kindness for everyone. I want children all over the world to be safe."

Those were nice answers, and in fact I'm sure they had some truth in them, but even as a child I couldn't help but realize that at that moment, for almost all of them, that wasn't what they really wanted most. What they REALLY wanted most was TO BE MISS AMERICA!

For all the metaphysical work that we do, when it comes to making a list of what we want, the list is almost always of things we want in the physical world. Success. Financial security. The realization of our "dreams."

If I stop and make a list right now of the things I want, this is what it would contain. (In no particular order)

— TO HAVE A HIT SHOW ON BROADWAY

— TO OPEN THAT SHOW IN LONDON AND THEN BRING IT TO BROADWAY

— TO WEIGH 175 POUNDS (At this moment, I happen to be on a diet, I've lost 47 pounds and have 8 to go.)

— TO BE DEBT FREE

— TO HAVE MY PARTNER LEARN SOME THINGS HE NEEDS TO LEARN ABOUT HIMSELF (Yeah, I know, I'm Mr. Thought Exchange and I know it's ALL going on inside of me, but that doesn't stop me from thinking that if HE changed, MY life would be different... and better.)

- TO WIN A TONY AWARD

- TO HAVE MY CDs BE BEST SELLERS

- TO HAVE THIS BOOK, AND ALL MY BOOKS, IN FACT, BE BEST SELLERS

- TO BUILD A LAP POOL IN OUR BACK YARD

- TO BUILD A GUEST SUITE ABOVE OUR GARAGE

- TO FINISH THIS BOOK (SOON) AND GET IT PUBLISHED

- TO MAKE A MOVIE OF NANCY LaMOTT'S LIFE

- TO HAVE A SUCCESSFUL INDIEGOGO CAMPAIGN WHICH ALLOWS ME TO PRODUCE THE NEXT NANCY LaMOTT CD AND ALL FUTURE CDs

- TO FINISH TWO BOOKS THAT I STARTED YEARS AGO AND HAVE THEM PUBLISHED

- TO DO MORE CORPORATE SPEAKING

- TO SPEAK AT CERTAIN UNITY CHURCHES THAT I'VE BEEN WANTING TO SPEAK AT

- TO HAVE MY CLASSES EXPAND

- TO DEVELOP A THOUGHT EXCHANGE PROGRAM FOR INNER CITY KIDS AROUND THE WORLD

- TO DO MORE TEACHING IN COLLEGES AND OBTAIN SOME ADJUNCT FACULTY POSITIONS

- TO HAVE MY SHOW *LISTEN TO MY HEART* PRODUCED IN MORE VENUES AROUND THE COUNTRY

- TO HAVE MY SHOWS *CHASING NICOLETTE, FRONT PAGE GIRL, DESPERATE MEASURES,* AND *LINCOLN IN LOVE* PRODUCED ON AND OFF BROADWAY IN NEW YORK AND AROUND THE COUNTRY

- TO HAVE MY NEW SHOW, *MONEY THE MUSICAL*, BE PRODUCED IN OVER 300 VENUES AROUND THE WORLD

- TO FUND MY NON-PROFIT FOR MY SHOW, *LISTEN TO MY HEART,* SO I CAN BRING IT TO CITIES AROUND THE COUNTRY AND CONTRIBUTE THE PROFITS TO UNITY AND OTHER CAUSES

- TO WORK OUT SO I CAN HAVE GREAT ABS (Or more accurately, to have great abs without working out.)

- TO HAVE DIONNE WARWICK RECORD A SONG OF MINE

- TO MAKE A KILLING IN THE STOCK MARKET

- TO PAY OFF MY MORTGAGES

- TO HAVE A MILLION-PLUS DOLLARS IN THE BANK (This one used to be first. Interesting that I thought of it so far down the list.)

- TO HAVE FLOWERS AND COLORFUL TREES ALL OVER OUR PROPERTY IN CONNECTICUT

- TO WALK 10,000 STEPS A DAY

– Oh, yeah, and of course, it goes without saying (which is perhaps why I haven't said it) to have my friends and family be healthy and happy, have my dad comfortable and doing well, end poverty, hunger and illness in the world and HAVE WORLD PEACE.

Now before we go, "How shallow. I couldn't possibly want these things in that order. I should want the "important" things and not all these material things," or before we say, "I know these things are not the real thing and that achieving them will not get me anywhere," let's just play the game, take this list (obviously I'm talking about your own list and whatever may be on it) at face value, and realize how we can incorporate and utilize these material world desires (and the game of going for them) as part of our process of experiencing wholeness and healing.

> "For all the metaphysical work that we do, when it comes to making a list of what we want, the list is almost always of things we want in the physical world."

CHAPTER 28
What We *REALLY* Want

When we look at our list of "things" we want, the first question we must ask ourselves is, "Why do I want this? What do I hope to get from this?"

Knowing that the ONLY place in which we EVER can experience ANYTHING is on the INSIDE, in the world of Invisible Consciousness, and that the only way we experience these things is via thoughts and sensations, the only things we could ever REALLY want, the only things that would in any way be real, MUST exist on the inside, in the invisible world of experience and consciousness. In this world, the REAL world in which we ACTUALLY live, thoughts and sensations are the ONLY things we experience. So what we REALLY want MUST be in the world of thoughts and sensations.

Now this doesn't mean that the physical world, what we see "outside" of ourselves, doesn't have a purpose, or that it isn't an integral part of the process of "getting what we want." (I put "outside" in quotes because we really only see what's "outside" of our selves via thoughts and sensations that are "inside" ourselves.)

But the big transition we MUST make in order to get what we REALLY want, is to know that what we REALLY want is NOT IN THE PHYSICAL WORLD.

Now before you despair and say, "Does this mean I can't have the things I want in the physical world?" let me assure you that when you have the things you want on the inside, the physical world, whatever it contains, will appear to you to be chock full of everything you could ever want.

But first things first. Let's look at what you really want.

Taking our list of what we think we want and asking the question, "Why do I want this?" we can translate what we want on the "outside" to what we think it will do for us on the "inside," which, as I've said over and over, is the place we really live. Sometimes we have to ask the question several times to get to the bottom of what we're really after.

Often, our first few answers will still pertain to the "outside" having to do with other people's opinions of us or our possessions or achievements. We want to keep asking the question until we find out what we want on the "inside."

So let's look at the first item on my own list:

- TO HAVE A HIT SHOW ON BROADWAY

Why do I want this?

The first answers that come off the top of my head are: To be successful; to be rich; to not have to worry about how I'm going to pay my bills; to show other people that I can do it; to impress people.

All of these are still in the "outside" world, so they are not yet the real answer.

What do I think having all these things would give me on the "inside?"

A feeling of safety? The thought that I have value? The experience that I have infinite possibilities? To be at peace with myself and the world?

These are closer to the Truth, because these are things we can actually have because they take place where we REALLY live, in the invisible, interior, non-locational world.

So, when I say I want to have a hit show on Broadway, what I REALLY want is:

- A FEELING OF SAFETY

- THE THOUGHT THAT I HAVE VALUE

- THE EXPERIENCE THAT I HAVE INFINITE POSSIBILITIES

- A SENSE OF BEING AT PEACE WITH MYSELF AND THE WORLD.

Now let's look at these.

A FEELING OF SAFETY – In the interior, invisible world, we are truly safe, because no occurrence in the "outside" world can in any way penetrate or hurt our "inside" world. We are ALWAYS nothing more than an infinite possibility for experience, and nothing can either diminish or expand that. So we already have SAFETY.

VALUE is not something that is dependent on having or achieving anything. Value is BEING valuable. In the place where we REALLY live, the invisible, interior, non-locational world, nobody has more or less value than anyone else. There are no possessions and no achievements, just "is-ness" which everyone has.

So we already have VALUE.

INFINITE POSSIBILITIES – We ALWAYS have those, no matter what has happened. That's just a given quality of each present moment. ANYTHING can happen, no matter what has come before. So we already have INFINITE POSSIBILITIES.

PEACE – Peace is nothing more than being with what is. When we can be with what is, exactly as it is, and be with the way we are when what is is, we are at peace. So peace is something that is available to us at all times. We always have the ability to experience our sensations and notice our thoughts. WHATEVER THEY ARE. So we already have PEACE.

So, I want to have a hit show on Broadway so I can have things I already have!

But the interesting thing is, if I want to have these things, it follows that the only reason I would want them is that I think I don't have them. To put it another way, the thought I'm holding is that I don't have them. Otherwise I wouldn't want them. And if I think I don't have them, I CANNOT see them in the world. The world is a mirror of our thoughts and CANNOT reflect something that's not in front of it.

So, when we want something, we first have to know that we want it because we think we don't have it, "inside."

Then we must ask ourselves what we REALLY want.

When we realize what that is, we must then realize that we already have it, regardless of what we are seeing on the "outside."

When we can stay in this position, the "outside" MUST begin to look like the "inside," no matter what's going on, because the only place in which we experience the "outside" is in the context of the thought we're holding on the "inside."

You know how they say, "Be the thing you want to see in the world?" Another way of putting that might be, "Be the thing you want to GET from the world."

> "The only things we could ever REALLY want MUST exist on the inside."

CHAPTER 29
It's All Inside

Now that we understand that our lives are lived completely on the inside, in the world of experience, the purpose of "problems" and how we go about "solving" them, of "dreams" and how we go about "achieving" them, of "manifestation" and what it actually means, shifts radically.

We think what we want is "things." That's what it looks like. But what we really want is the experience we think those "things" will bring us.

This is where the illusion lies!

The Truth is, "things" can't bring us an experience, they can only reflect what we are already thinking, reflect the part of the infinite consciousness that we are willing to open ourselves up to.

This does not mean that dreams and manifestation are useless. They are, in fact, important tools that we use to achieve the true purpose of life, which, in my opinion, is not to expand the number of "things" we have, but rather to expand our capacity to experience everything, inside of ourselves (which is the ONLY place we can ever have experience) with a sense of wholeness, and to be in touch with the fact that infinite experience is ALWAYS available to us.

For example, living in a mansion has no intrinsic value. You will experience the mansion according to your consciousness. There are people who live in mansions who do nothing but complain about them. There are people who live in smaller houses who think they live in the most beautiful home in the world.

When we choose a dream, we immediately begin to experience where our consciousness is, and how willing or unwilling (afraid) we are to be open to the infiniteness of invisible experience that we are.

By setting out to "achieve" that dream, move toward it, wrestle with it, succeed or fail, we are constantly confronted with opportunities to expand our ability to think more of the infinite thoughts that are always available to us. The way this expansion is achieved is by our being more and more able to be with the "uncomfortable" sensations that arise when we take on some of the thoughts we wish to hold.

This is the interesting paradox. The thoughts we wish to hold, the "positive" thoughts, are often the ones that create the most "discomfort."

> "'Things' can't bring us an experience, they can only reflect what we're already thinking."

CHAPTER 30
The Most Challenging Thoughts to Hold Are "Positive" Thoughts and Thoughts of Success

Common logic would tell us that the most challenging thoughts to hold would be the thoughts of upset, the thoughts of failure, the thoughts of lack. But in fact, given that these are all "protective" thoughts, it's the thoughts they protect us from that are the most challenging to stay with.

The thoughts that are the most difficult to hold can be the "positive" thoughts. Why? Because if these "positive" thoughts were associated with "uncomfortable" sensations in the past, when we try to hold them in the present they will not only bring up the most "uncomfortable" sensations, but we will find ourselves constantly jumping to our old "protective" thoughts to get away from those sensations.

The "protective" "I can't; It's dangerous; It will never..." thoughts come with their own discomfort, but we have actually run to them to lessen the discomfort that the "positive" thoughts bring.

This being so, when we DARE to dream, what we are often really doing is daring to bring up "positive" thoughts that we have not allowed ourselves to think since childhood. We try to hold these thoughts because we think they will give us an experience of success, an experience of fulfillment and an experience of wholeness.

And in fact they do. But here's the catch.

When you hold a thought of success, you ARE experiencing success in the only place you could ever experience success. Inside, in the world of experience.

"But," you might say, "Whenever I take on the thought of success, I feel "uncomfortable" sensations and I have thoughts that I can't succeed.

YES!!!!!!

If you have had any previous trauma related to taking on a thought of success, those "uncomfortable" sensations and thoughts that you can't succeed are what COME WITH IT.

In other words, what it feels like to have success is that you have the thought of success, you feel "uncomfortable" sensations, and have thoughts of why you can't have it. This is often THE ACTUAL EXPERIENCE OF SUCCESS.

For example, I'm a composer, and it's one of my dreams to have a show on Broadway. In fact, I've already been on Broadway, so more accurately it could be said that my dream is to have my next show be on Broadway.

Even though I've already been on Broadway, when I hold the dream of having my next show on Broadway, when I see it happening in my mind's eye, I immediately feel a sinking sensation in my chest and a disconcerting fluttering in my heart. In addition, I notice all sorts of thoughts arise like, "It will never happen; I'm not allowed to have a show on Broadway; I always get overlooked; Everyone else is allowed but not me."

These are all thoughts and sensations from my childhood. These all come with the EXPERIENCE of having a show on Broadway. I'm having that experience right now as I hold the vision of being on Broadway, since, as I have repeatedly said, the only effect of actually being on

Broadway would be that I would have an interior experience of it.

And here's the kicker! I have been on Broadway, and I can tell you that when a Broadway show has actually manifested, I feel JUST LIKE THIS! I have the thought that I'm on Broadway, I have "uncomfortable" sensations, and as paradoxical and ridiculous as it seems, I have thoughts that, "This can't happen; Nobody recognizes me; It's not enough," etc.

The interior experience is the same. Why? Because it's my Inner Child's experience and my Inner Child is stuck forevermore in that experience. No present experience changes that Inner Child's history. So I can only hold a dream and live it if I am willing to be with the sensations and thoughts of my Inner Child that come with it.

At first this notion seems hopeless. "You mean, I'm always going to feel this way? I'm never going to get over it?" But when we understand that, first of all, these thoughts and sensations can't hurt us, and more importantly, that by being with them we are being with our Inner Child and allowing the child to be seen in a way it has been longing to be seen for a lifetime, these thoughts and sensations become part of the fabric of success, as tolerable to an adult as aching feet are to a ballet dancer, as fatigue and leg pains are to a marathon runner, as doing push-ups are to a marine. When we understand the purpose for which we're going through this, we become able to tolerate the experience of success.

So the dreams, the physical world, the goals, the challenges, are not where life is really happening. They are tools to work with that are meaningless in and of themselves, but that help us to achieve experience, mastery and freedom in the place where life is really happening.

So, armed with the information that life takes place only on the inside and that our "positive" thoughts are often accompanied by "uncomfortable" sensations and "negative" thoughts, let's DARE TO DREAM!

PART VI

GETTING WHAT WE REALLY WANT

OK. Here, as promised, is the part many of you have probably been waiting for.

We've laid all the groundwork.

We know we live in the Invisible World of Experience.

We know that who we are is an invisible Observer/Noticer/Experiencer experiencing invisible Thoughts and Sensations

We know that the "uncomfortable" sensations and "negative" thoughts we experience are our Inner Child trying to get our attention so we can become whole and integrated.

We have developed the BASIC SKILL of being able to simply "be with" problems, "uncomfortable" sensations and "negative" thoughts without having to fix them, solve them, release them or do anything at all about them.

We know that those "uncomfortable" sensations and "negative" thoughts have no intrinsic meaning and no ability to harm us.

We know that the physical world is nothing more than a mirror which we can use to reflect back to us what we are thinking in the Invisible World of Experience in which we live.

We know that what we REALLY want is an interior experience of the unlimitedness that we already are.

We know that we already have everything we could ever want, in the only place we could ever want it....INSIDE.

So now we're going to talk about practical ways in which we can use these skills and understandings to solve "problems," hold visions, dream dreams and do whatever we need to do to see those dreams manifest.

Here we go!

CHAPTER 31

"Problems" Are Not The "Problem"

Most of us originally got into New Thought to try to solve our "problems." Common wisdom says, "I have a 'problem.' Something is bothering me. Something is lacking. Something is not right. I feel unhappy and uncomfortable because I have this 'problem,' but if I can solve the 'problem' I will feel better, be happy and be comfortable."

It is this thought that has sent us, and almost everyone else in the world, on an endless merry-go-round of frustration, disappointment and suffering.

The reason for this is that while we think that "problems" are the cause of our pain and must be removed in order for us not to have pain, in Truth "problems" are nothing more than "protective" thoughts that we take on to try to get away from the pain of our Inner Child.

It is when we begin to remove the "problem" and DARE to think that it could be solved, that all of the "uncomfortable" sensations and "negative" thoughts of the Inner Child arise.

Often, at this point, we begin to feel uncomfortable and think we're on the wrong track.

The only way we're going to be able to "solve" "problems" is if we are willing to experience the "uncomfortable" sensations and "negative" thoughts of the Inner Child that we created the "problem" to avoid.

If we are unable to do this, we will be right back in the "problem" before we know it.

Now that we know this, we are ready to exchange the "problems" we have for the dreams we wish to hold. We are ready to hold the Vision of what we want to experience because we are able to be with any "uncomfortable" sensations and "negative" thoughts that might come with the realization of that Vision.

> "Problems are nothing more than "protective" thoughts that we take on to try to get away from the pain of our Inner Child."

CHAPTER 32
Holding a Vision

The thought of a dream can be one of the most challenging thoughts to hold because it can bring up so many "uncomfortable" sensations and "protective" thoughts.

We all have dreams. We just have trouble staying with them when they bring up such discomfort.

In this chapter, we're going to work with what it takes to have a dream, hold a dream and live a dream.

The first thing I'm going to ask you to do is find a dream, in the place where all dreams are found. In the infinite, invisible world of "The Great Unmanifested." Just go into the invisible world of your imagination and see a dream of yours. Whatever comes up. You don't have to know how it's going to happen, you don't have to know if it's going to happen, you don't have to "believe" it. Just see it. Right there. In the invisible world of your imagination. You can find ANYTHING there. A baboon. You doing the twist on the rings of Saturn. A billion dollars. Whether you think it's possible or not, it's there!

When we're talking about all of your dreams being there, we're not talking about the physical world. Often we stop ourselves from dreaming because we can't imagine our dream actually manifesting.

We're not talking about a dream manifesting. We're just talking about seeing our dream in "The Great Unmanifested" (which is, in Truth, the only place a dream can EVER be, because the physical world is nothing more than a mirror.)

So, having found one of your dreams in "The Great Unmanifested," hold the Vision of it. I differentiate holding the Vision from holding the Thought, because the Vision is the Truth while the Thought is not. This is a very important distinction to make.

The Vision of your dream is the Truth because it MUST exist, it already exists, in "The Great Unmanifested" (which is the only place anything can ever exist...in your experience). There's no way it could not be there. No matter what you believe about it, no matter how uncomfortable you feel, no matter how many doubts you have, the dream is still there.

Any thoughts you might have about the dream not being there, not being achievable or not being possible are just that. Thoughts. These thoughts may limit your ability to see the dream, but they do not in any way change the fact that the dream is, always was, and always will be, in "The Great Unmanifested."

The existence of your dream is UNAFFECTED by any limiting thoughts you might have. It's just there. Eternal. Unchanging. Ever-possible. (Like you!).

So, holding that Vision, knowing that it's there no matter what, notice the thoughts that arise. Especially notice the "negative" thoughts that arise when you hold the vision of what you see, what you wish to experience (and already are experiencing just from the fact that you're holding the vision).

Don't push these "negative" thoughts away! Look right at them. Have them. Allow them, WHILE HOLDING THE VISION.

These "protective" thoughts are the Inner Child part of holding a Vision. Remember that the Inner Child is only a memory, so it has its experience in the exact place that you have yours, in your thoughts and sensations. So YOU are experiencing these "protective" thoughts while holding the Vision of the dream you wish to hold.

This is where so many methods of new thought and positive thinking go wrong. They tell you that if you think a "negative" thought it will come true. NONSENSE. If you hold the VISION of a negative thought, if you focus on it in the "Great Unmanifested," then that is what you will EXPERIENCE. But if you simply allow yourself to think the "negative" thoughts that come up when you take on the Vision you wish to hold, what you're doing is, at last, being with your Inner Child instead of ignoring it or pushing it away. You MUST do this or you will not be able to hold the Vision. If you refuse to recognize and experience your Inner Child's thoughts (and that's what they are, just thoughts), your Inner Child will subconsciously present you with circumstances that are NOT the dream so that you can experience what the Inner Child is experiencing. Save the Inner Child the trouble. Just experience what the Inner Child is experiencing whenever it comes up.

So, you are now holding the Vision of the dream you wish to hold, and at the same time you are experiencing the thoughts of why you can't have the dream.

Now notice the sensations you experience when you are holding the Vision and thinking the thoughts of why you can't have the Vision. Some of these sensations may be comfortable. Especially look for the ones that are "uncomfortable," and be willing to have them.

Here's the thing about those "uncomfortable" sensations. You have taken on all your "protective" thoughts in order to get away from the "uncomfortable" sensations that arise when you dare to hold the Vision of your dream. When you can be with the "uncomfortable" sensations that come up when you hold your vision in mind, you will not have to jump to the "protective" thoughts. More accurately, you will probably see yourself jumping to the "protective" thoughts, and instead of staying with them, you will simply move yourself back to your "uncomfortable" sensations, and thus stay with your Vision rather than your "protective" thoughts."

So, holding a dream is going to "The Great Unmanifested," finding your dream, which MUST be there, holding the dream as a Vision of the Truth that it's there, thinking the thoughts of why you can't have the dream if they come up, and feeling any "uncomfortable" sensations that arise.

Next, remember that the thoughts and sensations are the Inner Child's thoughts and sensations. They are going on in your world of experience, but they have no power to diminish or block or destroy the dream. They're just there.

Since they are the Inner Child, one thing I like to recommend is that you wrap them in a baby blanket. So you are now holding a Vision of a dream while walking around with a child, wrapped in a baby blanket, who has "uncomfortable" sensations and "protective" thoughts.

You can do that!

You are now actually EXPERIENCING the dream.

Just stay there. There's nothing else to do. Nothing to do to "Make it happen." It's happening in the only place it can ever happen. And the mixed experience you're having is making the separate Inner Child and your present Adult one integrated Being, each aware of and accepting the other.

The question that often gets asked at this point is, "Well, what do I do now?"

The answer is not "Strive, work, target, push." The answer is:

LOOK IN THE MIRROR!

"Any thoughts you might have about the dream not being there, not being achievable or not being possible are just that. Thoughts."

CHAPTER 33

Manifestation As The Mirror of Your Dream

If you are holding the Vision of the dream, you will see the dream in the "mirror of the world." NO MATTER WHAT IS THERE.

If you are holding a "protective" thought, you will see the "protective" thought in the world. NO MATTER WHAT IS THERE.

Since all the work we ever do MUST be on the inside, do not try to make anything happen in the mirror. Rather, use it to see what's happening in you.

So, see what you see in the world. If it's not what you want, notice your thoughts and sensations. Then go back to your Vision of what you DO want. The discomfort may escalate. Allow whatever thoughts and sensations that may come up to arise and be there.

Align yourself to holding the Vision while being with whatever "uncomfortable" thoughts and sensations arise.

Then look back in the "mirror of the world" and see what you see now.

Manifesting a dream is the process of just doing this over and over and over.

Interestingly enough, when you KNOW you have the Vision and that it's here in the only place it can ever be here, inside of you, you may not even need to see the manifestation. But EVERYTHING you see in the world will be the dream.

So, whenever you have a "problem," whenever you have a dream, go to the Vision, not to the outside world, hold the Vision and experience the thoughts and sensations that come up when you do. That's it. What to do will come to you automatically. Things will appear to happen TO you. Just stay there, in the EXPERIENCE of the Vision and all that this entails, and watch what unfolds next.

> "Do not try to make anything happen in the mirror. Rather, use it to see what's happening in you."

CHAPTER 34
Taking Steps Toward Your Vision

In many New Thought disciplines we hear things like, "You have to hold the Vision, but you also have to move your feet."

In Thought Exchange we say, "When you are truly holding the Vision, your feet move." Naturally. By themselves. Ideas pop into your head. Calls and opportunities come in and you field them inside of the Vision you're holding. Automatically. Without "thinking."

The only reason we would not move (or not move in the way we want to move) is because we have let go of the Vision due to "uncomfortable" sensations that come up when we hold the Vision. The only way to get away from those "uncomfortable" sensations is to take on "protective" ("negative") thoughts. Living inside those "negative" thoughts instead of the Vision we wanted to take on, we take actions (or more accurately actions take themselves) based on those "protective" thoughts.

If we are "forcing" ourselves to take action or thinking we have to make ourselves do something to make something happen, the implication is that that something is not here right now. In short, we are thinking we are missing something and we have to do something to get it. But of course, the mirror of the world MUST reflect what we're thinking.

When we have taken on "protective" ("negative") thoughts, and are acting (or not acting) because of them, we will know it immediately because we will see those "negative" thoughts reflected in the mirror of the physical world in the form of our not seeing what it is we want to see.

When we see this, it is not a sign for us to DO more (which could only be coming out of more thoughts of lack and thus could only result in our seeing more lack). Rather it is a sign for us to go back to the Vision and just stay there.

Of course, when we go back to the Vision, we will automatically be presented with things to DO. Those things to DO may come with "uncomfortable" sensations and "protective" ("negative") thoughts. The more we do, the more chance we have of those thoughts arising.

Earlier, we talked about how if you want to hold a Vision, you have to be willing to experience any "uncomfortable" sensations and "negative" thoughts that come with it.

I hope you're now seeing that if you allow yourself to do things toward the manifestation of that Vision (which can only happen if you continue to hold the Vision) your "uncomfortable" and "protective" thoughts will most likely escalate.

This is where the BASIC SKILL of being able to simply be with "problems," "uncomfortable" sensations and "negative" thoughts comes in.

YOUR CAPACITY TO MOVE TOWARD YOUR GOAL IS DIRECTLY RELATED TO YOUR CAPACITY TO HOLD YOUR VISION AND TAKE ACTION TOWARD IT WHILE FEELING INCREASINGLY UNCOMFORTABLE.

And your capacity to reach and stay with your goal is determined by your capacity to be that uncomfortable!

CHAPTER 35

"Solving" Your "Problems"

This is a technique that I often use in corporate situations, but it applies just as well to anything personal we're going through.

Often, corporations call me in to "solve" problems. I do so by creating the following chart.

1	2	3	4	5
PROBLEM YOU SEE IN THE "OUTSIDE" WORLD	THOUGHT OF YOURS THAT THE PROBLEM IS REFLECTING	THOUGHT YOU'D LIKE TO TAKE ON (What you'd like to see in the world)	UNCOMFORTABLE SENSATIONS THAT ARISE WHEN YOU TAKE ON THIS NEW THOUGHT	NEGATIVE THOUGHTS THAT ARISE WHEN YOU TAKE ON THIS NEW THOUGHT

STEP 1: Pick a "Problem"

I start the session by asking people to list all the "problems" they see in the corporation. So let's say the first "problem" that comes up is, "There's not enough money to do the things we want to do."

We put that in column 1.

1	2	3	4	5
PROBLEM YOU SEE IN THE "OUTSIDE" WORLD	THOUGHT OF YOURS THAT THE PROBLEM IS REFLECTING	THOUGHT YOU'D LIKE TO TAKE ON (What you'd like to see in the world)	UNCOMFORTABLE SENSATIONS THAT ARISE WHEN YOU TAKE ON THIS NEW THOUGHT	NEGATIVE THOUGHTS THAT ARISE WHEN YOU TAKE ON THIS NEW THOUGHT
NOT ENOUGH MONEY				

STEP 2: When you "look at" this "problem" in the world, what thought of yours do you see?

As we discussed earlier in the book, it can be tricky to answer this question. We're not saying that your "negative" thinking is causing the "problem." We're simply asking you to notice the thought that comes to mind when you "see" the "problem" in front of you, in the "mirror" of the physical world.

So, as in the dating example I gave early in the book, when someone turns you down for a date, you must look at what you're thinking. Are you thinking, "I'm worthless?" Are you thinking, "Nobody would ever go out with me?"

This is what we're looking for here.

So, looking at the "problem" of "There is not enough money," we would most likely be thinking something like, "There's not enough money" if that's what we're seeing in front of us.

Here's the thing. It looks and feels like the condition is causing the thought, and the way we discover the thought we're thinking is to use the mirror of the world to show it to us. But now that we see what our thought is, we're going to work with our thought, assuming our thought is causing our experience of the condition, since we know that the world is just a mirror, and as such is not causative.

So we put the thought of ours that we're seeing in the second column.

1	2	3	4	5
PROBLEM YOU SEE IN THE "OUTSIDE" WORLD	THOUGHT OF YOURS THAT THE PROBLEM IS REFLECTING	THOUGHT YOU'D LIKE TO TAKE ON (What you'd like to see in the world)	UNCOMFORTABLE SENSATIONS THAT ARISE WHEN YOU TAKE ON THIS NEW THOUGHT	NEGATIVE THOUGHTS THAT ARISE WHEN YOU TAKE ON THIS NEW THOUGHT
NOT ENOUGH MONEY	THERE IS NOT ENOUGH MONEY			

Step 3: What thought would you like to exchange this thought for which might reflect as the result you want to see in the physical world?

The place we look for this thought is in "The Great Unmanifested," the invisible world of infinite possibilities that exists in our imagination. Every possible thought is there. Every possible solution is there. There is nothing that cannot be there. And since, as I repeatedly say throughout this book (because this is often hard for us to remember in a world that appears to be so physically real), the invisible world of experience is the ONLY place where ANYTHING can take place for us, so this is the place we want to look to find the thought we want to take on.

You don't have to believe the thought you take on. You don't have to feel comfortable taking it on. In fact, most probably you won't feel comfortable. You just have to know it's there (it MUST be) and find it.

So, looking at the thought we would like to hold, it would probably be something like, "Infinite money is available right now."

1	2	3	4	5
PROBLEM YOU SEE IN THE "OUTSIDE" WORLD	THOUGHT OF YOURS THAT THE PROBLEM IS REFLECTING	THOUGHT YOU'D LIKE TO TAKE ON (What you'd like to see in the world)	UNCOMFORTABLE SENSATIONS THAT ARISE WHEN YOU TAKE ON THIS NEW THOUGHT	NEGATIVE THOUGHTS THAT ARISE WHEN YOU TAKE ON THIS NEW THOUGHT
NOT ENOUGH MONEY	THERE IS NOT ENOUGH MONEY	INFINITE MONEY IS AVAILABLE RIGHT NOW		

Step 4: What "uncomfortable" sensations arise when you take on the thought you want to take on?

By taking on the thought you want to take on, you've taken on a Vision. This thought MUST be true in "The Great Unmanifested." There is nothing that cannot be found there. (Remember doing the twist on the rings of Saturn?)

But when you take it on, you will most likely feel "uncomfortable" sensations. This is most likely the reason you haven't taken on this thought (and thus are not seeing it appearing in the "mirror" of the world in front of you.)

So notice any "uncomfortable" sensations you experience when you take on this thought, and simply have them. Don't try to change them, don't run from them, don't try to do anything to get rid of them. Just have them.

(Some people don't notice any "uncomfortable" sensations. If that's you, don't worry about it. Just skip to Step 5, and you'll most likely feel them after doing that step.)

The sensations you experience when you hold the thought you want to hold might be something like:

1	2	3	4	5
PROBLEM YOU SEE IN THE "OUTSIDE" WORLD	THOUGHT OF YOURS THAT THE PROBLEM IS REFLECTING	THOUGHT YOU'D LIKE TO TAKE ON (What you'd like to see in the world)	UNCOMFORTABLE SENSATIONS THAT ARISE WHEN YOU TAKE ON THIS NEW THOUGHT	NEGATIVE THOUGHTS THAT ARISE WHEN YOU TAKE ON THIS NEW THOUGHT
NOT ENOUGH MONEY	THERE IS NOT ENOUGH MONEY	INFINITE MONEY IS AVAILABLE RIGHT NOW	TIGHT THROAT POUNDING HEART SHORT BREATH QUEASY STOMACH TINGLING HANDS	

Step 5: What "negative" or "protective" thoughts do you notice when you DARE to take on the vision of what you want to see in the world?

Usually, as soon as you take on a thought like "There is infinite money available right now," when what you're seeing before you is "not enough money," your mind comes up with thoughts about why you can't have money; why the thought you wish to hold is not true; why you're a fool to think it is true or even possible.

We bring these "protective" thoughts into play in order to avoid the "uncomfortable" sensations that arise when we DARE to take on the "dangerous" thought that there's enough money when we don't see enough money before us.

Often we are aware of having "uncomfortable" sensations when we take on the Vision we want to take on, but sometimes people are so happy with the thought that they can have what they want that they profess to feel no "uncomfortable" sensations, but rather, just warmth or fullness or joyful tingling.

When this happens we skip step 4 and go right to step 5. Invariably, if the thought we want to hold is not what we're seeing, we will immediately be aware of all the thoughts of why we can't have what we want when we think the thought of what we DO want.

Once you have these "negative" thoughts you will almost certainly become aware of discomfort. So what I'm saying is, it doesn't matter whether you do Step 4 or Step 5 first. It's different for each of us. The end result will be that when you hold your Vision, if it's a Vision you have not been able to hold or which has not appeared in the "mirror" of the world before you, you will experience "uncomfortable" sensations AND "negative" thoughts.

So, let's assume you've done Step 4 and now do Step 5. If you felt nothing on Step 4, go back to it after you do Step 5.

"Protective" thoughts you might notice when you dare to take on the Vision that "Infinite money is available right now" might be:

1	2	3	4	5
PROBLEM YOU SEE IN THE "OUTSIDE" WORLD	THOUGHT OF YOURS THAT THE PROBLEM IS REFLECTING	THOUGHT YOU'D LIKE TO TAKE ON (What you'd like to see in the world)	UNCOMFORTABLE SENSATIONS THAT ARISE WHEN YOU TAKE ON THIS NEW THOUGHT	NEGATIVE THOUGHTS THAT ARISE WHEN YOU TAKE ON THIS NEW THOUGHT
NOT ENOUGH MONEY	THERE IS NOT ENOUGH MONEY	INFINITE MONEY IS AVAILABLE RIGHT NOW	TIGHT THROAT POUNDING HEART SHORT BREATH QUEASY STOMACH TINGLING HANDS	I'M NOT ALLOWED TO HAVE MONEY MONEY IS SCARCE WHAT I DO IS NOT VALUABLE ETC.

So, you now have a chart that consists of:

1. THE "PROBLEM" YOU'RE SEEING IN THE WORLD

2. THE THOUGHT YOU'RE HOLDING THAT IS BEING REFLECTED TO YOU BY THAT "PROBLEM"

3. WHAT YOU WOULD LIKE TO SEE IN THE WORLD (THE THOUGHT YOU'D LIKE TO HOLD)

4. THE "UNCOMFORTABLE" SENSATIONS THAT COME WITH HOLDING THE THOUGHT (VISION) THAT YOU'D LIKE TO HOLD

5. THE "NEGATIVE" OR "PROTECTIVE" THOUGHTS THAT COME WITH THE THOUGHT (VISION) YOU'D LIKE TO HOLD

You now have Choices. But they each come with challenges.

If you wish to hold the Vision of there being infinite money, you have to be able to be with the "uncomfortable" sensations and "protective" ("negative") thoughts that the Vision produces.

If you're unwilling to be with the "uncomfortable" sensations, you will jump away from them to one of your "protective" thoughts (any one will do) and begin to hold that thought as your Vision, the result of which will be that you will see the reflection of the Vision you're holding in the world before you. In this case, you will see "not enough money."

This can be a little convoluted to follow, but I think it will be clearer when you see it in chart form.

1	2	3	4	5
PROBLEM YOU SEE IN THE "OUTSIDE" WORLD	THOUGHT OF YOURS THAT THE PROBLEM IS REFLECTING	THOUGHT YOU'D LIKE TO TAKE ON (What you'd like to see in the world)	UNCOMFORTABLE SENSATIONS THAT ARISE WHEN YOU TAKE ON THIS NEW THOUGHT	NEGATIVE THOUGHTS THAT ARISE WHEN YOU TAKE ON THIS NEW THOUGHT
NOT ENOUGH MONEY	THERE IS NOT ENOUGH MONEY	INFINITE MONEY IS AVAILABLE RIGHT NOW	TIGHT THROAT POUNDING HEART SHORT BREATH QUEASY STOMACH TINGLING HANDS	I'M NOT ALLOWED TO HAVE MONEY MONEY IS SCARCE WHAT I DO IS NOT VALUABLE ETC.

The thought (Vision) you wish to hold, "Infinite Money is Available Right Now" comes with the "uncomfortable" sensations and "protective" ("negative") thoughts in the next two columns. If you want to hold the Vision in the third column, you can only do so by being willing to have the "uncomfortable" sensations and "protective" ("negative") thoughts in columns 4 and 5.

So, you hold your Vision and notice that you have "uncomfortable" sensations and "protective" thoughts when you hold it. Remember, you are the Observer, Noticer, Experiencer of these sensations and thoughts. They have no power to hurt or diminish you in any way. They just feel "uncomfortable." Even calling them "uncomfortable" is a judgment, a thought about the sensations. Actually, they just feel as they feel.

The interesting thing about this is that, since, as you will remember, the ONLY place things can be experienced by us is in the invisible world of our experience, what you are experiencing now IS the experience of the dream coming true. In other words, when you actually see unlimited money in the world, your experience will be EXACTLY what it is now. You will see the Vision of the unlimited money, you will feel "uncomfortable," and you will have thoughts of why you can't have it!

People do careers, strive for success, seek out relationships because they think that by having these things they will get away from their discomfort and "negative" thinking. But in fact, you can only have these things when you can tolerate this discomfort and these "protective" thoughts, because they COME WITH IT!

If this seems discouraging, remember that what you're really doing by being with all this discomfort is being with your Inner Child, who has been "uncomfortable" all alone up to this point and has been trying to get your attention. So your ability to heal your life and become whole is directly related to your being able to be with the "uncomfortable" sensations and "negative" thoughts that arise when you live your Vision and see your dreams manifest.

So, when you're holding your Vision, when you're having trouble being with your "uncomfortable" sensations, you will notice "protective" ("negative") thoughts arising. If you can just notice these "protective" thoughts, you can direct yourself back to your sensations and be with them.

There are two basic ways to direct yourself back to your sensations. They are slightly different, but produce the same result of being able to stay with the Vision you wish to hold.

The first is to Exchange the "protective" thought you've taken on for the "positive" thought you wish to hold. This will immediately put you back in the "uncomfortable" sensation that you tried to avoid by taking on the "protective" thought.

The second is to go directly back to the "uncomfortable" sensation. Using this method, you think the thought you wish to think (your Vision), you experience an "uncomfortable" sensation, you notice you've taken on a "protective" thought, and you move your attention back to the "uncomfortable" sensation. When you can tolerate being with the "uncomfortable" sensation as a meaningless sensation that, because of your Inner Child's history, comes with the "positive" thought you're holding, there is no reason to reach for a "protective" thought, because you no longer need the "protection" your Inner Child needed. You have the ability to experience the sensation.

If, on the other hand, you think you can't be with your "uncomfortable" sensations, you will grab one of the "protective" thoughts, stay with it, and the "protective" thought will become your Vision, rather than the Vision you wished to take on.

When you do that, you are now thinking a thought similar to the one you discovered you were thinking in column 2 (the column in which we see the thought we're holding that's being reflected as the "problem" we see in the world). And the reflection of that thought will be seen in the world as the original "problem" that you listed in column 1.

The chart would look like this:

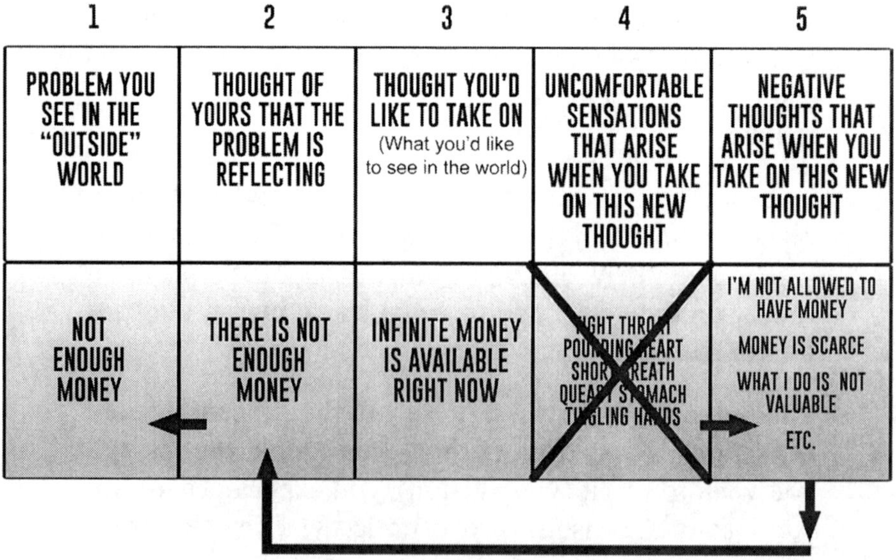

1	2	3	4	5
PROBLEM YOU SEE IN THE "OUTSIDE" WORLD	THOUGHT OF YOURS THAT THE PROBLEM IS REFLECTING	THOUGHT YOU'D LIKE TO TAKE ON (What you'd like to see in the world)	UNCOMFORTABLE SENSATIONS THAT ARISE WHEN YOU TAKE ON THIS NEW THOUGHT	NEGATIVE THOUGHTS THAT ARISE WHEN YOU TAKE ON THIS NEW THOUGHT
NOT ENOUGH MONEY	THERE IS NOT ENOUGH MONEY	INFINITE MONEY IS AVAILABLE RIGHT NOW	~~TIGHT THROAT POUNDING HEART SHORT BREATH QUEASY STOMACH TINGLING HANDS~~	I'M NOT ALLOWED TO HAVE MONEY MONEY IS SCARCE WHAT I DO IS NOT VALUABLE ETC.

The process of dealing with "Problems" is usually a combination of all of the above scenarios. You pick a "problem," you see the thought you're holding, you exchange the thought for a Vision you wish to hold, and you experience the "uncomfortable" sensations and "negative" thoughts that go with the Vision. At some point you think you can't experience the discomfort so you take on one of the "protective" thoughts and find yourself back thinking the thought you were thinking in column 2, which is revealed to you by the fact that you see the column 1 "Problem" again, at which point you notice your thought, exchange it, and start over again.

Gradually, as you do this, you are increasing your ability to hold the Vision in column 3 by staying with the discomfort it brings up and NOTICING the "protective" thoughts, rather than TAKING THEM ON to get away from the "discomfort." And when you can do this, what you see in the world is a direct reflection of the Vision you're holding.

Usually, when I do corporate events, we end up with a list of these issues. I then cut out columns 3 and 4 and give it to each event participant as a bookmark.

So in this case, it would look like this:

THE VISION	COMES WITH
INFINITE MONEY IS AVAILABLE TO ME RIGHT NOW	TIGHT THROAT POUNDING HEART SHORT BREATH QUEASY STOMACH TINGLING HANDS

They leave this on their desk to remind themselves that when they take on the thought on the left, they may very well feel the sensations on the right. After a while, like the marathon runner, like the marine, like the ballet dancer, they begin to accept that these sensations just come with the thought they want to hold, and they become used to them and think nothing of them. After a while, they often develop the understanding that when they have the “uncomfortable” sensations, it’s a sign that they’re on the right track.

> “If you wish to hold a Vision,
> you have to be able to be with
> the “uncomfortable” sensations
> and and “protective” (“negative”)
> thoughts that the Vision
> produces.”

CHAPTER 36

"Solving" ALL Your "Problems"

So, if you follow what we've been working with in the last chapter, any "problem" we could ever have can not only be solved, but IS already solved in the only place we can ever experience a "problem." In the invisible world of our experience.

A "problem" is nothing more than a thought of limitation which is thought inside of the Unlimited Invisible world of Infinite Possibilities. The "solution" to that "problem" also ALWAYS exists right alongside the "problem."

For example:

Let's say that your "problem" is that there is not enough money. As we said above, a "problem" can only be experienced as a thought, so your "problem" is that you have the thought that there's not enough money, and thus that's what you're seeing and acting upon.

If you look in "The Great Unmanifested" (The Invisible World of Infinite Possible Experience) there is, of course, unlimited money.

You are choosing not to see that. Why would that be?

Well, if we go back to the basic premise of Thought Exchange, we understand that for reasons related to your past, the thought that "Money is Unlimited" brings up "uncomfortable" sensations. Somehow, when you dared to believe that abundance or care or the help you needed was available, you got hurt or deeply disappointed. And you experienced that disappointment as "uncomfortable" or "painful" sensations.

To get away from those "uncomfortable" sensations, (by preventing yourself from ever again thinking the "positive" thought that originally brought them on) you took on a "protective" thought, which in this case would be, "There's not enough money." You are now living within that thought, so the part of the Invisible World of Infinite Possibilities that you are experiencing is "There's not enough money."

Here is a chart that illustrates what's going on.

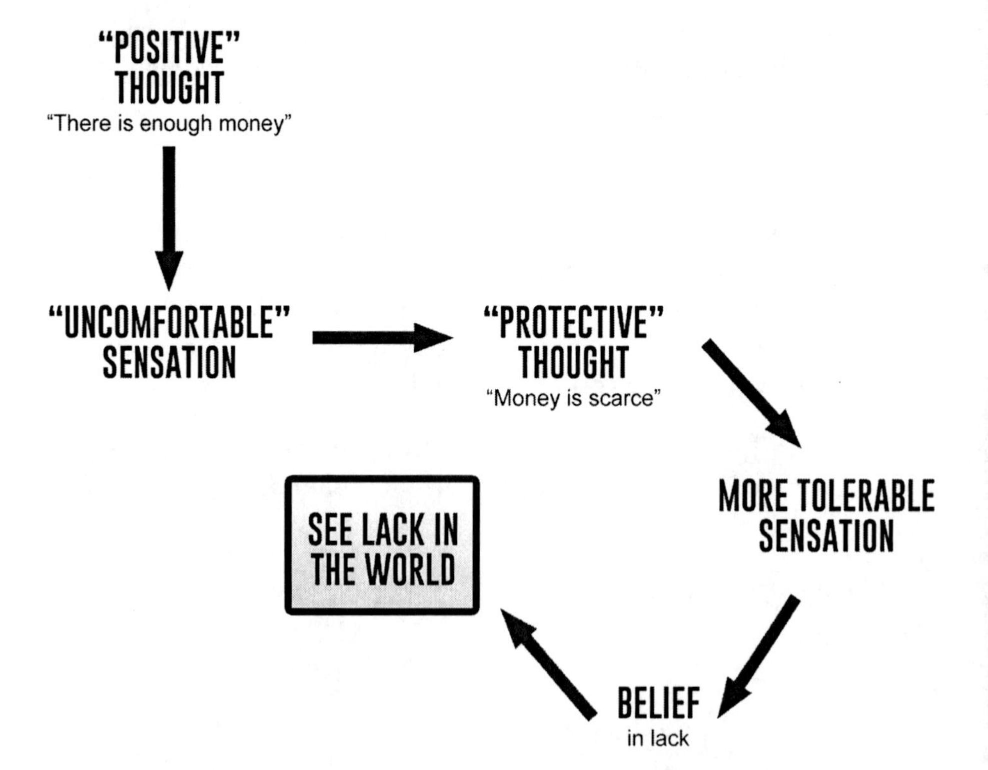

I think it's clear that what you've been doing is living in the "protective" thought, "There is not enough money" so that's what you're seeing.

In order to get out of that, all you would have to do is exchange the "protective" thought "There is not enough money" for the "positive" thought "There is enough money."

Since EVERY possible thought exists in "The Great Unmanifested" invisible world of unlimited possibility, the "solution" to EVERY "problem" MUST exist. All you have to do is take ANY "problem" ("protective" thought) into "The Great Unmanifested," find the thought you want to hold, and exchange your "protective" thought for the new thought.

Simple enough, and actually what almost any "Positive Thinking" New Thought method will tell you to do.

However, we know that the challenge in doing that is that when you "solve" your "problem" by taking on the "positive" thought, you will immediately be thrust into the "uncomfortable" sensations you've been trying to avoid by taking on the "negative" thought.

So the ONLY solution to this, the ONLY way to keep ourselves from going around and around an endlessly frustrating circle, is to be able to EXPERIENCE the "uncomfortable" sensations that come with the "positive" thought.

The interesting thing is this. Each time we "solve" a "problem" by looking in "The Great Unmanifested" and finding the solution, we are essentially taking on another "positive" thought. And as we know, "positive" thoughts that came with baggage create "uncomfortable" sensations.

So, strangely enough, in many cases, the more "problems" we solve, the more "uncomfortable" we get.

This realization gives us insight into why we create "problems" in the first place.

WE CREATE "PROBLEMS" TO AVOID "UNCOMFORTABLE" SENSATIONS

Knowing this, it would naturally follow that

WHEN WE SOLVE "PROBLEMS" THAT WE'VE CREATED, WE FEEL MORE "UNCOMFORTABLE" SENSATIONS.

In doing this work, on myself and with Thought Exchange clients, I've noticed that each time we solve a "problem," new "uncomfortable" sensations come up and we seem to create new "protective" thoughts to get away from them.

So, knowing this, let's see what the process of solving ALL our "problems" might look like.

I'll use an issue I'm having about money right now and share what goes on in me.

"POSITIVE" THOUGHT

"There is enough money"

"UNCOMFORTABLE" SENSATION

Foggy head
Sinking feeling in my stomach
"Weakness" in my legs

"PROTECTIVE" THOUGHT

"Money is scarce"

SOLUTION IN "THE GREAT UNMANIFESTED"

I exchange, "Money is scarce" for
"It is a fact that money is infinitely available"

"PROTECTIVE" THOUGHT

"The world is against me"

SOLUTION IN "THE GREAT UNMANIFESTED"

I go into the "Great Unmanifested" and find the possibility that there are people who are for me

"PROTECTIVE" THOUGHT

"I'm not allowed to have money"

SOLUTION IN "THE GREAT UNMANIFESTED"

I go into the "Great Unmanifested" and find the thought "I am allowed to have money"

"PROTECTIVE" THOUGHT

"Even if I had money, I'm too old" (Interestingly enough, I've had that thought from time to time even when I was 18, but NOW , I think I'm REALLY too OLD.)

SOLUTION IN "THE GREAT UNMANIFESTED"

I go into the "Great Unmanifested" and find the thought ""There is only NOW."

"PROTECTIVE" THOUGHT

"I'm going to die someday so what's the point of even trying."

SOLUTION IN "THE GREAT UNMANIFESTED"

We don't know what death is or what death means so that might not be a bad thing.

"PROTECTIVE" THOUGHT

(on and on)

I hope this makes it clear that ANY" "problem" ("protective" thought) can be immediately solved by going into "The Great Unmanifested" and finding the thought that is the solution to the "problem."

Since the thought of the solution will lead to more "uncomfortable" sensations and "protective" thoughts, it could be said that ANY "problem" can be solved as long as we are willing to be with the "uncomfortable" sensations and "protective" thoughts that come with our holding the thought of the solution.

From seeing this, can you take the leap of seeing that ALL of our "problems" are ALREADY solved, because the solution to the "protective" thought ALREADY and ALWAYS exists in the "Great Unmanifested?"

So now we can see why we create "problems" and don't want to solve them.

WE CREATE "PROBLEMS" TO AVOID DISCOMFORT.

WHEN WE SOLVE "PROBLEMS," WE FEEL DISCOMFORT.

So, you can solve all your "problems" as long as you're willing to FEEL YOUR SENSATIONS!!!!!!!!!!!

CHAPTER 37
You and Your Inner Child, Together at Last!

As I said earlier in this book, one of the big misconceptions in New Thought is that when you get what you want you will feel good. As we've discovered, when you get what you want (by holding the thought you want to hold) you will feel WHATEVER sensations come with holding that thought, and notice WHATEVER "protective" thoughts arise when you experience those sensations.

The same is true for "problems." Most of us live our lives thinking that if we solve our "problems" we will feel comfortable. And yet, as we experienced in the previous chapter, the more "problems" we solve (by knowing that the solution already is here, in "The Great Unmanifested") the more "uncomfortable" sensations arise and the more new "protective" thoughts we take on.

The process we discussed in the last chapter demonstrates that any "protective" thought ("problem") is already solved. Even though we may always notice "protective" thoughts (since there is always the possibility that they will arise in one form or another whenever we take on the thought we want to hold and experience "uncomfortable" sensations that come with that thought), we KNOW that the "solution" already exists in "The Great

Unmanifested" in the form of another one of the INFINITE possible thoughts that are ALWAYS there.

So, the more "problems" we solve, the more we are left with the sensations that arise when we are thinking the thoughts we wish to think. Were we to solve ALL our "problems" (which is a paradox since, on the one hand, "problems" will ALWAYS arise in the form of "protective" thoughts we take on when we experience "uncomfortable" sensations, and on the other hand, EVERY "problem" represented by these "protective" thoughts is already solved) what we would be left with is all the sensations, "comfortable" and "uncomfortable," that we were creating the problems to try to avoid!!!!

Another way of putting this is:

WHEN ALL OUR "PROBLEMS" ARE SOLVED, WHAT WE ARE LEFT WITH IS THE SENSATIONS OF OUR INNER CHILD THAT WE HAVE BEEN TRYING TO AVOID BY HAVING "PROBLEMS."

So the purpose of "solving" our problems is not to get away from our pain, but rather to connect to the pain of the Inner Child. To be with the Inner Child. To feel directly what the Inner Child felt.

When we can do this, we have, at last, gone back and gotten the Inner Child. The Inner Child is seen and heard and felt as it never was before. And we become integrated. We have the memory of the pain of our past, but it is held by an adult who is capable of feeling it. And as adults we can be with these sensations and do anything we want to do, think anything we want to think, and be anything we want to be.

All we have to do is be with our Inner Child's sensations, and we are whole and free!

This, of course, is easier said than done. When we are doing this, we find ourselves dealing with parts of ourselves that we've spent our entire lives running away from.

In the next section, I'm going to go into great detail about who our Inner Child is, what our Inner Child wants and needs, and how we can be with our Inner Child and experience wholeness, completeness and freedom by doing so.

"All we have to do is be with our Inner Child's sensations, and we are whole and free! This, of course, is easier said than done."

PART VII
UNDERSTANDING THE INNER CHILD

CHAPTER 38
How The Inner Child Works

For those of us who have spent the majority of our lifetime running from our Inner Child, trying to shut it up, trying to fix it, trying to overcome it, our encounters with the Inner Child can be puzzling, counter-intuitive, upsetting, frightening and surprising.

In this section, I offer insights into how the Inner Child thinks, how the Inner Child works, what the Inner Child needs, how the Inner Child goes about trying to get its needs met, and what we can do to meet those needs.

Whatever parts of the Inner Child have been disowned are parts of the "World of Infinite Possible Experience" that we have disowned. for ourselves. Our recognition and mirroring of the Inner Child's thoughts and sensations are crucial to our healing, our wholeness and our ultimate happiness in the largest sense of the word.

Suddenly, the impossible becomes possible, what we thought we couldn't have we find we already have, and our internal world, especially the "uncomfortable" sensations and "negative" thoughts we have not been able to come to terms with, not only make perfect sense, but, rather than stopping us, serve to move us forward.

As you will see when you read through this section, understanding and being with the Inner Child is more than just taking care of past damage. As you deepen your understanding and acceptance, you not only reclaim your past and open up your future (both of which take place only in your experience in the present) but you open the path to Love, Forgiveness, Peace and indeed to God or whatever you may call that Higher Power.

So read on, and meet, understand and grow to love your Inner Child.

IT'S THE "POSITIVE" THOUGHTS THAT SCARE THE INNER CHILD

Contrary to popular belief, it is not our "negative" thoughts that scare us. It is the "positive" thoughts that scare us. Not all of them, of course. Just the ones that became associated with painful sensations in our childhoods.

I heard a wonderful story from a grandmother on the West Coast that I think illustrates this well.

This grandmother's four-year-old granddaughter was visiting and was in the bathroom, standing up on the toilet seat. This particular toilet was quite high, and the granddaughter proudly stood on it and proclaimed, "There is no toilet that is too high for me!" Her grandmother applauded her and said, "You're right!" The little girl then jumped down from the toilet, threw her arms around herself and said, "I just love myself!" The grandmother smiled, threw her arms around her granddaughter and said, "I love you, too!"

This grandmother was allowing her granddaughter to express a positive thought, even if that thought seemed self-aggrandizing or had some bragging in it.

But imagine if the grandmother had said, "Get down from there before you hurt yourself!" Or, "Listen Miss Full-of-Yourself. Who do you think you are?" Or perhaps gave her a smack and said, "Go to your room until you learn not to show off!"

The child would have now associated pain with something that she regarded as "positive." In an effort to get away from that "uncomfortable" sensation, since the child is too dependent to refute the comment, and since the child actually, on some level, believes the comment because, after all, it came from her grandmother, the child would develop a strategy to make sure that she would never feel that "uncomfortable" sensation again.

And since the "cause" of that sensation was that she dared to have a "positive" thought about herself, she would try to prevent that sensation from ever happening again by taking on "protective" thoughts like, "I have to be careful; I'm not such hot stuff; I shouldn't brag; Being too confident will get me in trouble."

Any time she'd think a thought in the future that resembled the confident thought for which she was punished, she might experience the same "uncomfortable" sensations she experienced when she was originally punished.

THE INNER CHILD IS LIVING IN THE PAST (And Always Will Be)

When thinking of the Inner Child, people often get confused between the present and the past. They think that the object is to let the Inner Child know that it is safe now because what happened to it is not happening now. But to the Inner Child, it doesn't matter at all if it's safe NOW, because it wasn't safe THEN! And the Inner Child is living in THEN.

The reason for this is that what happened to the Inner Child happened, it will always have happened, it can never not have happened, and there's nothing that can be done to make it not have happened.

The Inner Child felt painful sensations when it had a specific "positive" thought, and the Inner Child will experience those sensations every time that thought comes up. The Inner Child may be living in the then, but it's living in the same body in which we are living now. What it feels, we feel.

No amount of logic, understanding, cajoling, teaching, reasoning, discipline, telling the Inner Child to get over it, correcting the Inner Child's perception, thinking positive thoughts, expressing oneself in the present, or trying to get other people to behave differently will make a bit of difference. The incident is past. It's done. A painful sensation went unseen, un-mirrored, and unrecognized in the past.

WHAT THE INNER CHILD IS WORRIED ABOUT IS NOT LIKELY HAPPENING NOW (And if it is, The Present Adult Has Different Tools to Deal With It)

The Inner Child is being experienced in the present, since that's the ONLY place it can be experienced. This means that based on the Inner Child's past experience, our present body is feeling the sensations that the Inner Child felt in the past, and our present mind is thinking the thoughts the Inner Child thought in the past.

It is VERY important to feel these sensations and think these thoughts, since this is the ONLY way in which the disowned, un-mirrored Inner Child can be contacted.

But it is EQUALLY important for us to remember that although we are experiencing EXACTLY what the Inner Child is experiencing, what the Inner Child is experiencing is related to the past and is NOT going on now.

It can be challenging to hold both these states of consciousness at the same time, but when we can do this, the Inner Child gets heard and felt and we, the adult living in the present, are free to be in the present.

HOW THE INNER CHILD BRINGS ABOUT INCIDENTS IN WHICH THE INNER ADULT CAN FEEL WHAT THE INNER CHILD FELT

As we've come to understand (see Chapter 11), the Inner Child's whole objective is to get the Inner Adult to experience the level of pain and the thoughts that the Inner Child experienced. To that end, the Inner Child will constantly be trying to generate incidents (or more accurately, the experience of incidents) in which our Inner Adult will experience what the Inner Child experienced, in hope that the Inner Adult will finally see, feel, hear and be with the Inner Child.

However, we must remember that the incidents that originally generated the Inner Child's sensations and thoughts would probably not generate those same sensations and thoughts in an adult. So the Inner Child has to generate incidents that are, to the adult, what the original incidents were to the child. And those incidents often have to be big.

Unfortunately, what we often do when these incidents are generated, is try to fight them off, rather than realizing that they have been generated by our Inner Child so that we can notice our Inner Child's thoughts and sensations. When we fight the incidents off and fail to notice the experience of the Inner Child, the Inner Child has no choice but to try to create bigger incidents.

Now, another thing we must remember is that WE DO NOT CAUSE THINGS TO HAPPEN. The only place anything "happens" is in our perception. So the Inner Child is actually trying to draw our attention to incidents that, in its perception, mirror the pain the Inner Child felt in the past, for the purpose of getting our Inner Adult to feel the exact pain and think the exact thoughts the Inner Child felt. Only in this way can The Inner Child get the mirroring that it failed to get as a child.

Recently, when something upsetting happens, I try to watch very carefully to see where I dropped a stitch, where I made a subtle choice, where I said something that supported the feeling of upset in coming about.

I've also thought back on times in my life when things seemed to be going "wrong," and can often see what it was I was unconsciously doing to contribute to that. In each case, with careful observation, I've been able to find an action that I took that supported and helped enact a "protective" thought that my Inner Child was holding.

I think it's very important to say here that when we discover that we have made an unconscious choice that has contributed to a problem or an upset, this is not something to beat ourselves up about. Many New Thought methods call these thoughts "sabotaging" or "negative," but if we can recognize that these thoughts and the actions they resulted in have been our Inner Child's way of getting our attention, we not only have compassion for them, but we are actually aware that these very thoughts and actions have been the road to healing.

Of course, this requires that we properly use these thoughts and incidents for the purpose for which the Inner Child has brought them to our attention: to recognize and be with the Inner Child, rather than to try and fix the incident or change the thoughts.

I remember, years ago, when I was single and holding the thought, "I'll never meet anyone," I used to jokingly say (though I actually believed it) that I could walk into a room with 99 people who were attracted to me and one who couldn't stand me, and immediately gravitate to the one who couldn't stand me, not noticing the 99 people who were wild about me. This was my Inner Child's "protective" thought based on years of disappointment and not getting what I wanted, especially if I asked for it.

In fact, it took me years to meet my partner, Shawn, because this thought I was holding was the way I was seeing the world. When Shawn finally "forced" his way into my life (in Truth I "allowed" him in because literally seconds before getting together with him I actually remember taking on the thought, "I deserve a partner. I'm a great guy. I would make someone a wonderful boyfriend") he confided to me that he had been attracted to me for six years. Six years! And I hadn't seen it. Not once! He told me that the moment we'd met, six years earlier, he had been drawn to me instantly and "knew" we would make great partners, although there was nothing he could do about it at the time because I was with another partner. He was in my purview all that time (even during the three years when I was no longer with my ex-partner), extremely interested in me, but I couldn't see it because the thought I was holding wouldn't allow it.

Now that I've been with Shawn for many years, when I notice a behavior in him that is upsetting to me, I've learned to notice the sensations I'm having, notice the thoughts I'm having, and then ask myself, "How does Shawn's behavior reflect a thought I am holding?" rather than "How could I change him so I won't be upset?" When I'm "upset with Shawn," I recognize that I'm not experiencing Shawn objectively, but rather, experiencing my Inner Child's experience of Shawn, based on my Inner Child's earlier experiences in life.

Strangely enough, whenever I'm with my thoughts and sensations around what "I" see in him, rather than focusing on changing him, he seems to change. We can't decide whether he actually changes or whether my perception of him changes. But it doesn't matter. I go from having a partner with whom I'm dissatisfied to a partner with whom I am extremely happy.

By going to my Inner Child's thoughts and sensations, rather than trying to change the incident or to change Shawn, I connect with my Inner Child's limited thoughts and am able to see all the other possibilities that exist in the present. Since the upsets are only going on in me, it could be said that my Inner Child is actually generating any upset I might be experiencing with Shawn, not so that I can fix Shawn, but so that I can see and be with the Inner Child. In fact, that's probably why I picked Shawn in the first place. (Or perhaps, my Inner Child picked him.)

This being the case, I've learned to almost welcome upsets (I still, of course, don't enjoy them) as opportunities to experience my Inner Child's thoughts and sensations, and by doing so re-open my experience of the infinite possibilities that exist NOW.

So, "Thank you," Inner Child, for the upsets you create so that I can see you, feel you, mirror you, incorporate you, and move through the world as an integrated, whole, limitless being.

THE INNER CHILD "CASTS" OTHERS AS PEOPLE FROM ITS PAST

My partner, Rev. Shawn Moninger, has a radio show called *The Good Show with Reverend Shawn*. Recently he had, as his guest, Nancy Napier, who has been a great mentor of mine.

Nancy is both a therapist and an Interfaith minister, so Shawn invited her on his show to talk about the subject of Transference and how it pertains to ministry.

Now, generally psychotherapists tend to define Transference as people transferring their issues onto another person, specifically the therapist, so they are seeing the therapist in light of their own personal issues instead of seeing the therapist who is actually in front of them.

But when Shawn asked Nancy for her definition of Transference, she gave an answer that I found extremely enlightening.

According to Nancy, "Transference is looking at the present and seeing the past."

This definition completely applies to our Inner Child. Since our Inner Child is actually living in the past (experiencing it in the present, since that's the only place the past now exists), the Inner Child looks at people in the present but sees them as people from the past.

So, if, years ago, our Inner Child was attacked by someone with a blue sweater on, we might find ourselves, in adulthood, sitting in front of someone wearing a blue sweater, and notice that we feel physically uncomfortable and are thinking fearful thoughts. There's very little likelihood that this person is going to attack us, but we're experiencing being attacked. This is the Inner Child looking at the present and seeing the past.

The Inner Child might cast your wife as its mother, your boss as its father, or someone making an innocuous remark as an attacker from the past. Because of its history, the Inner Child has expectations of outcomes and reactions to people that often have nothing to do with the present. No amount of explaining or rationalizing can reach the Inner Child because in the Inner Child's world (the past) there IS danger.

All we can do is notice the sensations and thoughts we're having and simply be with them, knowing and accepting that they're the Inner Child's sensations and thoughts, while interacting with the other person or circumstance as an adult. When we do this, we are not only using our adult capabilities, but we are acknowledging and mirroring the Inner Child's experience, which allows the Inner Child to be seen, heard, felt and thus taken care of.

THE INNER CHILD'S IMPOSSIBLE DOUBLE BIND

As adults, we often spend our lives trying to resolve our Inner Child's "problems" by getting something different to happen in the outside world.

But this cannot be done, because in areas where our child is stuck in the past, it's almost always because the child was in an impossible double bind. By this I mean a "damned if you do, damned if you don't" experience where no action could resolve it.

Examples of impossible double binds are thoughts like:

"If I reach for love I will be rejected."

(The child needs love, it reaches for it and gets rejected. So, to get away from the "uncomfortable" sensations that the rejection brought on, the child decides never to reach for love. This seems to keep the pain at bay, except the child never gets love, so it's in pain regardless.)

"The only way I can get love is if I feel exactly as the other person needs me to feel and give them exactly what they need."

(The child feels it has to change and suppress itself to get the other person's love. But, of course, if that's what the child is doing, the child isn't getting love. It's getting a person attaching to something the child is not, so the actual child is not getting love.)

"Things always get taken away from me in the end."

(Since there is never an end, it doesn't matter how much success we have, how much money we have, how many awards we've won, or how good our relationship is. Inside of this thought, we're ALWAYS in danger of losing everything, and in fact, the more we acquire the bigger the threat of loss.)

Interestingly enough, if we didn't have circumstances in our childhood that caused us to take on this "protective" thought, we might hold a completely different thought about things. One of my favorite sayings is, "Things always work out in the end, so if things haven't worked out...it's not the end."

NO MATTER WHAT WE DO IN THE PRESENT, WE CAN'T SOLVE THE INNER CHILD'S IMPOSSIBLE DOUBLE BIND

In our adult lives, the Inner Child's double bind is often manifested in our trying to get someone to love us while "knowing" that we cannot be loved. Or trying to make someone behave in a way that will allow us to feel good while "knowing" that we can't feel good. Or trying to get a parent to give us something that we "know" they can't give us. Or trying to get someone else to give us what our parents "should have" given us, while "knowing" that we will never be satisfied until we get it from our parents. (Actually, to be perfectly accurate, what we're really holding out for is for our parents to HAVE GIVEN us something that they didn't give us. And this, of course, is impossible, because it would mean changing the past.)

Even more frustrating is that should we, by some chance, feel that we are getting what we've been fighting for, we notice that we feel worse, because the feeling of emptiness or lack is still inside us.

As adults, we often try to become successful or rich or famous to "get away from" the emptiness the Inner Child feels, but it never works.

The reason for this is that the more we move out into the world to try to overcome the Inner Child, the more the Inner Child feels unseen and left behind. And since the Inner Child can't afford to be left behind, it will gravitate again and again to circumstances that cause us, as adults, to feel what the Inner Child felt like. Those circumstances often have to be quite dire to match, in an adult, the fear and pain the child felt.

So, for instance, let's say the Inner Child felt bereft because it didn't get a bicycle, and its bereftness was ignored or made fun of. We as adults, would not feel the same bereftness if we were refused a bicycle. In order for us to feel the same level of hopelessness and upset as the Inner Child, we might have to lose our job or be left by someone we love. So the Inner Child will unconsciously engineer situations in which those kinds of things will happen in our adult life.

The frustration for the Inner Child is that time and time again we walk into these circumstances, and instead of recognizing the sensations we're experiencing as the call of the Inner Child, we try to get rid of the sensations by trying to "resolve" the circumstance.

All this does is make the Inner Child try harder to get our attention, by generating more upsets and disasters.

THE INNER CHILD CAN'T GET WHAT IT NEEDS FROM THE OUTSIDE WORLD (It Can Only See What It Thinks)

Most of us have tried, for years, to get someone else, a partner, a lover, a parental figure to completely understand what we're going through, without success.

The reason for this is that the world is nothing more than a mirror, so rather than giving the child what it wants, the world will simply reflect back to the child what the child is thinking.

The world is not doing this on purpose. It HAS to, because, if you remember from earlier in this book, the whole world is ONLY going on inside of us in the form of thoughts and sensations that are observed by our Observer. So when we look at the world, all we can possibly see is our own thoughts.

Thus, when the child approaches the world with one of its inner double binds, the only thing that can happen is that the world will be experienced as responding within those double binds. So if someone who is holding the thought, "I can't have love" tries to get love from the world, the world's response will appear to the child to be, "You can't have love."

In relationship terms, the way it works is this. We, as adults, meet someone with whom we want to form an adult, romantic relationship. The other person feels the same way. Our Inner Child, however, begins trying to get the other person to perfectly give it everything it didn't get as a child. The other person is suddenly put in the role of having disappointed the Inner Child, withheld something from the Inner Child, etc. This is not something the other person had anything to do with, but he or she is saddled with that label. Instead of seeing an adult in front of him or her, the other person is suddenly dealing with a child. Not only that, the other person is dealing with a child from the past, so it is impossible for that child to be helped in the present. So the other person feels the impossibility of helping the partner, is saddled with a child instead of a partner, and reacts to the partner's Inner Child in the same way the partner's original caretakers did. The other person cannot help the child, rejects the child, tries to get away from the child, and the result is that the Inner Child once again goes through the rejection and impossible double bind it went through originally. To the Inner Child, this only serves to "prove" that what the Inner Child was afraid was impossible is, in fact, impossible. So the relationship breaks up, and the Inner Child goes on to try to find someone else who will fill what cannot be filled by an other.

THE INNER CHILD DOES NOT WANT TO FEEL AND DOES NOT WANT TO REMEMBER

So often, when people do Inner Child work, they try to say things to their Inner Child like, "It's OK, you can tell me." Or, "Let it out, I'm here for you."

When dealing with an Inner Child who has experienced trauma, we must understand that everything the child has set up has been for the purpose of protecting itself from painful sensations and painful memories which it is afraid it can't handle.

If the child is shut down, it's because it doesn't want to feel. If the child is in denial, it's because it doesn't want to remember. If the child is splitting into different personalities, it's because it is trying compartmentalize a pain that was too great for one child to handle.

If we try to break these defenses down too quickly, all we will meet is resistance.

A great example of this is found when we deal with what we call "multiple personalities." In the case of extreme early trauma, one of the mechanisms the Inner Child has for coping is to split into separate personalities. Each of these personalities handles a different part of the trauma, and one of the main features of this severe dissociation is that the personalities don't even know about each other. This can create great problems for the person in daily life, because they will suddenly "wake up" in a particular personality and not know how they got where they are. There are times when someone literally loses years of his or her life.

It would seem that the person suffering from this disorder would want to put him or herself back together. But the whole structure has been designed for protection, so each time you try to introduce two personalities to each other, what this means to the person is the re-experiencing of pain that they have spent their whole life trying to avoid.

So whether we're dealing with multiple personalities or early trauma that is either being acted out in the present or is being resisted through forgetting, professing to not have sensations, splitting off or other means, it is important that we not push the child, but that we simply create an environment in which the child feels safe to come to us at its own pace.

For the child to feel safe to experience more of its pain, it must be sure that it has us, the competent adult, with it every step of the way, not pushing, not controlling, not backing away, not needing it to move any faster or slower than it needs to move. Otherwise it will continue to hide and protect itself in any way it can. And by doing this, the child will continue to be alone in its struggle and healing will not take place.

WHAT THE INNER CHILD NEEDS

Something happened to the Inner Child. It had sensations that it couldn't tolerate, and there was no competent adult to be with it. The child was not misguided in its sensations. That's what the child felt. And the child wasn't misguided in the thoughts it took on. Taking on those thoughts was the only thing it could do to get away from "intolerable" situations.

The Inner Child doesn't need us to fix or change anything about it. We don't need to teach the Inner Child anything, or show it where it was misguided in its thoughts or sensations. In fact, to try and do so simply further invalidates the Inner Child's experience and drives it further into "uncomfortable" sensations, "protective" thoughts and acting out through the only body and mind it has. Ours!

We simply need to BE with the Inner Child, feeling its sensations and thinking its thoughts. This does not take away the Inner Child's sensations and thoughts, it just makes them safer to have because the Inner Child is now having them in the company of a competent adult who feels exactly what it feels.

This in itself is the healing.

As the Inner Child becomes able to feel and stay with these sensations (because they are being felt with a competent adult) the Inner Child does not have to jump away from them to "protective" thoughts, and thus the adult self can act in ways that are actually in keeping with what the adult wants, without leaving the Inner Child behind. Even when the Inner Child does jump away from the sensations with "protective" thoughts, the adult has the capacity to recognize that these are thoughts of the Inner Child from the past, think them, feel the Inner Child's sensations, be with the Inner Child and act as an adult while mirroring the Inner Child.

It would be like crossing the street with someone who's terrified to cross the street because, years ago, they got hit by a car. You can acknowledge their thoughts, acknowledge how they feel, be with them as they think and feel those things, and still take them across the street, since you know there's no danger in the present, or if there is some danger, it's something that can be navigated by you, the adult.

"HAVE" THE INNER CHILD'S THOUGHTS, DON'T "TAKE THEM ON"

As I've been saying throughout this book, the healing for the Inner Child occurs when our Inner Adult feels EXACTLY what the Inner Child feels, and thinks EXACTLY what the Inner Child is thinking.

Often, a problem occurs because as we are thinking the Inner Child's thoughts and feeling the Inner Child's sensations, which are occurring in our own mind and body, we begin to believe that those thoughts are real, for us, in the present. This doesn't work, because when we think we have become the Inner Child, the Inner Child is left without an adult to hold and mirror it.

Some people defend themselves against this possibility by essentially looking at the Inner Child from afar, saying things like, "Yes, I see how hurt you are but it's OK." Or, "I know how this feels to you, but it's not true." This REALLY doesn't work, because the Inner Child's experience is being distanced and disowned.

What we have to do is really "try on" the thoughts and think them, but always with the knowledge that we are "trying on," not "taking on," the thoughts of another person at another time (Our Inner Child).

It would be like asking a thin person to think of themselves as very fat. They know they're not very fat, but they would be taking on the thought, "I'm very fat," to experience what a "very fat" person would feel like. However, no matter how much they took on this thought, they wouldn't say, "My God, I'm fat!" because they know who they are today.

So when you are thinking the Inner Child's thoughts right along with the Inner Child, and feeling the Inner Child's sensations right along with the Inner Child, you must know that you are "having" these thoughts, not "taking them on" in the present.

THE INNER CHILD IS NOT RATIONAL

The Inner Child, like a dog or a cat, is not rational. It simply experiences sensations, has thoughts, and instinctively tries to protect itself from discomfort. Reasoning doesn't help.

I remember discussing, with my father, a painful incident from my childhood where I was physically hurt. He said, "You have to understand what was going on at the time." Now, of course, as an adult, I can understand what was going on and why what happened happened, but a child can't.

So I said to him, "Dad, suppose I'm walking down the street and there's a man on the roof of a building carrying an air conditioner. And the man has a heart attack and drops the air conditioner and it falls on my head. I can understand why it happened, and that he is not to blame, BUT I STILL GOT HIT ON THE HEAD BY AN AIR CONDITIONER! And I still got hurt. And until that pain can be dealt with directly, I will make up thoughts for the rest of my life about how I can't walk down the street, about how I always get hurt, or about imminent dangers that lurk in seemingly safe situations."

If, on the other hand, I can simply be with the historical

Inner Child's pain and thoughts around getting hit by an air conditioner, my Inner Child will not have to keep trying to reach me to get me to understand its pain by creating similar pain for me.

(Helpful hint: If you constantly find yourself unconsciously walking under falling air conditioners, you might, at some point, ask if your Inner Child is trying to send you a message.)

THE INNER CHILD THINKS THE PAIN WILL GO ON FOREVER

Have you noticed that sometimes when upsetting things happen to you, your mind immediately goes to thoughts like, "I'll never get out of this; This ruins everything; This will go on forever?"

The reason for this is that, for the child, an upsetting incident happened, pain happened, this pain went unseen and unfelt by a competent adult, and thus the child never had the experience of the incident being resolved, of the pain being experienced, or of being seen and understood. To this child, the pain is still going on. And, as far as the child knows, the pain will go on forever.

So, the thought that all is lost, that the pain will go on forever, is a natural thought for the child to have whenever something resembling the original incident occurs.

As adults, we must not push that thought away as ridiculous or unrealistic, but must notice and understand that of course the child has that thought. Then, we must be with the child as it's having that thought, by feeling what the child is feeling and thinking what the child is thinking. In this way the child gets seen, felt, heard and mirrored.

IT DOESN'T MATTER WHAT HAPPENED TO THE CHILD, IT ONLY MATTERS HOW THE CHILD EXPERIENCED IT

Often people will discount their Inner Child's experience because they either can't remember that something terrible happened to the child, or because they don't believe it could have happened.

The first step in healing the Inner Child is to BELIEVE THE INNER CHILD when it shares its experience with you, either through sensations and thoughts or through acting out. It doesn't matter what happened. It matters that the Inner Child had an experience, and continues to have that experience because it lives in the past.

Let's say, for example, that the child saw a movie and we didn't know that the child had seen the movie. And in that movie, someone was holding a knife in a certain way and ended up stabbing someone to death. Let's say that the child's parents just happen to often hold the knife in that way. They have no intention of stabbing the child, but the child is constantly terrified because it saw the movie. The parents are not doing anything terrible, the movie was just a movie, but nonetheless the child is having a constant experience of terror that it can't explain.

Only by being with that feeling of terror and those thoughts of fear do we have a chance of finding out what the child is afraid of. And even if we never find out, the child is protected because we are with it.

So don't make the Inner Child give you reasons or rationalize why it feels the way it does. Often the Inner Child doesn't know or is too scared to say. Simply meet the Inner Child at face value, wherever it is. BELIEVE THE INNER CHILD'S EXPERIENCE.

YOU CAN'T JUDGE A CHILD'S SENSATIONS, THOUGHTS AND ACTIONS BY ADULT STANDARDS

Recently, I was working with a client who had clearly had extremely challenging experiences as a child, for which her Inner Child was desperately trying to compensate.

From what she was reporting in terms of sensations, symptoms and actions, it was quite clear that some form of great trauma had occurred. Now, we must remember that great trauma is not always something horrifying or criminal or unconscionable. Great trauma is about how the child responded to something, not about what that something actually was. Sometimes something as seemingly innocuous as a mother leaving her infant child alone, either accidentally or to handle a pressing emergency with another one of her children, or a surgery or a situation or directive that was misunderstood, can create severe trauma if unprocessed.

(I'm smiling as I think of a picture I saw years ago of my aunt on a horse. She must have been about three years old, and at that time a photographer used to come around with a box camera and a horse and take pictures of small children sitting on the horse. My aunt had an absolutely terrified look on her face. When I asked her why she had looked so terrified, she told me that the nice photographer had said to her, "You sit on the horse and when I push this button you are going to go into this camera." She thought she was going to get sucked into the black box, so naturally, she was terrified. Because she could remember it, and because, AT THE TIME, she had been comforted and reassured, she could laugh about it. But if this incident had gone unremembered or un-mirrored, she might, in the present, experience an inexplicable fear of cameras, horses, sitting still, what other people say to her, anything.)

(Another incident comes to mind. It's a sweet story, but also could have been traumatic, left unheard and unnoticed. When my Godson was a small child, his family moved to a bigger house. When his mother asked him how he liked the new house, he replied, "I love it. But when is it going to start shrinking?" When she asked him why in the world he thought the house would start shrinking, he said. "Well, you said our last house got too small for us.")

These two stories are examples of fairly innocuous incidents that, unprocessed, could have resulted in an ongoing experience of trauma for the Inner Child. Often, the incidents are NOT so innocuous. But the point is, if the Inner Child is exhibiting symptoms of trauma, we MUST assume that the Inner Child EXPERIENCED trauma, and not withhold or adjust our compassion for the Inner Child based on whether we think something did or did not happen, on whether we think the Inner Child is telling the truth, on whether we think what happened is proportional to the reaction the Inner Child is having, on how others remember what happened, on the Inner Child's lack of compassion for itself, or on whether we think the Inner Child is remembering correctly. We must simply be with the Inner Child's thoughts and sensations. This is what accomplishes the healing, regardless of what "actually" happened. (I put "actually" in quotes because in the world of experience, there is no "actually." There is only EXPERIENCE.)

So, back to my client. She was noticing numerous symptoms and actions that had no explainable justification in the present.

She often reported that she had inexplicable and extremely uncomfortable sexual feelings whenever she felt endangered, and most often when she saw a man. She felt disgusting, and experienced a need to run or get out of her body.

She had eating disorders, including bulimia and anorexia. She would feel disgusting when anything went into her mouth and would feel compelled to throw it up. She knew she was severely underweight, but could not stop dieting, could not stop frantically exercising, and noticed she was frustrated because she wasn't losing weight fast enough.

She was aware that a part of her "wanted to die," although she was, fortunately, also aware of a part of her that wanted to heal.

She had strong symptoms of ADD, obsessive-compulsive thinking, and sometimes she even disassociated into different personalities.

Clearly, numerous incidents in the present were reminding her Inner Child of the past (a past her Inner Child couldn't remember – another sign that something traumatic happened that the Inner Child was trying to get away from).

All of this made perfect sense to me. Something really had happened that this Inner Child was running from, using whatever methods were available to her: not eating, throwing up, being disgusted, forgetting, going to ADD, obsessive-compulsive thinking, suicidal thoughts and disassociating.

The most striking thing I noticed was that although this made perfect sense to ME, every time one of these symptoms would come up, SHE would berate herself, saying things like, "I'm acting ridiculous again; Now I'm doing that stupid obsessive-compulsive stuff; I'm counting, disassociating, blah, blah, blah."

Now, to do this stuff in the present, as a present adult, in light of present circumstances, would be ridiculous. But THIS IS NOT BEING DONE BY A PRESENT ADULT. It is being done by a child, living in the past, with an unrecognized, un-mirrored incident. And the child's doing it makes perfect sense.

So you cannot judge a child's behavior by adult standards. Even though the child's sensations and thoughts are taking place in the present, in your own body, they are taking place in the PAST for the Inner Child and in that past EVERY ONE of these sensations and actions makes PERFECT sense.

What was challenging for my client to wrap her mind around (and what would be challenging for anyone for that matter) was that she was behaving this way in a present which didn't call for such behavior. I have had clients who truly insist that what their Inner Child is thinking and feeling actually IS going on in the present. But this is often a sign of even greater early trauma that the client is afraid to face. In this case, my client was aware that what was going on in the present didn't call for the reaction she was having. But she was judging and belittling the reaction that the Inner Child was having, forgetting that this was a perfectly legitimate reaction for a child who was living in the past to have, and that what the Inner Child needed was to be seen, felt and recognized.

So the challenge for this client, and for anyone dealing with unresolved childhood hurt, is to feel what the Inner Child is feeling, think what the Inner Child is thinking, and accept that this is a child, not a present day adult, that the child is in the past and not in the present, and as such, the child has every right to think and feel these things. We must also accept that because it is a child, the sensations may seem to come out of nowhere, the thoughts may be illogical and the conclusions may not make sense.

Make no mistake about it. Whether you want to or not, you ARE thinking what the Inner Child is thinking, and you ARE feeling the sensations the Inner Child is feeling.

There's no way not to. The Inner Child's thoughts and sensations are happening in your own mind and body, right now. The healing factor is how you hold them.

WHAT CAN WE DO IN THE PRESENT FOR THE INNER CHILD WHO IS IN THE PAST?

The only thing we can do in the present for an Inner Child who is in the past is acknowledge, accept, tolerate and be with the Inner Child's sensations and thoughts, no matter how painful, no matter how crazy they may seem. When we can do this, while knowing that these thoughts are the thoughts of our Inner Child and not our adult selves in the present, we can begin to gain insight into what the Inner Child is experiencing.

We can begin to understand what that Inner Child felt like, and really be with it and mirror it, by feeling and thinking what the Inner Child felt and thought.

We can begin to understand what happened and why the Inner Child felt, and continues to feel, the way it feels.

We can stop trying to suppress the Inner Child's past. We can stop trying to make it go away. We can stop trying to fix the Inner Child, or reason with the Inner Child. We can stop telling the Inner Child that it wasn't so bad. We can just "listen," REALLY listen, by feeling EXACTLY what the Inner Child felt and thinking EXACTLY what the Inner Child thought, while maintaining our link with the present and with our adulthood.

As we do this, the Inner Child will gradually begin to feel safer. Not safer in the situation it was in (the Inner Child will NEVER feel safe in that), but safer in sharing it with a competent adult. And as the Inner Child feels safer, it will begin to reveal its story that it has kept locked up for fear of repercussions, or fear of feeling the sensations that came with the story when the child was in it alone, or any number of other reasons. And as it reveals the story, we will understand it and we will not try to change it. It will not overwhelm us, since we are now adults. We will just be with it.

When we can accept what was and is for the Inner Child, and feel it in the present, as adults, knowing that what "is" for the Inner Child is not what "is" now (or even if it were, we have adult capabilities to deal with it) our whole life gradually begins to make experiential sense to us. Slowly we come to a point where we know that that Inner Child is in there, we know what happened to it, we know that it feels the way it feels, and ANY TIME something comes up for the Inner Child, we can be with it.

And when we can do this, our Adult is liberated to function as an adult in the world. We may, for the rest of our lives, be aware of the pain, aware of the regret, aware of the anger and the sadness, but as adults we can feel those things and live the lives we want to live.

There's nothing we can do to make the Inner Child's pain or the Inner Child's history go away or to make it not have happened. The very nature of the Inner Child's issues is that there was no "solution" in the past and there is no "solution" in the present. But although there was and is no solution, there is a way to be with what was and not have it get in our way at all.

YOU MUST LET THE INNER CHILD BE HOWEVER IT IS

Often, when I'm working with people who are trying to connect with their Inner Child's sensations, I will hear people say, "I'm not feeling anything. I'm not feeling the real stuff. I'm not in touch with what the Inner Child is feeling."

We must remember that the Inner Child's whole mission in life has been to get away from painful sensations that it felt it couldn't tolerate, using whatever tactics were available to it. In order to be with the Inner Child, and to really connect with its pain, we must connect to it wherever it actually is, not where we want it to be.

If we go to the sensations and find that we're feeling nothing, we must understand that it would be perfectly reasonable for the Inner Child, who was feeling too much, to suppress its sensations and feel nothing.

If we try to remember a painful incident and discover that we can't recall it, we must understand that it would be perfectly reasonable that when the Inner Child experienced something extremely painful that it could do nothing about, it defended itself by forgetting that it happened.

And should we notice that we're detaching, or disassociating, or even splitting into parts, this is not something the Inner Child shouldn't be doing. It only speaks to just how painful the past must have been that the Inner Child had to resort to these extreme "protective" devices.

We must not think of these things as pathology, as things to be gotten rid of. If we do that, we are ripping the Inner Child's defenses away and then the child is stuck with something it can't handle.

If we can just be with the deadness, the dissociation, the amnesia, whatever, we are connecting to the Inner Child, and eventually, in its own time, the Inner Child will feel safe enough to reveal whatever it needs to reveal in order to have us connect to the whole experience.

Don't push the Inner Child. Don't rush the Inner Child. Don't reason with the Inner Child. Just BE with the Inner Child.

I like to call this "Meeting the Child at the Outer Edge of its Resistance."

WHAT YOUR INNER CHILD IS THINKING IS STIMULATED BY THE PRESENT BUT HAS NOTHING TO DO WITH THE PRESENT

I've just begun a month-long tour, and I noticed in the weeks leading up to my leaving, I kept having the thought that I'm dying of some undisclosed illness. (Or, to be more accurate, my Inner Child kept having the thought that I'm dying of some undisclosed illness.)

I, of course, at first thought that I must be dying and so, perhaps, I should check into the Mayo Clinic or something and make sure I'm not.

I then sat with it for a while and realized that it's a tradition in my life to think I'm dying before I take a long trip or in fact commit to or do anything exciting. Years ago we were going on a fabulous cruise, and I was sure I had cancer before we left.

I recently did another long tour and I kept getting rashes that I was sure were a sign of some deep underlying diseases.

The association I had, when I sat still, was that when I was 12 years old, I was forced to go to camp against my will, so I must have some negative and fearful association with leaving home. I suppose my Inner Child must think, "If I'm dying, I won't have to leave home."

I've struggled with this all my life, always going to lots of doctors and getting checkups, always to find that there's nothing wrong (At least not physically).

So I was just sitting here thinking about this, having arrived at the beginning of my tour, and suddenly a light bulb went on! I realized that I've been struggling to get away from my Inner Child's thoughts and sensations, thinking that I had to invalidate them in the present, or else they would be TRUE in the present!

However, every time I try to make my Inner Child's thoughts and sensations invalid, either by ignoring them or going to the doctor to "prove them wrong," my Inner Child comes on more strongly with more thoughts and symptoms, because he feels I'm trying to disappear him. And every time I believe my Inner Child's thoughts and sensations, I get scared and spend a lot of time panicking and worrying, which only serves to frighten the Inner Child.

So what do I do?

Sometimes, when I have an issue like this and I bring it to my partner, Shawn, he'll pause for a moment, and then, keeping as straight a face as he can, ask, "What would a Thought Exchange person tell you to do?"

So much for me being Mr. Thought Exchange!

What I realized, sitting here, is what I need to do is let my Inner Child have the thought that I'm ill, and know that that thought has nothing to do with whether or not I am, in fact, ill. Like any human being going through life, I could be ill. I could not be ill. But my Inner Child's thought is neither causing nor preventing it. It's just a thought.

My Inner Child, when stimulated by certain circumstances in the present (many of which I may not even be aware) pulls up that "protective" thought. My job is to allow him to have it, notice it, feel it, think it, and go about my business as an adult.

This is the way I "got over" panic disorder. By having it. This is the way I "got over" fear of going on the stage. By having it.

The Inner Child is going to have lots of "protective" thoughts. When they arise, all we can do, all we should do, all we MUST do, is have the thoughts with the child and neither try to get rid of them nor act on them. That's the healing for the Inner Child and the freeing for the adult.

DON'T TELL THE INNER CHILD, "IT'S OK, DON'T WORRY"

Often, when people try to contact their Inner Child, they try to soothe it by telling it, "It's OK; It's safe; It's not so bad." But if we remember that the Inner Child is living in the past and not in the present, it's definitely not OK where the child is living. When we tell the Inner Child otherwise, we are negating its experience and giving it the impression that we don't understand what it's going through. The child will have no choice but to fight harder to show us how upsetting it really is (was) by creating more "uncomfortable" sensations and by walking us into more upsetting incidents in the present.

What the Inner Child needs is for us to be with how un-OK it was. The way we do this is to simply feel the Inner Child's sensations and think the Inner Child's thoughts, with the Inner Child. When we can do this, the Inner Child knows it's seen and heard, and the incidents can simply be felt and remembered as opposed to re-enacted.

DO NOT TELL THE INNER CHILD, "THAT WAS IN THE PAST. IT'S NOT HAPPENING NOW"

Often, when someone is trying to help someone else to "think positive" they will hear about an upset the Inner Child is having and say, "Yes, but now that you know that, you have to know that it's not happening now and you, as the adult, don't have to be or feel that way."

This, of course, is something that we, the Adult, must know, but it is NOT something the Inner Child should know. The minute the Inner Child hears this it will think, "I'm being left behind; I'm being forgotten about; They're trying to get rid of me." And the result will be that the Inner Child will kick up its "uncomfortable" sensations and "protective" thoughts to try and make sure that it has our attention and won't be forgotten.

The interesting thing is, it's natural for an adult to know it's in the present. The only thing that keeps us from being in the present is the voice of the Inner Child that we mistakenly think of as the voice of the present. That voice will always be there (because the Inner Child's history will never change), but when we can simply be with it, experience the Inner Child's sensations and think the Inner Child's thoughts, knowing that they're the thoughts of the Inner Child, we are automatically liberated to the unlimited possibilities of the present.

This is not an either/or situation. We do not have to get rid of the Inner Child's thoughts and sensations in order to be liberated as adults. In fact, we must do the exact opposite. HAVE THEM (That's why it's called Thought Exchange, not Thought Change).

PARADOX: WE "SOLVE" THE INNER CHILD'S PROBLEM BY ALLOWING THE INNER CHILD TO HAVE THE PROBLEM

This is one of the great paradoxes of healing. Let's say a child had something painful happen and took on the "protective" thought, "I can never be understood" to try and get away from the painful sensations.

The Inner Child may have tried every which way of Sunday to be understood, but ALWAYS, no matter what happens, experiences being misunderstood, because that is the thought the Inner Child is holding and thus the thought the child sees in the world.

No matter how much the Inner Child tries to get people in the outside world to treat it exactly how it wants to be treated, say exactly what it wants them to say, give it exactly what it wants, the thought the Inner Child is holding is still, "I cannot be understood." The misunderstanding happened in the past, and since the Inner Child is living in the past, nothing that happens in the present can erase that thought.

There is only one way to "understand" the Inner Child. Understand that the Inner Child holds the thought that it will never be understood, think that thought yourself, with the Inner Child, and feel the Inner Child's sensations as it holds the thought "I cannot be understood."

That thought may NEVER change, but if EVERY time the Inner Child has that thought, for the rest of your life, you go to the Inner Child and can be with that thought and the sensations it produces, you are, paradoxically, understanding the child by understanding and feeling its thought that it can never be understood.

You cannot tell the Inner Child "I understand," because in saying that, you are NOT understanding that the child is having the thought and the experience that it can't be understood. The Inner Child does not need you to fix it. In fact, it's impossible to fix it. The Inner Child needs you to experience with it what it was like for it to be in the predicament it was in. For it to be impossible for the child to be understood.

The Inner Child may never lose the thought, but it will not have to act out to get someone to understand, because it is instantly being understood in its thought that it cannot be understood. (You may have to read the last sentence a few times to get it, but it's at the center of how we heal past wounds without getting rid of them.)

IN ANY GIVEN SITUATION, OUR INNER CHILD AND OUR ADULT MAY HAVE DIFFERENT OBJECTIVES

Since our past and present are going on in the same body and mind, when handling any problem or incident, we must be aware that in places where the Inner Child has experienced earlier trauma, the Inner Child always has a different objective than the adult.

The adult's objective is to accomplish something, to hold a vision, to relate to the present. The Inner Child generally has one of two objectives. The Inner Child is either trying to get someone to mirror and feel its upsetting thoughts and sensations, or it is holding "protective" thoughts to try to get away from "uncomfortable" sensations. Both are futile, because the Inner Child is trying to get something in the present to fix something that's in the past. But nevertheless, the Inner Child keeps trying.

Neither the Inner Child nor the Adult are wrong. They're just living in two different worlds. The Inner Child is in the past and the Adult is in the present. The past cannot be changed, only recognized, acknowledged and felt...in the present. So if the Adult wants to deal with the present, part of what it must deal with is that the past remains, unchanged, as part of the experience of the present.

Only when the Adult can include the Child's experience in its experience in the present, can the Adult remain aware of the fact that unlimited possibilities always exist no matter what sensations and thoughts the child is having. This allows the Adult to function, in the present, as an Adult, and the child to be mirrored, seen and heard, which is really all it needs.

The Inner Child does not have to change in any way for the Adult to function. In fact, the Adult has to make this clear to the Inner Child.

THE INNER ADULT SHOULD ALWAYS PROTECT THE INNER CHILD

Once we have felt what the Inner Child felt, and thought what the Inner Child thought, in all its magnitude, exactly as the Inner Child felt and thought it, we never again need to ignore the Inner Child or fight off perceived outer circumstances in order to avoid feeling and thinking what the Inner Child was afraid to feel and think.

What this has meant for me is that the Inner Child is not only taken care of, but that it NEVER AGAIN has to face anything that appears to come at it from the outside world.

(As I say this, I must of course add the realistic caveat that nobody does this absolutely perfectly all the time, but most of the time it is true. Or at least, I always know that this option is available to me at every moment. I'm fond of saying that in my relationship with my partner, Shawn, I can almost always differentiate whether I am speaking TO his Inner Child or his Adult, but I'm not always so clear as to whether I am speaking AS my Inner Child or Adult. But I can usually catch myself pretty quickly.)

At any rate, for all intents and purposes, WHENEVER something comes at me that puts the Inner Child into "uncomfortable" sensations or "protective" thoughts, the FIRST thing I do, before dealing with what's coming at me, is to go to the Inner Child and experience the Inner Child's thoughts and sensations WITH the Inner Child.

Since ALL the Inner Child needs is for an adult to be with it, understand it, see it and feel it (and that adult DOES NOT have to be the OTHER person,...My INNER Adult will do just fine), my going to the child's thoughts and sensations and experiencing them right here and right now, in myself, effectively "puts the child to bed." The child is safe and does not have to try to act in the outside world to get something it can never get from the outside world. It's already gotten it. From ME.

With the Inner Child taken care of, my Adult can now field the problem in the present, with the adult capabilities of being disappointed, of problem-solving, of experiencing partial success, of protecting myself, etc. that the child doesn't have. Life is now being lived totally in the present (including the past that is being experienced in the present) but this past is now being experienced as what it is. THE PAST!

I actually have a visual image that I always hold of the relationship between myself, my Inner Child and the other person I'm dealing with in the world.

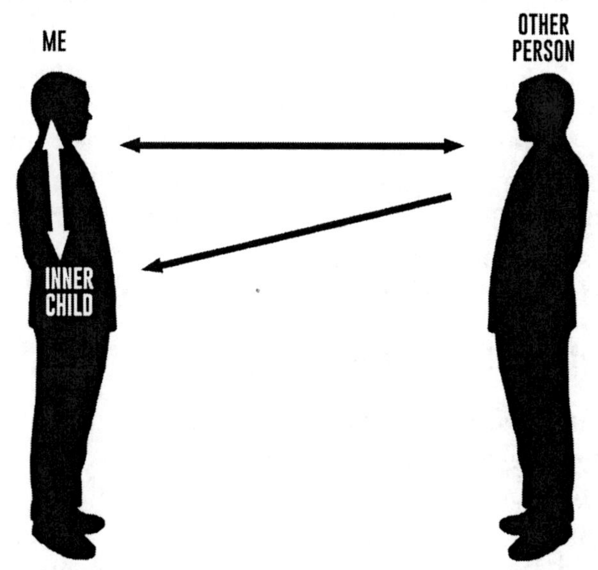

If you look carefully at the lines, you will notice that there is a two way line of communication between the adult "me" and the other person, a one way line of communication between the other person and my Inner Child (coming from the other person and going to my Inner Child, but not back from the Inner Child to the other person)

and a two way line of communication between me and my Inner Child.

When a communication comes in, it strikes me and my Inner child at the same time. Our responses may be quite different. Something that would be quite handleable to me as an adult living in the present might be extremely upsetting to my Inner Child because of its past experiences.

The FIRST thing I do is notice what my Inner Child is experiencing. I do this by experiencing my Inner Child's sensations and noticing and thinking my Inner Child's thoughts.

Now the Inner Child is seen and taken care of by an adult. ME. The Inner Child does not need to respond or try to get anything from the other person, because it's already gotten it from me.

With my Inner Child taken care of, I'm now free to respond to the other person as an adult. Albeit an adult who is feeling the sensations and thinking the thoughts of my Inner Child, but an adult who, being able to tolerate those sensations and thoughts, can handle the situation, in the present, with an adult's capabilities.

The Inner Child should NEVER speak to the other person.

(Of course, as I said above, this is the ideal situation. From time to time, especially in times of extreme activation or stress, we find our Inner Child speaking to an adult other than our own Inner Adult. The result of this interaction is usually that the Inner Child, who is seeing and treating the other person as someone from its past, gets treated by the other person exactly as the Inner Child was treated in the past. What usually happens next is that the Inner Child, feeling the old "uncomfortable" sensations, resorts to taking on its old "protective" thoughts, and either shuts down or attacks some more.)

Most marital fights are the result of each partner's Inner Child trying to get the other partner's Adult to take care of it. In fact, I might go so far as to say that most people get married because they think that the other Adult is going to take care of their Inner Child in ways that it was never before taken care of. The frustration is that the more we try to do this, the more our Inner Child experiences NOT being taken care of, because the Inner Child is living in the past and the other Adult is living in the present.

So, when uncomfortable or upsetting input comes in, we must, to the best of our ability, practice being with the Inner Child's experience first. Once we can do this, the Inner Child is taken care of, and we're free to act in the world as the adults we are.

EXPERIENCE YOUR INNER CHILD DIRECTLY OR SEE YOUR INNER CHILD REFLECTED AS THE WORLD IN FRONT OF YOU - YOUR CHOICE

As I've said repeatedly, your Inner Child's one mission is to be seen, heard and felt by you. One way or another, it's going to do that. It has no choice.

As we discussed in the last chapter, when a communication comes in that is disturbing to the Inner Child, if we can immediately connect, inside, with the sensations and thoughts the Inner Child is experiencing, the Inner Child is taken care of and we can deal with the situation as an adult who is holding a child, but whose behavior is not being governed or ruled by the child.

If we don't deal with the Inner Child, the Inner Child will be forced to "look elsewhere" for someone to understand it and feel what it feels. It will do this by acting out its "protective" thoughts in an effort to get rid of its "uncomfortable" sensations.

The transaction might go something like this. (I'll use myself as an example.)

Someone in a Thought Exchange class asks a question about some aspect of Thought Exchange, about something they don't understand or might even disagree with.

My adult hears the question and begins to think about it. My Inner Child hears the question and thinks, "Oh, no! They've found me out! I'm stupid. Why am I even teaching this? I don't know anything. I'd better not let them know that." Or, "He's so stupid for asking that. I hate him."

These thoughts, and the "uncomfortable" sensations that come with them, will rush through my head and body. I'll feel a sinking feeling in my stomach, or my heart might start to race, my "blood boil," or I might feel suddenly sleepy or wish I could go home. Even if the question is one that's fairly routine or innocuous, if it strikes my Inner Child as dangerous in some way having to do with the past, I will feel all these sensations and think all these thoughts.

If I, as an adult, can recognize these sensations and thoughts as those of my Inner Child, I can feel them, know that of course my Inner Child feels this way given his history, and simply be there with the Inner Child while answering the question as an adult. As an adult, I have the ability to discuss things, to be wrong, to compromise, to know that my whole life is not on the line if I don't completely know everything. So the question gets discussed and we move forward in one way or another.

If, on the other hand, I feel my Inner Child's "uncomfortable" sensations and think his "protective" thoughts and think this is really happening to me, in the present, I become my Inner Child and react to the person who asked me the question in the present as the Inner Child who is living in the past.

Thinking that I'm being attacked or that my life is over, I might resort to being defensive, aggressive, manipulative, evasive, frightened, desperate or any number of other things that my Inner Child might have reached for to try to get away from the discomfort of being in a situation where it felt there's no way out.

The other person, who simply asked a question, now sees before him not the carefully considered, intelligent, thoughtful, knowledgeable, yet vulnerable and open-to-the-possibility-of-learning-something-new or being wrong person that my adult is, but rather, a screaming, defensive child attacking him and accusing him of all sorts of things he didn't do or think, just because he asked a question.

Since the other person does not see that this is an Inner Child, but simply sees me as an adult who is acting this way, he will respond to me by dealing with me as he sees me... as the attacking, manipulative, defensive person that my Inner Child is being.

Can you see that my Inner Child, who was unseen by me on the inside, has now succeeded in putting its dilemma in front of me? What I refused to see on the inside (the initial "uncomfortable" sensations and "protective" thoughts my Inner Child felt when the communication from the other person first came in) is now being seen on the "outside" and is coming at me, "making" me feel what my Inner Child felt.

I now have two choices:

If I view the way the other person is treating me as something I have to fight off, I will essentially continue to fend off and ignore my Inner Child's "uncomfortable" sensations and "protective" thoughts by trying to fight the mirror. (Essentially, what I am trying to do, when I do this, is change the reflection I see in the mirror without changing what's in front of it, which of course, is impossible.) My Inner Child, who is still unheard, even though it has thrown its dilemma up on the "screen of the world" in front of me for me to clearly see, may now have to resort to escalating the "situation" with the person in front of me. And if that doesn't get my attention, the Inner Child will have to act out in bigger and bigger ways, always with the hope that I will finally recognize that the "problems" and "opposition" I'm seeing in the world are my Inner Child's dilemmas. This will go on until I make choice #2.

When I make choice #2 and choose to recognize the circumstance in front of me as the reflection of my Inner Child's "uncomfortable" sensations and "protective" thoughts that it is, I can stop and simply feel the sensations and think the thoughts that this "situation," that this "problem," that this "reflection" generates in me. When I do this, I am reconnecting to my Inner Child's experience, my Inner Child is taken care of, and my Adult becomes liberated to act as an adult, with all the capabilities and possibilities that being an adult entails.

THE LIBERATED ADULT

Did you ever see one of those great mothers who can be having a conversation with another adult while her small child is playing nearby? The mother maintains the conversation but always knows where the child is. The child may suddenly come to her crying, with a boo boo or a complaint. The child may fall down. The child may be hungry. The mother picks the child up or talks to it, recognizing its problem, empathizing, validating what the child is feeling while doing whatever is needed to alleviate it. She may hold and rock the child. She may give the child something to play with, a book to read or something to eat. She may gently explain that the child needs to be patient, they'll be ready to go in a few minutes, understanding that the child may have a hard time with that.

And all the while, she is maintaining her connection to the adult with whom she's talking.

This is how we must be with our Inner Child. We are in the adult world, but we neither ignore the Inner Child nor let it run wild. We're present with it. We "get" it. We understand that it's a child and will have thoughts and sensations that are "childish." When we can have this understanding and really be with the Inner Child, we can continue our adult lives. When we ignore or punish the Inner Child for being the way it is, the Inner Child runs wild in an effort to get our attention.

Your Inner Child is inside you. It's your past. There is NO WAY to get away from it. The only way to free your adult to be an adult is to be able to fully be with Inner Child, wherever the Inner Child is. This means thinking what the Inner Child is thinking and feeling what the Inner Child is feeling, WHILE KNOWING YOU'RE AN ADULT.

Challenging. But do-able. And necessary.

"MOTHERING" YOUR INNER CHILD

One of the most effective ways I've found of being with my Inner Child, especially when I'm going through something difficult, is to "mother" him when I get into bed at night and when I get up in the morning.

When I lie down in bed, I imagine my adult self sitting down on the bed next to the Inner Child and saying, "OK. Tell me. I'm all yours. Feel your sensations and I will feel them with you. Think your "protective" thoughts and I will think them with you."

I then go through my body and notice whatever sensations I'm having and simply have them. If thoughts of upset or worry come into my mind, I simply notice them too. If my mind begins to spin off, the "mother" part of me gently guides the Inner Child back to the sensations.

Essentially, I just sit there with the Inner Child until it falls asleep. If I wake up in the middle of the night, I do the same thing. Sometimes it takes moments, sometimes it takes hours, but the Inner Child is not alone, and in the quiet of the darkened bedroom, I can often connect to and experience the Inner Child's "uncomfortable" sensations and "protective" thoughts with a compassion, attention and focus that is harder to muster when I'm caught up in the issues of the day.

I don't try to help the Inner Child. I don't try to fix or figure anything out. I'm just there, experiencing the sensations that the Inner Child is experiencing, and thinking the thoughts that the Inner Child is thinking.

I do the same thing first thing in the morning. When I wake up, I lie in bed and simply feel my sensations, with the thought that there is an Adult "me" sitting with the Inner Child "me." Then WE get up and start the day.

Try it. It's often just what the Inner Child needs.

DON'T TELL YOUR INNER CHILD TO "RELAX"

When I was a kid and I would be upset about something, my father would often say, "Relax."

I always HATED that!

Often, in meditations on the body, we are told to go through our body and "relax" each part. In conjunction with doing the "mothering" exercise in the previous section, I tried one day to start at my feet and gradually "relax" each part of my body. In doing this, I had a revelation as to why I (and especially my Inner Child) hate to be told to "relax."

If we're going through our body to try to get rid of something, some discomfort, some tension, some sensation, the Inner Child is going to balk. When we "relax" and let go of holding, what we experience is whatever we were holding back by maintaining tension. So often, when we "relax" a body part, we may feel great sadness or great anger or great pain. The Inner Child needs to have these accepted by our Inner Adult or it will run back to holding, tension and "protective" thoughts.

I have found that if I go through my body with the thought "Accept" rather than "Relax," I can experience whatever is there with acceptance, and the Inner Child feels seen and experienced by me.

So when you go to "relax," be wide open to experiencing whatever is there. It may not be comfortable, but it is healing.

RECLAIMING DISOWNED SPOTS AND BURIED MEMORIES

As we go through the process of being with each part of the body and allowing what's there to be there, we will often come across places that either hurt or that we are "worried" about. You might find yourself having the thought, "There's something wrong there; There's something off there." (Being the hypochondriac that I am, I usually think that some bump or pain or anomaly is a sure sign that I have a fatal disease.)

When you hit these spots, try just being with them, not resisting them, not trying to figure them out, not trying to fix them, just experiencing them. Just let them know, "I am with you, I'm not resisting you, if you want to tell me what's there I'll listen, if not I'll just be with you." Nothing to force, nothing that needs to happen, just presence to see what's there.

Sometimes, when we do this, spontaneous memories will begin to come up. If they do, just let 'em roll. Follow them. Don't stop them. Don't steer them.

As with all this work, the important thing is not that you get a specific piece of information or have a breakthrough. It's that you develop a relationship with your Inner Child in which, wherever it is, you're willing to be there with it. Whatever it experiences, you're willing to experience it. It's the relationship we wish we'd had with our parents. It's a relationship that we can now provide for ourselves.

IMAGINE HAVING A HOME TO COME HOME TO WHERE YOU ARE ALWAYS SEEN AND HEARD

Imagine you've had a GREAT day. Wonderful things have happened. When you arrive home, there's someone there who asks you, "How was your day?" And when you tell them, they say, "Fantastic! That's wonderful. Tell me more. I want to hear all about it!" And you tell them and they listen and they hang on every word and feel just how you feel about it.

Now, imagine you've had a TERRIBLE day. All sorts of upsetting, disturbing things have happened. And when you arrive home, that same person is there, and once again they ask you, "How was your day?" And when you tell them, they say, "Oh, my, how upsetting, I can feel how painful that was. Tell me all about it. I'm here."

This is what we all dream of. A home where no matter how we're feeling it's received and seen, the other person is not burdened by whatever's going on with us, but can feel it with us. Can you see how, no matter what happened during your day, you would end up being OK, because you would always know that someone was with you, sharing it with you, not afraid of it, not trying to fix you? You'd always be connected. You'd always be loved, since love is really nothing more than seeing and being seen EXACTLY as you are.

This "home," this perfect "home" where the "other" can ALWAYS be relied upon to be there exactly as you need them to be, can only be found in one place. INSIDE OF YOU. When your Adult is willing to simply recognize and be with your Inner Child, no matter what it's feeling (or not feeling) you have this home. Always. It can't be lost. It's completely inside of you. Not dependent on anyone's behavior, on anyone having to do this or that in a particular way. Not capricious. Not up for grabs. ALWAYS there!

IN OUR INNER CHILD'S MIND, THE FUTURE AND THE PAST ARE THE SAME

Since the Inner Child is living in the past, and has never had the experience of having its thoughts and sensations in certain areas seen, the Inner Child knows NOTHING ELSE. The only thing it can see is what happened, and even though it's trying desperately to erase or get away from the past, it doesn't think that's possible.

What this means is that any time you, as an adult, are thinking about a future that is different than the past, the Inner Child will insist that the future IS the past. It will do this by coming up with "protective" thoughts of failure and lack and with "uncomfortable" sensations.

When we understand that our Inner Child may always come up with these thoughts and sensations, and that we can recognize them as the Inner Child's, the thoughts and sensations become part of the landscape of creating an experience of a different future, and do not interfere with or counteract the Adult's vision. The Inner Child, its thoughts and sensations, are just there, seen, felt, understood and allowed to be as they are, while the Adult moves forward in whatever way he or she wishes.

THE PAST AND THE FUTURE ONLY EXIST IN THE PRESENT

As we said before, your Inner Child is living in the past. But it is living in the past in the present, because the only way your Inner Child exists is in your present memory. It is remembering something that happened in the past by having sensations and thoughts in the present. That's the only place in which it can have sensations and thoughts. In the present.

The future doesn't exist in the future. It exists as thoughts (and sensations that accompany those thoughts) in the present. The future is a thought. The future exists only in the invisible world of your experience.

So EVERYTHING is happening here and now, the past, the present, the future, in the only place it can ever happen, in the invisible world of your experience. It's ALL just thoughts and sensations.

Sit still for a few moments and see if you can grasp this. Think of the past, and notice that you are thinking of it in the present. It doesn't exist in any other place. Now think of the future and notice that it too only exists within you. What's actually going to happen is not necessarily what you are thinking is going to happen, because you cannot be in the future in the future. You can only be in it now.

And whatever the future, whatever the past, you can act in whatever way you want to if you allow it to be what it is in the present, notice the thoughts and have the sensations.

THE THREE "REALITIES" – PAST, PRESENT AND FUTURE

Since there is no past and no future except as experienced in the present, all three are always simultaneously being experienced in the present.

The key to being able to live in the present is to be able to experience all three "realities," but to know which ones pertain to the past, which ones are about the present, and which ones have to do with the future.

Only in this way can we take care of our Inner Child and function as an adult at the same time.

When something disturbing or upsetting happens, our first instinct is usually to try to deal with the circumstance itself; try to get it to change or go away or resolve. The problem with trying to do this is that if we have not sorted out WHO is dealing with this, the Child or the Adult, we may find ourselves dealing with a present circumstance as though it were the past. When we do this, we never deal with the circumstance but rather recreate it as the same circumstance that upset us in the past.

Another way of saying this is that for the Inner Child, the circumstance is entirely different than it is for the Adult. And since the Inner Child is living in the past, the Inner Child is dealing with something that is not happening now, but rather with something that happened, that is not in the present and thus is over and done and CANNOT BE CHANGED, no matter what the child does in the present. (In Truth, the Inner Child can't even DO anything in the present, because it doesn't live in the present.)

Let me give you an example.

A client of mine was misguidedly struggling, as most of us do earlier in life or at the beginning of this work, to try to satisfy his Inner Child's past needs by trying to change the present. He would constantly assign motive and meaning to people and even to things that happened. These motives and meanings made perfect sense in light of his childhood experiences, but had almost nothing to do with what was actually happening in the present.

The problem is, when we assign and act on motives and meanings from the past, we keep turning the present out to match the past and we get nowhere. When we criticize people for doing things they're not doing, when we demand that people give us things that adults cannot provide to other adults, people tend to reject us, get mad at us or ignore us in the same way these things happened to us as children.

Now, one of the ways in which this client's Inner Child acted out his past was to almost always come to sessions at least ½ hour late. To the child, this was necessary, because he was rebelling against authority and had to "show" me, the adult, that he wasn't going to take it. By doing this, of course, he was missing half his sessions. And had I not been in a therapeutic relationship with him, but rather had been just someone in his life, I would have long ago stopped making appointments with him.

One day, I came to the session and waited for him to come at his usual late time. I waited. And waited. The whole session time passed and he hadn't shown up.

So I left, and sent him an email saying that I hoped everything was OK but that I had been there for the whole session (it was scheduled as a two-hour session) and left.

He called me a few moments after I had left, and told me that he was at the session, had been waiting for over ½ hour, and where was I? I called him back and told him that the session was scheduled for one and it was now after three. He said that according to his book, the session was at two. He had been there since 2:30 (his usual half hour late).

I checked my schedule, and sure enough, he was right! I had gotten it wrong.

I told him that I would head back and give him the hour and a half he would have had had I gotten the schedule right.

But here's the interesting thing. He was there at 2:30 and so was I. But when he showed up and I wasn't there, his child made all sorts of assumptions about why, and his child acted in ways that ensured that that point of view occurred.

Depending on the day and availability of rooms, we either met on the 3rd floor or the 7th floor. He had come to the 3rd floor. I was waiting on the 7th floor. His Inner Child made the assumption that I was somehow punishing him by not showing up, or that he had gotten the time and day completely wrong. Based on the Inner Child's assumption, he didn't check the 7th floor and didn't call me. When I asked him why he hadn't checked, he said that he felt that it was too much of a risk to call me and find out that I had abandoned him or was punishing him. This was, of course, his Inner Child running the show. An adult wouldn't be thinking I was abandoning him or punishing him, he would just wonder what happened. And an adult would also be able to tolerate that either he, or I, made a mistake. By functioning from his Inner Child, the client brought about the result he feared. He missed his whole session.

At some point, his adult took over, made the call, found out that indeed I and not he had made a mistake, and got the satisfaction of having the remainder of his session. This was progress.

Interestingly enough, his Inner Child, who sees everything from the standpoint that people are lying to him and abusing him (as his parents did), was even upset when I told him to wait right there, that I would be back to make up the time. Where the Inner Child went was to the fact that when I had set up the appointment with him, I had told him that this was the only time I had available. Now, suddenly, I was able to come back, so OBVIOUSLY I had lied to him when I said this was the only time.

In truth, when I had realized my mistake, I immediately called my next appointment and moved around the rest of my day so I could make it up to my client. I hadn't lied when I had said that this was the only available appointment, but when it turned out that it was "my bad," I made the necessary adjustments.

So, this client was taking an incident in the present, treating it as though it were in his past, and in doing so was predicting an outcome in the future totally in line with what had happened in the past. If he could have experienced his past as his past, experiencing his thoughts and sensations instead of enacting them, he could have chosen different actions in the present, knowing that in the present he could tolerate the thoughts and sensations that these actions might bring, and could have held a different future in mind where things worked out. The moment he did this (by his Adult calling me to find out where I was) the future did, in fact, work out differently.

FEELING ONE WAY/ACTING ANOTHER

When we are aware that the uncomfortable sensations and "negative" thoughts we're having are those of the Inner Child, and can allow those sensations and thoughts to be as they are, no matter what they are, we have complete freedom and choice of activity.

For example, when I was 20 I experienced what psychiatrists would call severe panic disorder. Every time I would get up to walk, the room would spin and my heart would pound.

I was sitting in a chair one day, furious and despairing because I thought I would never be able to do anything because I couldn't walk without having those sensations.

Suddenly I thought, "Fine. I'm going to feel this way forever. EVERY time I walk, the room is going to spin and my heart is going to pound. So be it." And I got up and walked. And the room spun and my heart pounded. But I walked, even while having those sensations. I was many years from coming to the understanding that this was my Inner Child, but it didn't matter. Through the act of walking WITH the sensations, I was, inadvertently, BEING with the Inner Child, allowing it to be just as it was. I now knew I could walk, WITH the Inner Child, so I kept walking. And I kept doing things I wanted to do, going places, eventually even conducting shows on Broadway. I often had those same sensations, but over the years I got so used to them, so accepting of them, that they ceased to be an issue. Now I hardly ever experience them, but if I do, I just keep doing what I'm doing. I know it's my Inner Child, I accept that it's remembering things that happened to it and that that's not my present reality, although it is the Inner Child's. The two of us now live together, in one integrated body and mind, present and past being experienced and acknowledged, past being seen and felt, present being acted on.

CHILDREN GET ABANDONED/ADULTS GET LEFT

So often when you ask an adult what they're afraid of in a given situation, they will say, "I'm afraid of being abandoned."

As soon as they say this, you know the Inner Child is speaking.

Children who are abused, physically or emotionally, rightfully fear abandonment. Children need a caretaker so that they can eat, so that they can live somewhere, so that they can emotionally and physically survive.

Often, you see children who are abused by their caretakers, still clinging to the very caretakers who are abusing them. The reason for this is that a child cannot survive without a caretaker, so even if the caretakers are abusive, the child will stick by them and try to get what it needs from them. In this light, I would define abandonment as being without a competent adult who can see your plight and take care of you. As adults, our Inner Child is NEVER without the possibility of having a competent adult recognize and feel its experience. It has US, the Inner Adult, ALWAYS with it, ALWAYS with the possibility of being available.

What this means is that as adults, if we're experiencing abandonment, it's we ourselves who are abandoning the Inner Child, not anybody else. Should a marriage break up, should someone close to us die, should we be kicked out of our home, we may have strong feelings and thoughts of being left, but we are not abandoned. We not only have resources and connections, as adults, that children don't have, but we have the ability to hold our Inner Child, feel and think what it feels, be with that and move forward.

Painful, yes. Impossible, no.

CARING FOR OUR INNER CHILD IS LIKE CARING FOR SOMEONE WHO IS OLD OR INFIRM

An analogy comes to mind that has to do with my dad.

My dad is 93, and although he's in excellent health, he has some of the challenges that come with being 93. He moves more slowly, shouldn't be driving, forgets words. No matter what I do, I am not going to be able to make those things not be there. That's the way my dad is.

In looking at the Truth of dad's life, my brother and I found we had two basic choices:

We could rail and complain, wish things were different, pretend that dad's condition wasn't what it was, even ignore it altogether. This would not only not make the condition go away, but would probably cause upsets, changes of plans, worry and things like that as my dad's unmet needs surfaced.

The other possibility was that we could experience our thoughts and sensations around the condition. In other words, be with it, like we would be with our Inner Child.

We chose to do the second, and as soon as we really experienced our thoughts and sensations around it, ideas began to spontaneously surface as to how we could best take care of my dad, giving him an independent life and yet seeing that his needs were met. The fact that my father had certain special needs was not unbearable or unhandleable to us as adults.

After a bit of research, we found a place for him to live where he's near us, where he lives in a beautiful apartment with his own furniture, where he gets his meals taken care of, where he has friends, where we are notified if he needs anything, and where he has all of his issues recognized and taken care of. With this in place, I can function as an unfettered, full-fledged adult, doing things I want to do and accomplishing what I want to accomplish, knowing that my father's issues are taken care of. They are still there, but they're not at all in my way.

It's the same thing with the Inner Child. We cannot change its history, we cannot make things not have happened that happened, but we can make it comfortable and safe by acknowledging its condition, being with its condition, and internally meeting its needs. And when we can do this, our adult is free to live an adult life, have adult relationships and accomplish adult things.

FORGET ABOUT "CANCEL, CANCEL"

So much New Thought work has been directed at releasing "negative" thoughts and "uncomfortable" "sensations, getting rid of them, canceling them, sending them away, getting over them (or under them or around them). If we think of these sensations as the Inner Child's experiences, in the present, that are stuck in the past (and ALWAYS will be because what happened, happened) then trying to release them or let go of them or get around them would be like having a child in pain in front of you and telling the child "I'm releasing you; I'm forgetting you; I'm canceling you; I'm moving on without you."

What could the helpless child who is being treated like this do?

Well, it could scream louder and exhibit more pain to get your attention (resulting in more "uncomfortable" thoughts and sensations.)

Or, it could shut down and try not to feel anything or not remember what happened (and since the child lives in you in the present you would experience being shut down and would not know why you feel this way).

Or, it could vow never to think certain thoughts again so it would never feel certain sensations again (in which case you would not be able to think certain thoughts.) Most likely the thoughts that would become unavailable to you would be thoughts like, "I can do it; I can have this; It's possible," since those were the thoughts that were originally thwarted which generated the painful sensations which were not seen, resulting in the "protective" thoughts that the child (and hence you) are holding in the present.

THE "BAD" NEWS – YOU'RE NEVER GOING TO GET OVER THIS

Often, we spend our lives trying to get "over" the Inner Child or "away from" the "uncomfortable" sensations and "protective" thoughts the child is having. There are many ways in which we try to do this; by thinking that we could be so successful or "in control" that we will never have to feel these things again; by trying to get someone else to behave perfectly toward us so we will never be hurt or disappointed as we were in childhood; by trying to be so rich that we can "buy" happiness; by doing every sort of therapy or New Thought method imaginable to try to release, let go of, overcome or "positive think" our way out of the past.

But none of this works, because the past is the past, it already happened, it cannot be taken away, and the Inner Child is living in the past because in the past disturbing things happened and it was unseen and un-helped.

The only thing we can do is feel what the Inner Child feels and think what the Inner Child thinks. In this way, it's as if the child has the perfect mommy with him or her at all times. Things are still experienced as they were experienced, but now they're experienced with "mommy" present.

THE "GOOD" NEWS – YOU DON'T NEED TO GET OVER THIS

When we practice being with the Inner Child, what we're practicing is being with the sensations and thoughts that we couldn't tolerate as a child that stopped us from doing what we wanted to do. When we can truly be with the experience of the Inner Child, our adult self automatically realizes that it's just an experience in the present of something in the past, it doesn't in any way prevent us from doing anything we want to do, and doesn't even prevent us from enjoying things, as adults, while the Inner Child is feeling what it's feeling.

Years ago, I was working on a Broadway Show with Alan Menken, the composer of *Beauty and The Beast, Aladdin* and many other hit Disney movies. We were having a big presentation in front of important backers, and I was conducting. I arrived at the studio that morning and said to Alan, "I just came from a really upsetting therapy session, and I'm feeling so bereft, I feel like I'm going to cry through the whole presentation." To which Alan said, "So cry through the whole presentation. Let's go."

What Alan was doing was supporting me in giving my Inner Child permission to be however it was. He was, in the present moment, which is the only place you can parent anyone, being a good parent. He was saying, "I know that you have the adult skills to conduct this and that you can do so while being with your Inner Child's sensations and thoughts."

In fact, I conducted it beautifully, had a good time, and didn't cry. My Inner Child was safe in feeling however it felt, and I didn't have to curtail myself. I just had to be willing, at any moment, to have it cry if that's what it needed to do.

So we don't need to suppress or forget or get rid of the Inner Child in order to act like adults. It's just the opposite. If we try to do that, we are essentially saying that we fear the Inner Child, we are abandoning the Inner Child, and it will act up and act out to get our attention.

This is especially important when we're being successful or stepping out of our comfort zone. When we're doing this, we're going right to the place where the child is afraid, and the child will feel its sensations more than ever. If we can feel them with the child, we can keep going. If we can't, we'll stop.

THE "EVEN BETTER" NEWS – YOU WOULDN'T WANT TO GET OVER THIS

The fact is, this Inner Child is a part of you. It's the part of your past where you were hurt and where you developed strategies to avoid that hurt, thinking that you couldn't tolerate it. Until you can be with that hurt, you're limited by your past. When you can be with any sensations and thoughts that come up, and simply experience them, you are reclaiming unlimited possibilities and nothing can stop you.

WE HAVE LEARNED TO TALK TO OUR INNER CHILD THE WAY OUR PARENTS TALKED TO US AS CHILDREN

So often, when we "hear the voice" of the Inner Child, or experience the "uncomfortable" sensations of the Inner Child, we respond to it with fear, anger, frustration or attack. At these times, we will often blame our issues on our parents and on the way we were treated by them in childhood.

It is true that our childhood treatment at the hands of our parents or caretakers was most likely the source of these issues. Our parents, out of their own fears and inability to be with their own Inner Child, often did constantly, clearly and consistently treat us and think of us in ways that were, shall we say, less than encouraging and supportive.

But here's the thing. At a certain point, we learned the lessons they taught us well, and WE TOOK OVER. It is not our parents saying those things now. It's us.

It reminds me of Anna Russell, the hilarious opera satirist, who said, "At one time or another, every famous voice teacher has ruined my voice...and I now feel in a position to do the same for yours!"

It's as though our parents said, "We have done our best to train you to criticize yourself, to not think highly of yourself, to feel guilty and ashamed, and now we're sending you off in the world with full confidence that you have the inner tools to maintain this state of consciousness without our help."

It is a crucial step in our healing for us to realize that it is no one other than ourselves who is maintaining this state of affairs, and the way we're doing it is by responding to and treating our Inner Child exactly the way we were responded to and treated.

I think this is best said in one of my favorite song lyrics, written by one of my favorite songwriters. In his song *Forgiveness' Embrace*, Stephen Schwartz, perhaps best known as composer and lyricist for such shows as *Wicked, Pippin* and *Godspell,* and movies such as *Pocahontas, The Hunchback of Notre Dame* and *Prince of Egypt,* wrote:

I HAVE SERVED A FULL LIFE SENTENCE
AS A PRISONER OF MY PAST
AS A VICTIM OF A VICTIM OF A VICTIM*

This is true, but what it really points to is that the one who is presently victimizing us is none other than ourselves.

We may not immediately know what to do about this, but knowing it's happening is the first step.

THE INNER CHILD IS NEVER MALEVOLENT

I was working with David Grand, the brilliant and innovative creator of Brainspotting, a technique that elegantly and efficiently helps people to pinpoint, incorporate and heal childhood and adult traumas.

As I was doing the work, I noticed that there were two thoughts that always "screamed" in my brain.

The first was,

"You Can Never Have Anything You Want... Everything Will Be Taken Away."

* "Forgiveness' Embrace", Music and lyrics by Stephen Schwartz, Copyright © 2001 Stephen Schwartz

And the second was,

"You Will NEVER Know Why This is Happening."

These voices tended to come up most strongly when I was going for something I wanted, or succeeding at something.

Recently I had been about to finish my second book, was downsizing financially to give myself more freedom to do the theater projects I really wanted to do, was about to sign a deal for a third book and was having successful meetings with producers and publishers, and was even approaching my weight goal through diet and healthy eating.

You would think I would be happy about all this, but in fact, I was having all sorts of physical symptoms, feeling exhausted, imagining I was dying of some disease and thinking, "I'm too old and I should just give up." (By the way, I've ALWAYS thought I'm too old, even when I was 18)

When I reported these voices to David Grand, I described them as vicious, punishing, malevolent voices that were out to get me. When he asked me, "Who is speaking?" my knee-jerk reaction was to say, "It must be my father." When he suggested that my father could not possibly be speaking to me here and now at this moment, I realized that, of course, these were voices inside of me speaking. That being said, these voices had to be my Inner Child, who had been hurt by the experiences he'd had with my father. But this Inner Child could not possibly be malevolent or out to get me. This Inner Child was hurt, frightened, protecting itself, and feeling lost, scared and disenfranchised inside of my own psyche, just as it had felt lost, scared and disenfranchised inside the "care" of my father.

David Grand then asked me to invite the Inner Child who was saying, "You Will Never Have Anything You Want... Everything Will Be Taken Away" into the room. When he asked me how old the child was, the number 2 came into my mind. When he asked what the child was wearing, I saw a diaper. He asked me to look at the child, who was standing in the corner.

(Where the child or the memory of the trauma is located is a very important part of David Grand's Brainspotting work. To find out more about this, I would suggest reading his book, *Brainspotting: The Revolutionary New Therapy For Rapid and Effective Change.)*

What I saw was a wide-eyed, frozen, terrified baby. All sorts of memories of what happened to this child began to flood in, and I cried and felt tremendous empathy for this terrified two-year-old. David Grand asked me if the baby would let me move toward it. I actually saw the baby slowly move toward me, still wide-eyed and terrified. Eventually he sat down next to me on the floor, and a few moments later climbed into my lap. I could really understand how, given what this baby had been through, how he had been viewed at that time, and what he'd had to close off against and lose, he would have taken the frozen position of, "You'll never have anything. Everything will be taken away."

This voice no longer seemed anything resembling malevolent. I had empathy and sympathy and love and compassion for this little child, and as I felt that, the wide, frozen eyes gradually softened and the baby went to sleep on my shoulder.

Next, we called in the Inner Child who was saying, "You Will NEVER Know Why This Is Happening."

He turned out to be 17, and as I reviewed the traumatic events that had happened to him at that time (which also contained a lot of the fallout from the events that had happened to the two-year-old), I realized that this 17 year old had shut off his knowledge of his talents, of his value and of his ability to go for things, express his own wishes and live authentically, in order to protect himself from the pain that trying to be himself had brought up in the household in which he was raised.

I had always assumed that something horrible (sexual abuse or severe loss or physical abuse that I couldn't remember) must have happened in order for part of me to say, "You Will Never Know Why." But when I stopped focusing on "What must my father have done, what must my mother have done?" and focused instead on the Inner Child who had had the experience, I realized that my Inner 17 Year Old had taken that stance because he felt responsible for "ruining my life." He had made decisions to shut down that resulted in my being in a mental hospital three years later, that resulted in my getting married when deep inside I knew I was gay, that resulted in me postponing what I really wanted to do for over 25 years and resulted in my current sense that I haven't accomplished nearly what I could have.

Now, rather than seeing his voice as a malevolent voice keeping crucial information from me, I could see him as a hurt, terrified teenager thinking he had to protect me from himself (or more accurately, protect himself from what he thought would happen to him if he didn't protect me (his current caretaker) from himself.

Of course, I could have compassion for this kid and know that he'd had no ability to make any other decision at the time. And in knowing this, I now knew "why" these thoughts were happening, even as I knew that this child might continue to think this thought. It was OK.

I had now incorporated two injured parts of my Inner Child, and in doing that, had made the important shift from focusing on what my parents had done, to focusing instead on what I was doing to myself in response to my experiences with my parents.

And with that, possibilities that have always been there for me but that I couldn't allow (because I had been ignoring the pain of my Inner Child by misconstruing it as the malevolence of an adult voice) returned to my awareness. I could take actions I couldn't take before, because I could feel the intense pain and fear of my Inner Child, as represented by these warnings of failure and danger, and know that they were the thoughts of frightened parts of my past. They had become parts of me that, as an adult, I could see feel and hold without having them stop me from being an adult.

THE INNER CHILD CAN BE ANY AGE

From the last section, I think it's clear that our Inner Child can be any age. Inner Child is, of course, a metaphoric term for an experience that is frozen in the past. As such, something unprocessed as recently as yesterday would be experienced today as our Inner Child. Usually, when we think "Inner Child," we have a vision of a little baby. It's important to understand that the Inner Child is actually whatever age at which the trauma occurred.

SHIFTING OUR FOCUS FROM "WHO DID THAT?" TO "TO WHOM WAS THAT DONE?"

Often, in therapy, we tend to focus on how awful our parents were, what they did to us, how we were hurt. It's, of course, important to know this, but the healing actually comes when we pay attention to the part of us that was hurt, and to our becoming the parent to that part. There is no way we can punish our parents or make them really see what they have done and how awful they were. In fact, we wouldn't want to do that. It would do no good and would only make us feel guilty. And it's something the Inner Child couldn't tolerate, because we would be "killing off" the very thing the Inner Child couldn't live with out. A parent. No matter how punishing and abusive they were.

So we want to get the focus onto the Inner Child's experience, and be with that. The Inner Child has been trying to get rid of its "uncomfortable" sensations by taking on "protective" thoughts. Only when we can recognize this, by being with those "uncomfortable" sensations and "protective" thoughts and seeing them for what they are, can true healing happen.

WHEN YOU HEAR A PUNISHING, CRITICAL OR MALEVOLENT VOICE, ASK, "WHO IS SAYING THIS?

In areas in which we are stuck as adults, I think we all hear voices in our heads saying things to us like, "You can't succeed; You're not allowed; You're no good."

As I said a couple of sections ago, we often remember and regard these voices as the malevolent and punishing voices of parents and caretakers. If we regard them in this way, it is impossible to do anything with these voices except futilely struggle against them and feel put upon and beaten by them.

It is only when we realize that these voices are coming from us, and are in fact, not malevolent adults, but hurt parts of the Inner Child inside of us doing their best to avoid their own pain and ward off our adult pain, that we can begin to know the voices for what they really are and incorporate them.

So whenever you hear a voice warning you of danger, telling you you're bad, telling you that it's a fact of life that you can't have something or that the outcome is going to be bad, ask, "Who is saying this?" And when you meet the Inner Child who is speaking, look at it, listen to its story, listen to what happened, feel what it feels and think what it thinks, and your fear and frustration will change to empathy and compassion.

I began writing this section on a plane ride to Tampa. My partner Shawn and I have had a home in Tampa for a number of years, and as part of our downsizing, we took a good look at the fact that, although we love it, we hardly use it, and the financial freedom we would have in not having to pay for it would allow us much more time to do projects we really dream of doing in New York.

As I landed in Tampa, I noticed how much I love the place, and at the same time had the thought, "This is good that we're selling this. I can see myself in New York, opening my shows on and off Broadway and traveling around the country developing new shows."

As I had that thought, I heard a voice loud and clear say, "Yeah, but the minute you clear the way for all that good stuff, everything you've been developing in New York is going to disappear. All the excellent meetings you've had are going to go south. All the projects you've been developing will turn to nothing." In short, the voice was saying, "Everything will fall apart if you go for what you want."

This is a voice I often hear, and I often feel extremely discouraged and begin to think, "What's the use of trying?"

But this time, having just finished working on the first part of this section, I stopped and asked, "Who's saying this?" I then waited quietly to see what would come up. I didn't rush. I didn't push. I knew it was some Inner Child part, and that that Inner Child part might be timid about coming forward.

After a couple of minutes, I remembered an experience I had had with Disney. I had conducted movie scores for them for many years, and had made the decision to taper off my conducting and be a full-time writer. Shortly after

I'd made that decision, I planned a trip to L.A. where I had a little conducting booked, and a lot of writing meetings and projects planned. Right before I went out there, EVERY writing meeting and writing project fell through and I was left with only the conducting.

As the months went by, I persevered, and I got a couple of writing projects. I wrote two great songs for the first project and yet I wasn't given the entire film to write. Then, on the second project, I wrote one of the greatest songs I'd ever written and right after I wrote it, the producing team changed, they decided to go in a "different direction," and I was fired.

So, here was a memory of an Inner Child's experience of preparing the way, letting go of one thing only to have the other fall through.

Now, here's the thing. I knew about this memory and had spent a lot of time being upset about it. But as I looked at it in light of what I was now working on, I realized that I had always looked at it from the point of view of what "they" did to me. This time, I decided to really look at the Inner Child who had experienced the pain of going through it. As I saw and felt that person, I understood that, of course, he would take on the "protective" thought, "Everything will fall apart if you try to go for what you want," to keep himself (and me) from ever going through that experience again. When I could really feel for him, in his pain, he was seen, and simultaneously, my Adult could see that this past experience doesn't necessarily mean that it is destined to happen again. My Adult could also see that even if it did happen again, I had tolerated it once and could tolerate it again.

Knowing this, it was still scary to contemplate what I was giving up in hopes that something new would happen, but it lost the absoluteness of the Inner Child's pronouncement, "Everything will fall apart if you try to go for what you want."

Now, having spoken to this Inner Child part, it was clear to me that this couldn't have been the earliest occasion on which this thought arose. So I sat and waited to see if an earlier incident would appear. And it quickly did.

I was brought back to an incident I knew a lot about, as it was one of the significant, psychologically formative incidents in my life. To summarize it briefly, I was 10, I wanted a bicycle, I asked all my relatives who usually gave me birthday gifts if they would give me money toward a bicycle, they did, I put the money in my piggy bank, went away to camp, and when I came back, the money was gone. My parents had taken it and put it away for college and said they didn't want me to have a bicycle. They also had no empathy for the fact that I might be upset and that I couldn't understand and be happy with the fact that college was better than a bike.

Now, I'd of course, worked on this incident in therapy for years and years, but again, from the standpoint of how awful and wrong my parents had been. This time, I simply worked with the Inner Child's experience of the incident. I saw how he would naturally take on the thought, "Everything will be taken away from you at the last minute (A variation of the thought, "Everything will fall apart if you try to go for what you want")."

When I could really feel what he felt, I had great empathy for him, and no longer saw this voice as coming from my parents, but from my own hurt Inner Child.

I'm sure we could go further and further back (my father once told me that when I was three I used to do something "so cute." I used to watch my brother building a big tall building out of blocks, and at the last minute I would walk over and kick it down. Hmm. Wonder what THAT was about.)

We don't always know exactly what incidents the internal voices we hear pertain to, but if, when we hear them, instead of believing them or railing against them as malevolent, we can simply ask, "Who is saying this?" and feel the sensations and think the Inner Child's thoughts that are coming from inside of us, we can transform these thoughts from certainties about our future being dished out by tyrannical parents, to fears being expressed by our Inner Child based on things that happened in its past.

If our parents could have done this with us when we were children, we wouldn't have these stuck, scared Inner Child parts inside of ourselves. But they couldn't, because they couldn't be with their own Inner Child parts. Fortunately, your Inner Child now has a new parent who can do this. YOU. What happened will never not have happened, but your Inner Child parts are finally seen, heard, felt and incorporated.

GETTING PAST BEING TERRIFIED OF OUR INNER CHILD

I spent the first part of this morning, as I often do lately, sitting in a quiet spot in my home with my eyes closed, looking at where I'm physical or mentally "uncomfortable," and simply being with the discomfort.

As I moved through the upper chest and shoulder that felt stuck, the right foot that felt "weird," the burning pain that suddenly arose in my right hand, the thought that I'll never finish this book, that I'll never be recognized, that the apartment we're selling won't sell, I noticed that each of these things scared me. Even though they're just thoughts and sensations, I'm afraid to even look at them.

I noticed that I jump to, "I'd better go to the doctor, this could be a sign of a serious illness," or, "It's too late. I've made too much of a mess of my life to ever have anything good," or, "Everything I've been working on is going to lead to nothing."

As I was noticing all this, I reminded myself that all these sensations and all these thoughts are not here to attack me. They are the sensations and thoughts of a child who is scared and worried and hurt and needs someone to be able to listen to it, not someone who is terrified of it and trying to get it to shut up.

As I sat with this, I realized that probably the way I'm feeling right now is exactly how my parents must have felt when I, as a child, had problems. My problems activated their own Inner Child, and they, unable to tolerate their own Inner Child, recoiled from or tried to fix mine.

And now, I WAS DOING THE SAME THING!

As I realized this, and became able to view these sensations and thoughts as the thoughts of a hurt child, I decided to slow down, take time and just sit with them, whatever and however they are. Not judge them, not try to run from them, not be impatient with them, but instead, to suspend my thoughts of having to "save myself" by fixing something or going to the doctor or even saying that nothing is wrong. And I just looked. Just felt the pain, not as my pain, but as the pain of an Inner Child who was trying to show me something.

At first it was just pain, but then there was a sort of thawing of the Inner Child. I could literally feel the Inner Child feeling accepted. "Oh, you're going to sit here with me? You're going to be able to stay with me and not be afraid and run? I have time. I have room."

And as that started to happen, I began to feel closer to the Inner Child. In some places, insights as to what was underneath the pain began to come in. In other cases, I just said, "OK, you don't have to tell me what this is, I'm just sitting here with you." Then creative ideas about other things started to arise. I noticed them, but went back to the child, saying, "Thanks, I'll keep those for later, but right now I'm just with you."

The sum total of this experience was that I realized that I have spent a lifetime being terrified of my Inner Child. And this terror has translated itself into hypochondria, anxiety, hopelessness, inaction, frustration and failure, as my Inner Child tried again and again to get my attention.

Often, when we first sit down with our Inner Child's sensations and thoughts, our habitual modes of getting away from them kick in.

See if you can get underneath your terror, and simply experience the Inner Child as it is. A scared, hurt child whose pain cannot hurt you in any way. It just needs you to see it and be with it.

And watch your terror turn to curiosity, your curiosity turn to awareness, your awareness turn to compassion and your compassion turn to love.

WORKING WITH OTHER PEOPLE'S INNER CHILD

One of the remarkable things I've found is that as I've become able to experience and understand that these "malevolent" inner voices are actually the voices of my Inner Child, I've been more and more able to experience the "malevolent" voices of other people as their Inner Child.

This has been especially useful in my relationship with my partner, Shawn.

Shawn can have quite a tendency to be prickly and to snap and say things in a cutting tone of voice. Early in our relationship, I would feel very hurt by these comments, thinking, "He doesn't care about me; He's not taking care of me; He's doing this to hurt me." I would think these things because his comments (even if they weren't about me at all) would sting and cut to the injured Inner Child part of me that had been hurt in similar ways when I was young. How frustrating that, rather than my partner being the antidote to my childhood (which is what I think most of us secretly hope our partner will be) he was, in fact, repeating it.

But as I began to shift my focus on my own Inner Voices from thinking of them as voices of a punishing adult to voices of a hurt child, a strange thing began to happen in relation to my reaction to Shawn's behavior. I began to experience his snapping as the voice of his scared Inner Child, rather than as the behavior of an adult, and I began to look for what was frightening him rather than what he was doing to me. In short, I began to be able to have the same compassion for his Inner Child as I had for mine.

This shift in me had several effects.

First of all, in some way, it gave Shawn more room to have compassion for himself, in that I was not escalating and recreating the painful experiences he'd had when he'd expressed himself in his childhood.

Next, as Shawn had more compassion for his own Inner Child, he actually began snapping less. Which meant that I was snapped at less.

And, most important for me, I began to realize that Shawn, rather than being the wrong partner because he was always activating my Inner Child, was the perfect partner in that he gave me constant practice in being empathetic to HIS Inner Child, which I could only do if I was being empathetic to MY Inner Child.

THE ONE WORD THE INNER CHILD NEEDS TO HEAR

Years ago (fortunately, MANY years ago) I was having an argument with my father about something he'd done in my childhood that I'd never gotten over. I was trying to get him to admit that what he had done was wrong or bad, and he was defending himself. He was saying things like, "When are you going to let this go? Do you want me to apologize? What do you want me to say?"

When he asked these questions, I stopped and thought, "What is it I really want my father to say?" And I realized that there was only one word that I wanted him to say, and that word was, "Oh."

Essentially what that "Oh" would mean was, "Oh, I see that that was your experience. I see that inside of you that's what happened." That's all the Inner Child needed. It wouldn't make the incident go away or not have happened. It wouldn't change the sensations that came up when I thought of the incident. It wouldn't necessarily even change the thoughts I would have when memories of the incident came up, or when things came up in the present that brought the incident to mind. But it would make everything make sense, and the child who felt unrecognized or hurt would now be recognized because someone would recognize how it felt and let it feel the way it felt.

SAY "OH TO YOURSELF

No matter what sensations the Inner Child is experiencing, no matter what thoughts the Inner Child is having, try saying "Oh" to them. "Oh, this is what you're feeling. Oh, you're having this thought. Oh, your stomach is churning. Oh, you're thinking you'll never have anything. Oh, you're thinking you're all alone. Oh, you're thinking you're going to run out of money."

Just say, "Oh" as if to say, "Oh, I see. Oh, I get it. Oh, I'm feeling it too."

Don't fix it. Don't give the child advice. Don't tell the child it's really alright. (It isn't alright where the child lives.)

Just be with it. Be with whatever comes up in each moment. Watch it stay the same. Watch it change.

When you can do this, your whole life will change.

EVERY UPSET IS AN OPPORTUNITY TO CONNECT TO YOUR INNER CHILD

When something upsetting happens, we feel the Inner Child's sensations and think the Inner Child's thoughts. In fact, this is the ONLY effect of the upset.

So:

Knowing that we have an Inner Child in us who had things happen that were too upsetting to experience, all alone, at the time;

Knowing that this Inner Child created "protective" thoughts to get away from those sensations;

Knowing that we are still holding those "protective" thoughts in the present and that they're keeping us from doing the things we want to do and fulfilling the dreams we wish to fulfill;

Knowing that all this child needs is to have our Inner Adult feel exactly what it's feeling and think exactly what it's thinking;

It stands to reason that EVERY time one of these upsets comes up, rather than trying to get rid of it (which leaves the Inner Child as isolated as before, since the Inner Child can NEVER get rid of it) EVERY upset becomes a new opportunity to be with the Inner Child, tolerate, with the

Inner Child, a sensation that it could not tolerate on its own and that we could not tolerate before, and thus open up new possibilities of thought because, as we know, the only way we can stay with a new thought we want to take on is to be able to stay with the sensations and "protective" thoughts it brings up.

So welcome ANY upset as a chance to do this, and EVERY upset will be experienced as a healing and expanding opportunity.

THE INNER CHILD, THE INNER ADULT AND THE OBSERVER

It's easy to say that we should welcome upsetting experiences as chances to heal, but it's easier said than done. In order to do this, we have to position ourselves so that we can tolerate and be with, as adults, the sensations and thoughts of the Inner Child that come up when present situations mirror past hurts.

It is only when we are in the position of knowing that who we are is an Invisible Observer, located nowhere, seeing, feeling and observing thoughts and sensations but not in any way being affected by them, that we can stay with our painful sensations and "negative" thoughts.

So we have an Inner Child who is living in the past (but experiencing the past in the present, since the present is all there is).

We have an Inner Adult who has the capability of being with the sensations and thoughts that the child couldn't be with, and of taking actions the child couldn't take in the world, because the Inner Adult has autonomy, has choices, has skills and has experience.

And we have the Noticer, Observer, Experiencer which is who we really are; an invisible consciousness located nowhere, having no opinion, just watching the Inner Adult and the Inner Child, just noticing all the thoughts and sensations and opinions and fear and acting out. No judgment. No opinion. No action taken. No criticism. Just noticing.

Our healing of our past and our integration as full beings with access to our unlimited potential, depends on how these three parts of ourselves interact.

OUR OBSERVER HOLDS THE SPACE FOR THE INNER ADULT TO BE WITH THE INNER CHILD

In order to allow the process of our Inner Adult experiencing our Inner Child's sensations and thoughts, simultaneously, in the same body, at the same time, there must be that part of us holding the space that although we're experiencing those uncomfortable sensations and thinking those "negative" thoughts, who we REALLY are is not, in fact, affected by any of this. This knowing who we REALLY are is what prevents us from acting out, running away or suppressing the process which is so essential to our healing.

Once the Adult can completely be with the Inner Child's sensations and thoughts, the Adult is free to take on any thought and do whatever he or she wants to do, because the ONLY consequence of having ANY problem is that the Adult will experience sensations and thoughts which the Adult is now able to tolerate.

So freedom in our adult life is achieved by the Adult being able to be with the sensations and thoughts of the Inner Child while being "held" by the invisible, located-no where Consciousness that we truly are.

PART VIII
LIVING AS AN ADULT

When you have reclaimed your connection with your Inner Child by practicing the four steps that constitute the BASIC SKILL of being able to be simply be with a problem and be with the "uncomfortable" sensations and "protective" thoughts that come with it, "problems" and challenges are handled completely differently. EVERY "problem" that arises is nothing more than an opportunity to be with whatever sensations and thoughts you're having. Our Inner Child does not have to keep the "problems" in place, because the Inner Child is immediately seen and felt by us. Now, we are free as adults, to, as they say in the famous Alcoholics Anonymous Serenity Prayer, "Accept the things we cannot change, change the things we can, and have the wisdom to know the difference."

The following are some examples of how this works. A few of them are from my life. Some are from other people's lives, in which case either permission to tell the stories using their names has been granted, or the names have been changed to protect people's anonymity.

CHAPTER 39
When We're With The Inner Child, The Adult Kicks In (12 Stories From Real Life)

DONNA & DONNITA

Donna, a woman in her sixties, had experienced a childhood filled with abuse that came in numerous forms; being ignored, being rejected, in fact not being allowed to speak for long periods of time.

When she first came to Thought Exchange, she came to work on her singing. Although she was a marvelous singer and very well liked by all the people in the class, she always experienced extremely "uncomfortable" sensations when she got up to sing. Her "interpretation" of these sensations was that nobody wanted to hear her sing, that it was hopeless for her to get up and sing at all, and that she should just give up, go away and disappear. The words "This is not for me" kept coming to mind.

Since these thoughts made no sense in relation to how talented and personable she was, or to how the class actually felt about both her and her singing, we could assume they were "protective" thoughts, taken on by a child who, when she had dared to express herself, had been tormented and criticized. This torment and criticism had resulted in the child experiencing "uncomfortable" sensations, which, to a child, were intolerable. With no competent adult to be with her, the child had no choice but to try to get away from those sensations. Since the thought that had produced the "uncomfortable" sensations was something in the area of "I can express myself" (the thought that, in fact, caused her to want to get up and sing) the "protective" thoughts she chose were; "It's hopeless; I'm awful; Nobody wants me; It's not for me."

As we worked on being with these sensations and being with the "protective" thoughts, Donna became more able to get up and sing, tolerate the sensations (which were still there, they just didn't stop her from singing) and accept that she was thinking these thoughts. It became clearer and clearer, as she was able to be with her thoughts and sensations, that these were the thoughts and sensations she had experienced practically all the time as a child. No adult had paid attention to this child, but now there WAS an adult who, after 60 years, WAS paying attention. It was Donna herself.

She decided to call her Inner Child Donnita. At first she would talk to Donnita and try to comfort her from an adult perspective, but gradually she began to be able to simply Observe when she was feeling Donnita's sensations and thinking Donnita's thoughts.

And an interesting thing began to happen. The more she could allow herself to feel the sensations Donnita was feeling and think the thoughts Donnita was thinking, the more she was able to realize that these were just sensations and thoughts among many possible sensations and thoughts. Gradually, as the Inner Child got taken care of, Donna's adult got liberated to be able to function as an adult WHILE the Inner Child was feeling the sensations she was feeling and thinking the thoughts she was thinking.

The proof of the pudding came in a taxi cab ride. Donna had taken a short taxi ride, and when she arrived at her destination, she gave the cab driver a credit card to pay for her $5 cab ride.

The driver began berating her, saying, "Lady, you can't give me a credit card for a $5 fare. I'm not gonna accept that. You gotta pay cash!"

Donna instantly felt a sinking feeling and a sense of anxiety, and noticed that she was thinking, "I'm bad; I'm wrong; All is lost; I'm in danger." But she was able to observe that she was thinking this, and was aware that these were Donnita's thoughts. She didn't try to suppress them or run. She just felt them. For about 10 seconds.

And then, an adult thought came to her, and inside, with a sort of smile, she turned to Donnita and said, "Don't worry honey, I'll handle this." And she turned to the cab driver and in a harsh voice said, "Listen you S.O.B! It's my right to pay any damn way I want and either you're gonna take the credit card or I'm going to call the police."

To which the cab driver shot back, "I'm gonna just drive away with you still in the cab."

To which she answered, "Fine, but you're going to do it with the door open, because I'm not shutting it!"

The cab driver took the credit card payment and Donna and Donnita got out of the cab. Donnita, of course, was having sensations and thoughts as this was happening, but because Donna had been able to be with her, Donna had been able to take care of her and act as an adult at the same time.

The whole experience proved to be quite exhilarating.

THREATENED BY THE MOVERS

This one happened to me.

For many years, I had stored about 20 plastic containers of scores, CDs and other items that were valuable and important to me, in a storage bin in my dad's basement in New Jersey.

When my dad moved to Connecticut to be nearer to us, we had to find a new place to store the containers. We found an inexpensive storage place about 20 miles from our home, and arranged to have the movers take the containers there after delivering my dad's stuff to his new home. The price for the entire move was all-inclusive.

The initial move to my dad's new place ended up taking much longer than expected. By the time they moved my dad's stuff in, it was 3 AM, and they hadn't delivered the containers to our storage space. Since the storage place closed at 7 PM, it was way too late to deliver them that night. The movers mentioned that they would be passing near there on the following Sunday, so I gave them the code to the gate and a key to the storage bin and told them to just deliver the containers on Sunday and mail us back the key.

A few weeks went by and we didn't get the key. I called to find out that they had not, in fact, delivered the boxes, and they said they would call me when they were delivering them.

I had sort of forgotten about it until one night, about two months later, I left a class I was teaching in New York and found that I had six texts and three phone messages. The movers had been trying to get in touch with me to tell me that they were delivering the boxes that night, had lost the entry code and the key, and needed me to be there. The calls came in at 8:15. They wanted me there by 10:00. I was teaching in New York and didn't get the messages until 9:45.

They had asked me to call the driver, and when I did, he told me that he was at the storage space and I needed to get up there. I told him I was 65 miles away and there was no way I would come up there. He said, "This is the second trip we've had to make on this move. We have to deliver this stuff tonight. If you don't come up, we're going to take it back to your father's house and leave it there." I told him he was not to do that. It wasn't my father's stuff. He then said, "Well you're going to have to pick it up in New Jersey or pay us to redeliver." I said that it wasn't my fault that they didn't deliver when they said they would, and this move was done on a flat fee basis. And on and on it went.

We got off the call with no resolution.

When I hung up, I noticed that I felt helpless. These movers had my stuff, they were going to toss it away or make me come and get it and pay more money. It was all so unfair and infuriating.

And then, I stopped and just felt my sensations. And as I felt this hotness in my chest and emptiness in the pit of my stomach, I realized that this kind of thing, where someone was terribly, crazily and irrationally wronging me, with me having no recourse, had been a recurring theme throughout my life.

I stayed with the sensations and the thoughts for a few minutes, just being with what it felt like to be wronged in this way. I was being with my Inner Child, who had felt this way many times.

And, as happens when we do this, since I was able to stay with the child's sensations and thoughts, adult thoughts came to mind.

I left a message for the mover saying that under no circumstances were they to deliver the stuff to my father, as the delivery would not be accepted. I called my dad and told him to call the desk and make sure they didn't accept any deliveries of containers. I called the desk myself to make sure. And I had the thought, "I'll deal with this tomorrow. I'm in the right so I should get what I want, and even if I had to pay something or, at worst, pick up the stuff in New Jersey, it wouldn't be a catastrophe.

By the time I got home, I was fine and it was a non-issue.

I got a good night's sleep, and the next morning I got up and spontaneously wrote a friendly email to the mover. I said, surely they didn't think they could call me at 8:15 and expect me to be home and available to drive 20 miles to the storage space. I said I understood how frustrating it must be for them too, and suggested that they hold the stuff until the next time they were passing the storage space, give me a couple of days advance notice and I would be there.

After four days, when I didn't hear back from them, I wrote a brief email saying I was just checking to make sure they'd gotten my previous email.

They wrote back to say that was fine, and gave me a date when they'd be up there.

Settled. When I took care of my Inner Child by being with his sensations and thoughts, I was able to find adult solutions to the "problem."

THE TONY AWARDS

Although I write books and lecture on metaphysical subjects, my lifelong career has been spent as a composer and conductor, working on Broadway, in the movies, on recordings and on TV.

I had co-written a show that had played briefly on Broadway. It was, to say the least, not a critical success. However, like any show that runs on Broadway, it was eligible for a Tony Nomination.

I truly didn't expect to get nominated, but of course in the back of my mind I hoped I would. On the day the nominations came out, I checked online and, as expected, I didn't get a nomination.

In the first conversations I had with people calling me, they either told me, "You were robbed. You should have gotten one," or they said things like, "Well, you knew you weren't going to get nominated so I'm sure you're not surprised," or "Well at least you were eligible," or even "Too bad. Sorry about that."

I noticed that although I was not terribly upset, there was a gnawing sensation that was uncomfortable, and NONE of the things that were being said were helping. In fact, I couldn't take them in.

So I went to my sensations. I felt a sinking in my chest, a little numbness in my arms and an emptiness in my stomach.

When I sat with those sensations, I began to become aware of thoughts like, "I never get recognized; I'll never have a hit; Nothing good happens for me; I'm always out of the loop," etc. I recognized these as all very familiar thoughts that I have thought frequently throughout my life.

I just stayed with the thoughts and sensations for about 10 minutes. And then my adult came into play. To the extent that I was able to feel the sinking sensations and think the thoughts my Inner Child thought, I was able to become aware of adult thoughts. The first thought I became aware of was, "Wow, I've always thought I was completely out of the loop, but this year I actually was in the running to be nominated. That's real progress." I then thought, "Now I'll be able to go on the cruise." (I was scheduled to be performing a show of mine on a cruise at the same time the Tony's were being presented.) Then I noticed that the Tony's didn't seem like such a big deal, like something out of my reach. It was just an award. I could win it in the future. Or not. And the next thing that happened was I got a call saying that the producers we were negotiating with about my next Broadway show were sending over a contract.

The point is, every once in a while I still get a little pang about not getting nominated, but whenever I get it I simply notice my sensations, notice my thoughts, do a little more bonding with my Inner Child by feeling his sensations and thinking his thoughts, and I'm very quickly back to my adult self that has a present-day understanding of the situation, not a living-in-the-past experience.

It hardly bothers me at all now, and I'm on to all sorts of other exciting projects. And who knows. Maybe one of them will lead to a Tony Award. Or not. My Inner Child's life, understandably, may be about that (although, of course, winning a Tony Award would not in the least bit change my Inner Child's past) but my adult has the ability to dream, the ability to want, the ability to enjoy success and the ability to experience disappointment and put it in perspective.

A BAD REVIEW

A friend of mine had put out a new book and his publicist had suggested that he ask his friends to post positive reviews about it on Amazon.

When he looked on Amazon, he saw one mediocre review and no others. The review wasn't bad, it was three stars out of 5, but some of the comments felt disparaging.

My friend went into a spin: He'd never sell his book; He was a lousy writer; This always happened, that he worked so hard on things and then they failed.

Being a Thought Exchange student, he went to his sensations and felt a kind of tingling numbness all over his body and a "tired" sense. He noticed he had thoughts like, "What's the use; I never have success; Everyone will either laugh at me or ignore my book because of this review."

He had gotten this information late at night, so he got into bed, just being with his sensations and thoughts, and went to sleep.

In the morning, he woke up, still feeling some of the sensations and thinking the thoughts, and he just stayed with them.

And...his Adult kicked in.

The first adult thought he had was, "Gee, anyone who's in show business or who is a writer or who is in the public eye has lots of ups and downs, gets lots of bad reviews. It goes with the territory, and they recover."

With this thought in mind, he instinctively sat down at his computer and wrote to numerous friends who he knew loved the book and asked them if they'd be willing to write reviews on Amazon. A slew of five-star reviews appeared, which were not only excellent but which directly contradicted the complaints the three star reviewer had.

Within a couple of days the whole thing seemed like a distant small incident and he was onto publicizing the book and doing his next creative projects.

DONNA AND DONNITA'S DIET

Donna, whom you met in the first story in this section, had had a weight issue all through her adulthood. She had tried everything; been to live-in diet programs, had a lap band installed, been on every diet known to man, and still she could neither break through to being thin, or keep whatever weight she had lost off.

We began working on her diet together, using Thought Exchange principles. What we noticed was that she could stay on a diet for a period of time, lose some weight, and then all of a sudden she would "go wild," "have to eat" and gain some weight back. Since we were working every week, we were able to catch why that was happening.

In every case, she had hit a new weight low and some sensation would arise that was so uncomfortable that she had to get rid of it by eating. (Mind you, by eating eight muffins, or a plate-full of French fries, or everything in sight.) We came to understand that at each of those weights, whatever uncomfortable sensation she had originally had (based on things that had happened in her childhood) she had made the same associations to it in her adulthood and thought she HAD TO get rid of them by eating. When we would sit with the sensations and simply feel them (a sinking, an emptiness, a backache) and notice the thoughts that came up (my life is empty, I'll never get what I want, I'll never be happy) she was able to stay on the diet.

One evening, Donna called me at home and said that she had been having the most physical pain she'd ever experienced, in the form of agonizing spasms in the muscles of the left side of her back and hip. She said she had been to her physical therapist, who said that all the muscles in her body were tightening up and wouldn't let go. They had given her three strong painkillers and they had done NOTHING to relieve the pain.

This was the clue that something else was going on. If the spasms were indeed just physical, the pain killers would have done something. I flashed on a time when I had suddenly developed a pain in my left leg that was so strong that I couldn't walk. I had tried all the doctors, all the painkillers, and nothing had worked. I then remembered reading Dr. John Sarno's groundbreaking book, *Healing Back Pain* (a book I highly recommend to anyone experiencing unexplained physical pain).

Dr. Sarno's theory is that when we don't want to experience certain thoughts or emotions, our body takes a little oxygen away from certain areas and we experience agonizing pain that distracts us from the thought we don't want to think or the emotion we don't want to feel.

I called Dr. Sarno, and when I went to him, he gave me a thorough physical examination and told me that my leg pain was indeed not physical (or not physical in the sense that it was not being caused by what the doctors were saying had caused it).

The moment he told me this, my leg pain ceased, but it was replaced by such a profound depression that I had to go into therapy with one of his psychotherapists to work on this deep depression that had been revealed. The result was that I didn't have the symptoms anymore, nor did I have the depression.

Back to Donna. I suggested to Donna that perhaps this pain was the deep pain that Donnita had experienced that was coming to the surface so that Donna could be with it and the Inner Child could finally have an adult recognize fully what the Inner Child had gone through.

The thing about this work is that we often start out very excited, making a lot of progress, because when we're able to be with the little pains of the Inner Child, the child is taken care of and feels better. But as we go along, the Inner Child begins to reveal the big things that stopped it, the unfathomable, un-feelable (for a child) pain, and if we want to heal, we have to be with that pain 100% and be with the thoughts that go with it.

So, on the phone, I asked Donna to sit down and close her eyes and go to where the pain was. It wasn't hurting the way it had when it was at its height but it was definitely there. She said she was afraid to go to it because she was afraid it would spread ("protective" thought). I told her to go to it anyway.

At first she said, "It's getting worse. I'm afraid it's going to hurt ("protective" thought). I asked her to stay with it and see what happened.

All of a sudden she said, "Oh, my God. I feel the most profound sense of emptiness and hopelessness." I asked her to stay with it, which she did. I asked her how her pain was, and she said, "It's not there. "

We sat together on the phone for a while, just me being with her being with Donnita feeling as an adult the Inner Child's sense of hopelessness while her Inner Child felt it as a child. They were feeling it as one. I asked her if she was OK to keep on feeling these sensations and thinking these thoughts and she said, "Yes." I told her that if the pain returned or if she had the urge to "eat the deep sense of emptiness and hopelessness away" she should call me at any time, day or night.

The next day we had a session, and she reported that she had no pain and was feeling more hopeful and excited about life than ever before. And she was back on her diet.

It turns out that she had hit a low weight that she hadn't seen in decades, and it was at this weight that the deep pain of the Inner Child came up. Her life had been spent avoiding this pain, not only by eating, but by making sure that she didn't succeed at certain things, she didn't step out and take a stand or live fully (which would have brought on the wrath of her mother when Donna was a child).

She was now no longer afraid of the pain because she had faced it with Donnita, her Inner Child. And because that pain had been part and parcel of a lot of thoughts of possibility that she hadn't dared to think for fear of the pain, she was now free to think those thoughts and life opened up wide, in the only place life can ever open up wide, in her INTERIOR EXPERIENCE.

As she continues working with her weight, she knows that there may be other "pockets of pain" where something comes up that she has to be with. But she now has more experience being with the pain, and also experience knowing that when she is with the pain, it may be extremely difficult, but the opening and the freedom that follow are what she's craved all her life and been unable to achieve. Until now.

LETTING AN UPSET BE UPSETTING

Mary Jo was taking a walk with her 20-month-old granddaughter. Her granddaughter had brought along her baby doll and was wheeling her in her baby doll carriage.

They came to a staircase, and when Mary Jo went to take her granddaughter's hand, her granddaughter lost control of the baby doll carriage and it went tumbling down the stairs.

Mary Jo's granddaughter burst into tears and was inconsolable. Mary Jo, finding it upsetting that her granddaughter was upset (another way of saying this is that Mary Jo could not tolerate, within herself, that her granddaughter was upset) tried to console her granddaughter by saying, "It's OK. Look, the doll is fine. Nothing happened. There's no reason to be upset."

The child only cried harder and louder.

Suddenly, Mary Jo had an inspiration. She knelt down, put her hands on the child's shoulders, looked her in the eye and said, "That must have been very frightening for you."

The child nodded her head and said, "Yes." She immediately stopped crying and they went for a lovely walk. All the child had needed was for her upset to be seen, felt and acknowledged by a competent adult.

TALKING TO ADULTS WHO HEAR YOU

I was visiting my best friend from childhood, Pat, and we were having an "adult" conversation. Her nine-year-old son Ben, who is my Godson, walked into the room and tried to join the conversation. Pat turned to him and said, "Honey, this is adult time." I could see that he was a little dejected at not being included, so I said, "We'll do something together later." Ben left the room.

After Pat and I had talked for a while, we joined the rest of the family, we all had dinner together and talked in the living room. When it came time for Ben to go to bed, we could see that he was in a bit of a snit, and we didn't know why.

The next day, Pat called me and said, "We have a problem. Ben is upset because you said you would do something with him and you didn't." I answered, "I thought I said we'd all do something together later, and we did all have dinner and sit around and talk." Pat responded, "Well, Ben didn't see it that way. He assumed you were going to do something specifically with him. And when I asked him if he wanted me to talk to you about it he said 'no,' so I'm not sure what to do here."

I said, "Well, when you get off the phone, why don't you tell Ben that you were just talking with me so you know I'm home, and see if he wants to call me to talk about it."

Now, I don't know about you, but I can't imagine myself, at nine, calling up my parents' friends and telling them I was upset. And frankly, I can't imagine my parents allowing me to do it. In such circumstances, I would have been told things like, "No, don't be silly. You heard it wrong. You shouldn't be upset."

Pat and I hung up, and two minutes later, my phone rang. The conversation went like this.

"Hello."

"Hi, David. It's Ben"

"Hi, Ben. How are you?"

"Well, actually, I'm not so good."

"Why not?"

"I'm upset with you."

"How come?"

"Well, you said you were going to do something with me yesterday and you never did."

"Gee, what I meant by that was that we would all have dinner together and spend time talking."

"Well, that's not what you said."

Pause.

"You know, Ben. You're right. I'm so sorry. Would it be OK if I make it up to you next time?"

"Sure. That would be fine."

"OK. See you soon. Love you."

"Love you, too."

The next time I came over everyone left me alone at the pool with Ben, and for an hour I taught him "G" language. ("G" language is a language we used to speak as kids where you inserted "dg" in between each syllable to make what you were saying unintelligible to adults or other kids who didn't know "G" language.) Ben and I had not only spent an hour together doing something all by ourselves, but he now had a nifty new skill to show for it.

What was fascinating to me was, that evening, Ben sat down next to me and said, "Did you remember that you were going to spend time with me?" My response was, "Yes, that's what I was doing when I was teaching you "G" language. "OK, just wanted to make sure."

It wasn't the time spent that was as important to Ben as the fact that I had remembered my promise and was being with him because I had promised.

The cherry on top of this story is that Ben, who is now a 27-year-old journalist and graduate of Yale, HAS NO MEMORY OF THE INCIDENT. By hearing him, being with him, mirroring him and acting on his thoughts and sensations, we essentially erased the trauma.

Another interesting thing is that this can only happen when an adult, mirroring presence is on the scene at the time. I have many such childhood traumas that were not handled in this way, and even though I spent years in therapy on them, I still remember them vividly. They don't affect me in the same way because my Inner Adult is now with my Inner Child any time they come up, but my Inner Child, who lives in the past and experienced the un-mirrored trauma, still experiences the trauma and probably always will.

ALLOWING YOURSELF TO THINK, "THIS WILL **NEVER** HAPPEN"

This one happened to me. I had spent a year with various shows of mine (I'm a composer by profession) falling through and losing their producers. They were all shows that were worthy of Broadway and somehow they weren't getting there. In addition, recently I had watched several contemporaries get shows to Broadway and I was really feeling depressed and frustrated.

I was at my wits' end as to what to do next, so using the techniques in this book (even I don't always do that. I get as caught up as anyone else in trying to FIX things) I simply sat with the sensations that arose based on this latest series of "failures."

I felt a sinking sensation in my whole torso, a kind of squirmy sensation in my groin (that my mind wanted to call "embarrassed and humiliated") and an overwhelming sense of fatigue.

I sat with it.

I then noticed that the predominant thought in my mind was, "I will NEVER get my shows to Broadway." (Interestingly enough, I had just had a show on Broadway the year before, but that didn't in any way stop me from thinking, "It will NEVER happen.")

That was the thought that came up, so I sat with it. And then an interesting thing happened. I suddenly remembered that after my partner of 15 years had left me (that's another book) I had spent three years KNOWING that because I was such an awful, leave-able person, I would NEVER have another relationship.

I've now been with my partner Shawn for 12 years. And it's the most wonderful, fulfilling, interesting, amazing relationship I've ever been in.

So I suddenly re-contextualized the thought as, "This is one of the stages of thought that I always go through on my way to having great success."

In this way, I could comfortably have the thought, knowing that all that was happening was that I was re-experiencing something that my Inner Child had felt and thought that had never been seen and felt by an adult. A hopelessness that the Inner Child took on because he had no options in certain circumstances where he had dreamed of having something, and had to take on "protective" thoughts to keep him away from those dreams.

Knowing this, my adult kicked in. The adult, who knows that there are always infinite possibilities and also knows that my value as a person is not dependent on whether my show gets to Broadway, immediately came up with a whole bunch of new people to call, and new tacks to try. In addition, things also seemed to start coming at me from outside me. Those things, of course, were always possible, but they were now revealed to me because my perception had changed.

EXPECT THE WORST AND MAKE THE CALL

Recently, I had an experience which really demonstrated the potential discrepancy between the Inner Child's experience (and predictions) and what actually happens in the present.

I had been working with a high powered deal broker who was a fan of mine and had stepped in to try to connect me with some major players to invest in my music and produce my shows.

My Inner Child, of course, thought, "This is ridiculous. I'm nothing. These people are not going to give me the time of day."

My deal broker friend handed my scripts and scores to one of the high-up associates of major producer who said she would read them and pass them on to the producing firm's New York representative.

A week later, I got a call from the deal broker saying that I should call the New York representative and try to get an appointment with him.

I felt an immediate sinking sensation (obviously coming from my Inner Child) at the thought of how humiliating this call would be.

I emailed the deal broker and asked if she knew if this guy had read the material, if they were interested, if I could ask him to call her? She called me back and said that what she does is put people together and then it's up to me. She said she was too busy (with REALLY big and important deals, my Inner Child was sure) to get involved in having this producer call her and get her in the middle, and that I should just make the call and see if I could get an appointment. She said she didn't know if this person had actually received the material or not.

In truth, this deal broker is someone who is very supportive of me, a very big fan, and had sought me out in the first place. And, quite frankly, I'm a successful and beloved songwriter.

This did not make a bit of difference to my Inner Child. I hung up the phone and noticed what I was thinking.

"Well, that was a brushoff. She just wants to get rid of me. There's no way these people are going to be interested in me. I should just call the deal broker back and say, 'Thanks for trying, but I'm too pathetic to even waste your time on, so I'll just give up.'"

My Inner Child assumed that I would be lucky to even get someone on the phone, and if I did, they would be nasty, say, "Who are you and why the heck are you bothering me?" and hang up.

As I sat there, I realized that I was now in the emotional position I would be in if the Worst happened. If, in fact, I did call and get a horrible brushoff, I would feel and think just like this.

So, I was already at the bottom.

I had nothing to lose.

I picked up the phone.

A receptionist answered, very pleasantly, and I said, "Hi, this is David Friedman. Is David around? (That was the producer's name.)

The receptionist said, "Oh, hi David! You know, the other David is in London at the moment. But what can I do for you?"

(Well this was not how I'd foreseen the conversation going, but of course, it could still go sour).

I said, "The deal broker told me she had given my scripts to one of your producers who was going to give it to David and that I should call David and see if we could have a chat about them."

She said, "Oh, listen. Let me shoot him a text and see what he wants to do. Give me your number. I'll call you back."

I gave her my number, my Inner Child assuming I would never hear from her again.

Five minutes later, she called back. "David said, why don't you set up an appointment to meet in person."

WHAT??? (That was my Inner Child's thought)

She then said, "He's moving his office to London so he'll be running back and forth a lot, so it would work best for him to have the meeting after July 15th.

(Ah, there it was. I was leaving town for five weeks on the 11th.)

I said, "Ooh, I'm leaving town for five weeks on the 11th to go on tour. I have a reading of a new show in Connecticut on the 9th and I'll only be in town on the 10th before leaving."

She said, "That sounds exciting. Let me see what we can do. We'll at least get you a phone meeting. Let me call him."

(OK. That's the end of that.)

She called back and said, "Did you say you were going to be in town on the 10th?" "I did." "Well David was planning to stay home and pack that day, but he said if you can do it at 3:30 in the afternoon he'll make a trip in to the office.

WHAT THE HELL IS GOING ON? (My Inner Child again.)

I hung up, amazed at the discrepancy between what my Inner Child thought would happen and what actually did happen. Of course, my Inner Child immediately went to the thought that this doesn't matter because nothing will come of it and he'll just do a courtesy meeting, maybe out of respect for the deal broker.

But at any rate, I realized that I was able to make that call and at least leave the possibilities open, because I was able to be with the enormous fear and doubt and hopelessness that my Inner Child felt. I didn't have to stuff it or hide it. Had I done that, it probably would have gotten enacted.

Now, to follow up, the day of the appointment arrived, I showed up at 3:30, and the secretary said, "Hi, you must be David. We had you down for 2:30 and the other David has a 4:00 appointment out of the office." I said I was quite sure we'd said 3:30 though I could be wrong (actually I was QUITE sure we'd said 3:30 because we had purposely pushed it toward the end of the day and I was coming from another appointment that would have been too close for me to ever have set a 2:30). She was abjectly apologetic and said it must have been her mistake. She said, "Well, let's at least get you two together for a few minutes."

David came in, apologizing for the mistake, asked if I could possibly come in tomorrow (I couldn't, I was flying out at the crack of dawn) and said, "OK, let's just meet and greet and when you get back we'll have a proper sit down."

He then said, "Listen, before we start, I wanted to say, I'm sure you've heard this many times before....."

(My Inner Child KNEW that what I was about to hear was that they're not really doing new musicals or there's no money around or there are no theaters around or I'm not famous or successful enough.)

"...but your music has meant the world to me. In fact, a singer who is a close mutual friend of both of ours sang your song 'Listen To My Heart' at our wedding. "

(WHAT???????)

And so we had a conversation in which he asked me about the history of the shows, I told him what we were looking for and why I thought this one show would be a perfect fit, and he said he'll bring it to London, give it to the partners and we'll talk further.

Now this doesn't mean that I'm going to get my shows produced by this company, and of course my Inner Child has had enough experiences of "Everything's going to be taken away at the last minute" to not be at all surprised if, in fact, nothing comes through, but it is, to me, a great example of how it's the inclusion of the Inner Child that allows the adult to function.

Once you can tolerate being with the Inner Child's fear and dire predictions, the outcome can only be as dire as you expected, or better. If it turns out to be as dire as you expected, you already know how to be with that. And if it turns out better, your adult is on the way to getting what it wants without deserting or losing the Inner Child.

"I CAN GO OUT THERE WITH THAT!"

I was being honored with a Lifetime Achievement Award, and my friend Lucie Arnaz was presenting it to me.

We were backstage, waiting to go on, and we were both nervously pacing the floor. Lucie had to go out there and spend five minutes speaking intelligently, amusingly and glowingly about me and my achievements. Then I had to go out there, speak, sing and receive an award.

We were experiencing the usual jitters that one experiences before going onstage. The fact that Lucie is a star who has performed on stages thousands of times, and that I am a very experienced musician and speaker who was there to be honored by all in attendance, did nothing to diminish the uncomfortable sensations and resultant "protective" thoughts ("I'll make a fool of myself; I don't know what I'm doing; They'll all hate me").

Suddenly, Lucie turned to me and said, "OK. Thought Exchange. What are my sensations? My throat is tight, my stomach is churning and my hands are shaking."

Just at that moment, the announcer said, "Ladies and Gentlemen, won't you welcome the one, the only, Miss Lucie Arnaz!"

Lucie paused, looked at me, and said, "I can go out there with that," strode onto the stage and was delightful, charming and funny.

I took her lead, felt my sensations, and went out, sang beautifully, spoke eloquently and received my award.

SENSATIONAL!

USING CRITICISM, FAILURE AND OPPOSITION TO HEAL

So far, we've been talking mostly about how to deal with our Inner Child's thoughts and sensations. Often, however, when we try to point out to someone (or even to ourselves) that whatever pain or upset is going on is going on only in the Inner Child, they (or we) will say, "But no! It's actually happening in the world. Look what that 'other' person said. Look what that 'other' person did! Look at the 'failure' I'm seeing. Are you saying I caused this to happen?"

Whenever we're criticized or opposed by the "outside" world, it's a natural reaction to either feel guilty, ashamed, frustrated, angry or to refute what the person or event is telling us as untrue, unfair, wrong, incorrect, idiotic, etc. Of course, this will often be our first reaction, but if we hold onto it and think of is as the objective truth, we lose a valuable opportunity to use the "negative" criticism and "unwanted" events to heal our Inner Child.

Often, traditional "positive" thinking will say things like, "Don't let those comments get you down. Tell yourself that's not true, it's just 'their' problem. You're not going to let them stop you like the others did. That's just like your horrible mother but now you're an adult." In short, "positive" thinking is telling you to push your Inner Child's reaction aside and REPLACE it with "positive" thoughts and "positive" actions.

I say, "GOOD LUCK TRYING TO DO THAT!"

If we remember that what we see in the world is just a mirror that reflects our own thoughts back to us, we understand that our reaction to whatever has been done or said is revealing thoughts that WE have often long-held. It is these thoughts that are producing our experience of the world, not the other way around. So the world, just like a mirror, is HELPING us to experience what our Inner Child is thinking. This being so, we certainly don't want to CANCEL those thoughts.

The important thing is to be with the Inner Child, NOT THE INCIDENT OR COMMENT. When we can do this, we finally get to be the hearing, seeing, feeling parent to our Inner Child, who wasn't seen when incidents like the present incident happened earlier in life. And if you're receiving the criticism now, you can be sure that it's because YOU are holding the thought. Otherwise it wouldn't even appear, or if it did appear, you'd experience it much differently.

When we can really be with the criticism or failure, and transfer that to being with our Inner Child, we often find that we are actually grateful that the person said what they said or that the incident happened.

A wonderful example of this came up in one of our Thought Exchange classes.

George (not his real name) had spent his life being a successful entrepreneur. But even with all his success, there was a level of great success that continually eluded him. Recently, he had found himself facing a lot of opposition in raising money for a project he wanted to develop that would move him to a new level of "bigness" (his word) in the world.

George was someone who was used to pushing, targeting, moving forward, feeling the fear and doing it anyway. This had gotten him very far, but it wasn't bringing him to the level he hoped to achieve.

In class, George was a very hard worker and made great progress, but there were some qualities of his that many other class members found irritating.

When we would finish the opening meditation and I would ask what people's reaction was to the meditation, you could see (or so it seemed to me and to members of the group) that George, rather than really being involved with people, was just biding his time until he could speak about his own issues. A class never went by when he didn't take the floor, usually early on, to make sure he got to work on what he wanted to work on.

He also had a habit of interjecting his own observations when other people were working with me, which many in the class experienced as his interrupting the flow in order to work out his own issues rather than the issues of the person who was talking.

George was feeling that one of the other class members, Kay (not her real name), was irritated with him, and he confronted her and asked if he had done anything to upset her. Kay told him, in clear but not attacking terms, how she felt about some of the ways he was behaving in class.

George's reaction was to say that Kay was wrong about that, that he did this for a living and thus was very tuned in and connected to other people's issues, and that he was uncomfortable being in class with Kay feeling that way about him.

In looking at this, it was clear to me that being able to "get" this rather than fight it would actually be the answer to George's breaking through to the experience of success he desired. These behaviors were clearly coming out of a sense of inadequacy that his Inner Child held, and the more George pushed to overcome it, the more the mirror of the world reflected it back to him. In meetings, even though he was experiencing himself as working hard, going for the goal and being helpful to others, what was reading was his tension, his desperation and his thought that he didn't deserve the success he desired.

This could be the ultimate shift that would allow him to break through, but in order to make that shift he would have to, in essence, re-experience the most painful parts of his childhood; the rejection, the misunderstanding of his motives, the feelings of invisibility. The world, in this case in the form of other class members, was here to help him do it, if he could only allow it.

George chose to leave the group, saying that he didn't feel safe or supported there. I suggested that the group WAS supporting him by safely and lovingly reflecting back to him what he needed to see about himself, but he insisted that they were "wrong" and that it was their problem. I said that it was fine if he wanted to leave the group and not deal with this at this time, and assured him that he would have other opportunities to deal with it in the future, since when we leave one mirror and step in front of another, we will always see the same reflection.

In my own life, I also have areas of success that have eluded me. I actually have noticed that I have always held thoughts like, "The world will not recognize my talents" or, "I will not be remunerated for my talents."

The reason I was able to notice these thoughts is because that's what kept happening. For years I would fight to get the world to recognize and remunerate me, but that was as impossible as trying to get a mirror to reflect something that's not in front of it. Finally, after getting so many rejections that I couldn't ignore them, I began to see that the work had to be done on the inside, not on the outside. As I've done this, I've seen the reflection change. My Inner Child may always think those "negative" thoughts, but I can be with them, see, feel and hear them, so I don't have to have them reproduced in the mirror of the world for me to see them. This way of being helps me in several ways. First of all, it leaves my adult free to think and act in ways that allow me to see the world as I wish to see it. And, should I revert to ignoring my Inner Child's thoughts and sensations, they will immediately appear in the mirror of the world so I can work on them.

So when you receive criticism or repeated failures keep occurring, of course allow yourself to feel them and think the "negative" or defensive thoughts you're thinking. Then do what the title of this book suggests. Use your "negative" thoughts (and this includes "negative" circumstances) to see, incorporate and thus heal your Inner Child.

YOU HAVE MY COMPLETE ATTENTION

A couple of years ago, I experienced several traumatic events, within a short time period, that generated all sorts of symptoms and sensations. The most upsetting one was a persistent itch in my chest which, when I scratched it, would develop into an "angry" dry, crusty, itchy rash.

I would go to dermatologist after dermatologist, trying to get rid of this rash, to no avail. Creams and treatments that were "guaranteed" to work, didn't.

I then began to think that I must have some serious underlying disease. Lymphoma. Bone cancer. Kidney or pancreatic cancer.

Having had no success with conventional doctors, I took the nutritionist and homeopathic route. They told me I had a leaky gut and was allergic to dairy, soy, sesame, eggs and a host of other things. I began to take 30 vitamins a day to cover all my "deficiencies."

I didn't feel better.

One of the other "symptoms" that appeared was that my singing voice began to not work properly, which was extremely upsetting because I'm a songwriter and have many occasions on which to perform my songs around the country.

Gradually, I noticed I was feeling hopeless, like my life was over, like I was being persecuted, like nothing good would ever happen and I might as well just end it all right now.

Practitioners began telling me that my meridians and systems were congested and not working properly, especially the ones that had to do with grief and anger. So I began writing about that every morning, getting in touch with feelings I had "skipped" over the years.

I still itched.

One day I thought, "OK. Put your money where your mouth is. You are having a sensation, your Inner Child is trying to tell you something, trying to have you feel what it feels, and you're trying to stop it, get away from it, 'heal' it, 'cure' it. In short, you're trying to get rid of it and ignore it. "

"You're hearing your Inner Child's helpless, tortured, upset, hopeless voice, you're regarding it as a malevolent voice that's trying to hurt you, and you're trying to KILL IT. So naturally, to survive and keep trying to get heard by you, it keeps trying to get your attention, with itching, with fatigue, with a voice that doesn't work, with thoughts of hopelessness. And you keep trying to push it away."

With that realization, I said to myself, "OK. You've just written a whole book on the importance of being with your sensations, however 'uncomfortable' they may be. You MUST be with your sensations, no matter how 'uncomfortable,' no matter how painful. And you must be with them without any effort to get rid of them or get away from them. Even if they last forever."

And with that, I turned to the itching in my neck and just itched.

At last, I was saying to my Inner Child,

YOU HAVE MY COMPLETE ATTENTION.

Having now given my Inner Child my complete attention, what I noticed next was really interesting. As I just allowed myself to experience itching, and viewed that itching as my INNER CHILD'S discomfort that needed to be seen and felt, rather than as MY discomfort that needed to be taken away, I began to notice that I was not only getting new information, but that my thoughts were shifting.

Rather than thinking of that part of my body as attacking me, I began to think of it as a part that I had disowned. When I looked at it that way, I began to think of my chest and neck area as the passageway between my heart and my head and my mouth. And I began to understand that somewhere along the line I had blocked that area so that the painful feelings in my heart would not reach my consciousness and would not come out of my mouth.

As I looked at this, I realized that this was actually a lifelong way I'd had of dealing with difficulties. Gradually, memories of difficulties began to surface and I stayed with my Inner Child. My perception of the itching began shifting. Rather than thinking of it as something that was attacking me and could hurt me, I began to think of it as a "coming back to life" of that area, as a sign of feeling, as a sign of awareness of upset. The more I did this, the less I itched and the more "upset" I began to feel.

Over the next period of time, my physical symptoms gradually began to shift and disappear, to be replaced by a conscious knowledge of the pain that they had been created to cover. Instead of focusing on the symptom, I was now focusing more and more on being with the pain of the Inner Child.

The interesting thing is, the more aware I was of the Inner Child's pain, the more liberated I became to be able to function as an adult. My being with these "negative" thoughts and "uncomfortable" sensations did not, as people often fear, mean that "negative" things happened. In fact, it was quite the opposite. I was able to move forward with numerous things I'd been afraid to do, WHILE having the "uncomfortable" sensations and "negative" thoughts of the Inner Child. I became clearer and clearer about what was the Inner Child and what was the Adult, and the fact that I could hold them both at the same time and distinguish the two from each other allowed the fearful child to be fully held and seen while the adult me became more fearless.

USING THESE STORIES FOR YOURSELF

As I'm sure you noticed, all these stories have the same pattern. We have an upsetting incident happen, the Inner Child's sensations and thoughts are stimulated, and when we can be with them, our adult capacities become available to us and we resolve the problem in one way or another. As adults, we have powers of tact, negotiation and creativity that are not available to a child. We have more freedom of choice. And we have the ability to be with disappointment and accept losses without globalizing them.

As we begin to understand this, EVERY challenge becomes an opportunity to connect with our Inner Child, strengthen our capacity to be with thoughts and sensations, and regain our capacity to function as adults.

As you go through life, see if, instead of fighting off upsets, you can move as quickly as possible to experiencing your sensations and simply thinking whatever thoughts come up.

Just stay with them, and watch your adult thoughts, which contain both solutions and acceptance, rise to the surface.

PART IX
PRACTICAL MATTERS

So, we don't live in the physical world, but only in the world of experience.

But, we do have the physical world (whatever it is) at our disposal, to use for the purpose of expanding our awareness of the infinite possibilities for EXPERIENCE that exist inside us.

Many people, including New Thought students, often think that the goal of life is Manifestation. That would be like saying that the "goal" of putting on a new outfit is to see it in the mirror. The mirror allows you to see the outfit, but the EXPERIENCE of what you see is within you.

As you read through the next section, it's very important to remember that all of these "practical" activities that have "goals" attached to them are, like the games we talked about earlier in the book, being participated in not for the purpose of Manifestation but for the purpose of Inner Awareness of the Infiniteness that we are. Manifestation is just the mirror to show us which part of that Infiniteness we're holding in mind.

TWO IMPORTANT TRANSITIONS

In the course of our studying New Thought, there are two important transitions we have to make in our understanding that will help us to use all of these "practical" pursuits as pathways to Enlightenment.

When I first began studying New Thought, I, like most people, thought of the physical world as the Source. Things in the physical world, like success, relationship, money, even where I lived and how I looked, would determine my value as a human being and would also determine how happy and fulfilled I would be in life.

I, like most of us, was raised with the idea that the object of life is to achieve and have things in the physical world.

Even "emotional" things that seem to be interpersonal, like a "relationship" or "love" were still often thought of as things to "have," things to check off, things to possess as part of the REAL package of having success and money and comfort and notoriety. Things.

As we live and grow, we usually, at some point, run into the "invisible" world of Spirituality. The world that does not contain "things," but rather contains experience.

The misconception is that many of us think that Spirituality is something to be "used" for the purpose of getting the "things" we want in the REAL world, which we think is the physical world.

Even religion is most often thought of in this way. I can't tell you how many Fundamentalists I've heard say things like, "I prayed to God to get me this job and God came through." Or, "God is so good, He cured me of this disease or sent me money or sent me a boyfriend or girlfriend." In this concept, God is here to give us "things." We "worship" God so that God will show us favor and give us "things," and if we don't, God will punish us and not give us "things."

The Spiritual world is thought of as a tool to get us "things" in the physical world.

In fact, the exact opposite is true.

The first important transition I had to make in order to begin to be able to live out Spiritual Principles was to realize that Thought is the Source of the "things" I see in the physical world. That these "things" that we see in the physical world are reflections, out-picturings, manifestations of thought. The revelation was that Thought must come first.

This new perspective definitely brought me closer to the Truth, and gave me a new way to work with life. Holding "positive" thoughts, being aware that what I envisioned would be reflected in the world, I thought I had mastered the "art" of living life. The Secret, as it were, was to hold the thoughts I wanted and watch "things" appear. The goal was to have "things" appear... and then I would be happy.

However, as I went along, and did in fact see a lot of great stuff appear, I began to realize that there's a big fallacy to this way of thinking, and it's one of the major pitfalls we meet when studying New Thought.

In this way of thinking, I thought of spirituality as a technique to use that would get me the "things" I truly thought were important and that I wanted and needed in the physical world. The physical world was still where I thought I lived, what I thought of as the REAL world, and spirituality, or the invisible world, was a tool that I could hopefully use to get to the goal of having "things" in the REAL, physical world.

If we're truly to understand, practice and reap the enormous benefits of New Thought, there's a second crucial transition we have to make, and this can be the most challenging one, because it not only flies in the face of what most of us have been taught through all of our earlier lives, but it flies in the face of what we think we see before us, where we think we live, and what MOST humans agree is the Truth.

In order to truly utilize and live New Thought principles, we must make the transition from thinking that we're doing all this "spiritual stuff" so that we can have something in the REAL, physical world, to understanding that the "spiritual stuff" IS the REAL world. The "spiritual stuff" is the point. The WHOLE point. It's the ONLY world that exists, or at least the ONLY world we can experience.

So, with this new perspective in mind, let's take a look at some of the areas that people often find challenging in various ways.

And in light of the fact that this book is called "The Healing Power of Negative Thoughts", let's look at those challenges as pathways for us to get in touch with and connect to our Inner Child, rather than as problems that need to be solved or overcome.

By looking at challenges in our lives in this way, we can hold every challenge as another opportunity for us to be with our Inner Child, and by doing so, to heal.

USING DIETING TO HEAL OUR INNER CHILD

Want to feel what the Inner Child is feeling, and think what the Inner Child is thinking? Easy. Go on a diet!

One of the most common methods we use to try to escape "uncomfortable" sensations and the thoughts that go with them is eating. (Drinking is of course another one. Want to find out why you drink so much? Stop drinking!)

But let's look at eating. We have "uncomfortable"sensations and we stuff them down with food. The thing is, when we do that, we gain weight.

But the tactic works in that, at least temporarily, we don't feel the "uncomfortable" sensations. So we begin to get into a cycle of using eating to assuage or even to circumvent "uncomfortable" sensations. And we get fatter.

When we begin to control what we eat, usually we are happy for the first few days. We're losing weight, and isn't that what we want to do? We're having thoughts that when we're thinner, we'll be more attractive, healthier, our lives will be better.

And then we hit the first spot where some sensation from the past that we didn't want to feel got covered by eating and the subsequent weight gain that went with it. And bingo! We feel that sensation. We experience the sinking feeling, the emptiness, the butterflies, whatever, and we think the thoughts that go with it. Often our first thoughts are thoughts like, "I need to eat; This won't work anyway; I'm not getting enough carbs" (I actually had that thought while I was dieting once, and did what I thought was perfectly sensible at the time – I ate eight ice cream sandwiches!) Another one of my favorite thoughts at times like this is, "I'm losing weight too fast. I must be sick. I'd better test that by breaking the diet and seeing if I gain weight." (I always do!)

Have you ever noticed that there are certain weights which you keep approaching and "bouncing off" of? Those are generally weights at which something happened which we didn't want to feel. I recently lost 50 pounds, and at 198 and again at 187 I hit them three or four times, bounced up a few pounds, came down, bounced up, and did that several more times. At a certain point I went into feeling truly empty and having hopeless thoughts. When I was able to stay with those sensations and thoughts, my weight started to drop again.

So yes, diets are great because they are physically healthy and because we look and feel better. But a possibly even greater benefit is that they force us to connect to the sensations and thoughts of our Inner Child. And when we can finally be with these sensations and thoughts instead of having to run from them or suppress them, we become whole, we become able to choose our actions no matter what sensations and thoughts we're having, and in addition we look and feel physically great.

Another way of saying this is, you can't be thin unless you can tolerate the EXPERIENCE of being thin. If you're trying to get thin to get away from your Inner Child, the Inner Child will keep throwing "uncomfortable" sensations and "protective" thoughts in your way until you recognize it. Being thin is not necessarily feeling comfortable. It's feeling whatever you're feeling and noticing whatever the Inner Child is thinking when you're thin. Only when you can do that can you actually be thin and stay thin, if that's what you want to do.

BEFORE YOU EAT, TAKE A SENSATION BREAK

The sensations that come up when we diet can be so strong that often the food is in our mouths before we even realize it. Sometimes we just feel that we can't tolerate the sensations, and even though we know better, we eat.

We must be gentle with ourselves and notice that dieting can be really challenging, not because it's difficult to know how to lose weight (we all know how to do that) but because what dieting really is is a process of reclaiming our ability to be with the sensations and thoughts that we could not be with as children.

So even if you feel you have to eat something that's not on your diet, and decide you're going to do it, I suggest a five-minute Sensation Break. When you see something and say, "I don't care. I'm going to eat it," say to yourself, "OK. I'm going to eat it. But before I do, I'm going to go to my body and experience my sensations. Experience whatever pain, emptiness or shaking is there, and also notice the thoughts I'm having of hopelessness or upset or whatever."

Now, before you eat, simply be with those sensations and thoughts. In this way you're spending time being with your Inner Child's experience, both in terms of sensations and in terms of thoughts. This, in itself, is healing to the Inner Child. After five minutes, even if you eat, you have practiced, for five minutes, being with sensations and thoughts you have not been able to be with before. By simply doing this for five minutes, you and your Inner Child have experienced healing, and more possible thoughts have opened to you.

After the five minutes you may not even feel like eating. But if you do, don't worry about it. Eat, knowing that you have practiced being with sensations and thoughts, and that as time goes on and you incorporate more of these childhood experiences into your adult self (where they can be tolerated) you will experience more and more unlimited possibility in your life, because you will be able to think any thought, have the sensations that go with it, and be able to do anything you wish to do.

And you'll be able to stay on your diet.

NOTE: When we hit certain extremely challenging sensations, five minutes may seem too long a time to have to tolerate them. If this is the case, take a 30- second break. Or a one-minute break. Whatever you can tolerate. But set the amount of time before you begin the break and try to stick to it. And if you don't succeed, try again next time.

USING TITHING TO HEAL OUR INNER CHILD

Want to experience what your Inner Child is thinking and experiencing around money and prosperity? The quickest way to connect with the Inner Child's sensations and thoughts around money is to tithe.

Tithing is the practice of giving 10% of all you earn to your church. In traditional Christianity, tithing has often been treated as charity, as an obligation and as a responsibility to support the church.

In New Thought, it's viewed quite differently, although even in New Thought circles, tithing is one of the most feared and misunderstood practices. In New Thought, tithing is giving 10% of the "spiritual food" you've received at your church, or from anywhere in fact, back to the Source of that Spiritual Food, so that that Source can thrive, prosper and continue to dish out more Spiritual Food.

The underlying concepts around Tithing are:

- Abundance is infinite.

- The experience of abundance is an interior experience.

- Thought is the cause of how much of the infinite, ever-present abundance you are able to experience.

- Your church (as well as people, teachers, organizations, etc.) is a source of New Thoughts that allow you to experience more abundance.

- Since the "outside" world is only a mirror of what you're thinking, you have to already be thinking you're abundant in order to see abundance.

- By tithing, (or conversely, not tithing) you are taking an action that, as it were, puts your money where your mind is.

I think most of us would agree, as we look around our world, that one of our biggest problems, our biggest challenges, seems to be MONEY. Money of course, like everything else physical, is nothing. But our thoughts about money create, in most of us, tremendous limitation in what we think we're allowed to think, what we think we're allowed to do, what we think we're allowed to have. And those thoughts come from our earlier life, from our earlier experiences and from what we saw and were taught.

Our thoughts about money, in many cases, reflect in our seeing the world as a place of limitation and lack. This is because we erroneously think that money is limited, hard to get, and that money, which we think of as so scarce, means things about our lack of value or worth. So we hold these thoughts about OURSELVES and the result is that what we see around us is lack.

In fact, money is no scarcer than water. It's all around us, EVERYWHERE. If you asked me for a glass of water, I would give it to you immediately. I would give you 50 glasses of water. Why? Because I know water is infinite. SO IS MONEY! It's everywhere. But we only see that portion of it that is in our consciousness.

If you lived in Biafra or some other drought-ridden nation, you might be unwilling to part with a glass of water because the consciousness there is that there is a great lack of water. And yes, they're seeing no water around them, but there's plenty of water in the world. It's only our consciousness that creates ANYONE lacking water. There's not only plenty of water in the world, but there are plenty of ways to get it to everybody. Often the only thing in the way of getting water to everyone is our consciousness that money is scarce and that we can't "afford" to get water to the people who need it.

So one of the biggest issues we have is our consciousness about money, which is showing up in the mirror as our experiencing our lives as limited. And TITHING is the greatest and most efficient way I know to break open that consciousness and experience abundance.

The way tithing does it is this. By taking on the thought "money is abundant and flowing," (which we must be thinking in order to tithe, otherwise we would NEVER give away 10% of our money) by taking on this thought and taking an action on it, we bring up every doubt we have about money, every fear, every uncomfortable sensation. So tithing is not fun, it's not easy, it's not comfortable. It's about as much fun and as easy as doing 100 push-ups or running the marathon or...being married. It brings up "negative" thoughts and "uncomfortable" sensations.

But these "negative" thoughts and "uncomfortable" sensations, or more accurately, the fear of them, the avoidance of them, are what are keeping us from seeing the infinite abundance that already exists inside our invisible consciousness. Just as doing 100 push-ups gives us inner fortitude. Just as running the marathon is not so much a physical exercise as a mental one where we learn that we can stick with something no matter how uncomfortable and painful it feels. Marriage can be the same thing. If it's something we desire we must be able to be with the "painful" thoughts and "uncomfortable" sensations that go with it.

So when we tithe, we experience what it's like to hold the thought that money is abundant and plentiful. And very often, it's frightening to hold that thought and to feel the great discomfort and fear that our Inner Child feels when we hold that thought of abundance. The Inner Child most likely has this fear because when it dared, at an earlier time, to trust abundance, it was hurt. But when we tithe, we ARE holding that thought and honing our ability to experience abundance, which is the only way to HAVE abundance.

So, can you see that there's another paradox? We tithe in order to experience abundance. So when you experience abundance, it's important (and natural) to tithe to express and keep that experience going. But perhaps it's even more important to tithe when you're NOT experiencing abundance. To give when you think you have nothing. This is the way to return to the experience of abundance, to open your vision wider to see more of the infinite abundance you already have. It can be VERY scary, but walking through that fear is the most effective way I know of returning to an experience of abundance.

Like so many other "successes," wealth and an abundance of money is not necessarily comfortable to be with. (Ask most "rich" people you know and they will tell you how challenging it can be.) The thing is, when you take on the thought of tithing and actually do it, you are actually experiencing what abundance feels like. The surprise, for many, is that the experience of abundance frequently comes with the Inner Child's "uncomfortable" sensations and "protective" thoughts. If you cannot be with the Inner Child's thoughts and sensations around unlimited money, you WILL NOT BE ABLE TO EXPERIENCE ABUNDANCE. You may keep yourself from having money, or you may have money, but either way you will still feel "poor."

If you want to experience the Truth, that you are unlimited and that abundance is always here and available to you, you have to practice being with the way it feels to experience that abundance.

Tithing is one of the best ways I know to practice this. It's not for the church. It's not for others. It's for YOU, to have the opportunity to hold the thought of abundance and practice being with what your Inner Child experiences when you hold that thought.

It's not about money.

Money isn't even about money. It's a mirror in which we get to see where we're holding "protective" thoughts that are limiting our EXPERIENCE of unlimitedness.

USING RELATIONSHIPS TO HEAL OUR INNER CHILD

Recently I was on a Caribbean cruise with my partner Shawn, and since I was working on this book, and in close proximity with my partner, I was watching our relationship carefully to see what I could learn about the principles about which I'm writing.

One day, Shawn and I decided to meet two friends for breakfast and then go into town in Jamaica to shop with them. We were meeting at 8:15 in the morning, and I had something to do, so I told them I would be there at 8:30.

We were planning to leave the ship at 9:00.

When I arrived, they'd just finished breakfast. Shawn said he had to go back to the room, and our two friends said they wanted to go outside and smoke. They told me to stay and have my breakfast and they would come back and pick me up and we would all go down to Shawn's and my room and get off the boat together.

I had a tiny sensation in my chest which I ignored, and I said, "OK."

The moment they left, I thought, "Why did I say I'd wait? I'm going to be finished with my breakfast in three minutes. I should have gone down to the room with Shawn and told them to meet us there."

I waited in the dining room for 15 minutes and the guys didn't show up. I finally decided to go to the room, thinking perhaps they had gotten confused and gone down there.

When I got to the room, Shawn was sitting there and said, in a disturbed tone, "Where are the boys? You were supposed to bring them! Now we're going to have to wait or go shopping without them and I'm going to be late, this is very upsetting," and on and on.

I told him they hadn't shown up, and that I thought perhaps they'd come to the room. Shawn said that they didn't know what room we were in. He hadn't given them our room number.

Being the brilliant observer of behavior that I am (other peoples' behavior that is, not necessarily my own!) I immediately thought, "Ah. Shawn carries the thought that he can't do what he wants, that he HAS TO get to shopping on time and will be stopped, and that he can't depend on people. And the way in which he brought that about was by skipping the beat of giving them his room number. He had unconsciously done something small that assisted in things working out the way he feared.

I tried calling the boys' room and they weren't there. So I told Shawn to wait in our room and I would go back up to the restaurant and see if I could find them.

On my way up, I began to think, "OK. I understand what Shawn did to bring about his thought. But what did I do to bring about mine?"

I realized that I carry the thought that I will be blamed for things I didn't do and that Shawn will unfairly chastise me. As I thought about it, I realized that I, against my better judgment, had said I would wait upstairs, thus setting up a situation where I was at the mercy of someone else and if they didn't come through I would get blamed.

Realizing this, I was able to know that I had done nothing wrong, know that it was MY thought that I'm misunderstood and will get yelled at, and I was able to simply be with the sensations that came with that. Now I no longer feared it. If Shawn snapped at me, the only result would be that I would have an "uncomfortable" sensation, which I knew I could tolerate.

Knowing this, I also had compassion for Shawn, understanding that just like me, he carries thoughts and sometimes unconsciously reacts to them.

The boys never showed up, so I went down to the room, relaxed in being able to experience my sensations and fully prepared to allow Shawn to have whatever reaction he had.

I walked in and said, "Sorry, I couldn't find them," to which Shawn said, "That's OK. It's not your fault. I just want to go shopping and would have liked to go with them. "

So I suggested we get off the ship and wait for them. After two minutes of waiting, Shawn said he couldn't wait anymore. I felt the sensation that goes with him saying that to me, so I was able to respond, "No problem. You go on ahead and I'll wait." He went shopping, the boys arrived in 10 minutes explaining that somehow it had taken them more than 15 minutes to get to the smoking area and back (it was a big, crowded ship) and we met up with Shawn a few minutes later and had a lovely day shopping.

This may seem like a fairly innocuous story, but when we are seeing ourselves being treated a certain way or when we see things happening that are upsetting, we must look for the thought WE'RE having, because that thought is unconsciously controlling the most subtle choices in our behavior, our tone of voice, what we think of the other person (which will read in the vibration we give off) etc.

If we can just remember that whatever we're seeing coming at us is nothing more or less than what the Inner Child thinks, we can turn our attention to being with the Inner Child's sensations and thoughts, rather than to trying to change what's before us (which would be like trying to change our reflection in the mirror without doing anything ourselves.)

The Buddhists say that a relationship is one of the highest and most challenging forms of spiritual growth, because you are ALWAYS in front of a mirror. When we can take the opportunity to use the mirror to see our own thoughts, a relationship becomes valuable and fulfilling, no matter what's happening.

USING HYPOCHONDRIA TO HEAL OUR INNER CHILD

In my last book, *The Thought Exchange – Overcoming Our Resistance to Living a SENSATIONAL Life*, there was a whole section on Panic Disorder.

When I was 20 years old, I was hospitalized for Panic Disorder. Although it seemed, at the time, like the worst thing that could happen to me, in that it robbed me of the ability to feel comfortable, to enjoy anything, or to move forward in my career and personal life, I am now, in retrospect, actually incredibly grateful for it.

There's no doubt in my mind that my early challenges with extremely "uncomfortable" sensations were the root of my eventually creating The Thought Exchange. In wrestling with these "uncomfortable" sensations, and in trying every way I could think of to get rid of them, I was finally forced to surrender to the fact that they weren't going away.

Ultimately, my only choice, if I wanted to live any sort of life, became to BE with my "uncomfortable," frightening sensations. And in being with them, I was, perhaps for the first time in my life, being with, seeing and feeling my upset, unseen Inner Child (which was the source of these "uncomfortable" sensations in the first place). This was not only the source of my healing and reconnecting to the unlimited possibilities that the invisible world inside of us always contains, but it naturally, over the years, expressed itself in the healing work I do for myself and with others.

So it could be said that through the intense experience of "Panic Disorder" I became an expert in sensations.

In this book, I want to talk about another area in which I feel that I can truly say I am an expert, because I've spent a lifetime experiencing it. Hypochondria.

Hypochondria is a way of being in which we translate "uncomfortable" sensations into the thought that we have some serious illness. A slight numbness immediately becomes Multiple Sclerosis. Every headache is a brain tumor. A bump on the skin is cancer. We read about some disease, or hear that someone else is sick, and we immediately have it.

Since my childhood, I have spent a lifetime doing this.

I cannot tell you how many diseases I have created in my mind over the years. I like to joke that I have a terrible doctor because I've been seeing him for over 25 years and he STILL hasn't diagnosed the serious illness I OBVIOUSLY have.

It reminds of the joke about the tombstone that reads, "See? I told you I was sick!"

People often make fun of people with hypochondria and tell people who experience it things like, "That's ridiculous; Get over it; You're fine; There's nothing wrong with you. It's all in your head." But there's nothing funny about it, for a number of reasons.

The first, and most obvious, is that we are constantly tormented and distracted from our lives by thoughts that death is imminent. Who would want that?

But if we remember the basic Thought Exchange principle that the ONLY way to get rid of an "uncomfortable" sensations is to take on a "protective" thought, then we can see that the thought "I am dying" is a "protective" thought, taken on to get away from an "uncomfortable" sensation that we think we can't tolerate.

There's something that the Inner Child is experiencing and trying to get us to see that we are afraid to see, so we take on the "protective" thought, "I am sick."

Why would we take on this upsetting "protective" thought? I've come to understand that when we have a sensation that we think we can't tolerate, we think that we MUST make it go away. By translating it into a disease, we can then have the hope that if the doctor can cure the disease, the sensation will go away and we'll be rid of the sensation forever.

The trouble is, of course, that the sensation is our Inner Child calling to us, so it's impossible to make it go away. So the more we create the thought of disease in our mind, the more the Inner Child will have to reach out to us by giving us "symptoms." If we keep insisting we are sick, the Inner Child might actually have to make us sick to get our attention.

So, as we do with any "protective" thought, whenever we experience it, we have to go to the Inner Child. And the way to do this is to FEEL OUR SENSATIONS. This can be extremely frightening, since we created the condition of hypochondria in the first place to get away from these very sensations. But feeling them, being with them, is the ONLY way to connect to, see and feel the Inner Child who needs us to be with its predicament.

When we can connect and stay with the "uncomfortable" sensations of the Inner Child, we find that they are an "exact" representation of what the Inner Child went through, once removed because the Inner Child had to "get away from" the impossible double bind of what was going on. When we can be with this experience, our history and the reason why we took on hypochondria often becomes clear.

Recently, I was working with someone who, at various times in his life, had experienced all sorts of "strange" physical symptoms and was constantly concerned about being sick. He had been under a lot of stress during the last couple of years, and he developed a feeling that could best be called "disembodiment" in his right leg. It wasn't numbness, it wasn't weakness, it was just a feeling of his "not being in his leg."

He kept thinking this must be Multiple Sclerosis, but it

didn't seem to "progress" to that. I asked him if he could just spend the next few days simply "being" with the "disembodied" leg and notice what happened.

This seemed like a risk to him, but he agreed to try it. And interestingly, when he just stayed with the leg and didn't jump to the "protective" thought that he was ill, he got great insight into why the thought of being ill was "protective."

As he stayed with the sensations in his leg and noticed where his thoughts went, he began to spontaneously remember beatings he'd received as a child. One in particular kept coming to mind. He knew about these beatings, had worked on them for years in therapy, so they weren't a surprise. He wasn't consciously holding anger or the thought that they shouldn't have happened, so he was able to find it interesting that this memory came up around this sensation in his leg, and simply observe himself. The more he stayed with the sensation in his leg, the more clearly this particular beating came into focus. Where he was. The position of his body, on his back with his legs flailing to try to protect himself. The pure "ouch" of what it felt like.

And interestingly enough, as he stayed with the experience he was having in his leg, he got a lot more insight into why he had chosen "hypochondria" as an escape.

The beatings hadn't happened very often, but the particular nature of his beatings was that once his abuser got started, there was no stopping him. If my client cried, he was hit and told not to cry. If he didn't cry, he was hit until he did. If he fought back, he was "creamed." And if he didn't fight back, he was hit until he got angry.

The last one gave him a real insight into his hypochondria. To simply be with a sensation (which was a "dramatization" of the child's pain) would mean, in this system, that he wouldn't be fighting back, and if he didn't fight back, that meant he would be hit more. So his Inner Child was thinking that if he just sat with the pain and didn't think he had Multiple Sclerosis, he would get Multiple Sclerosis!

The ONLY way to avoid Multiple Sclerosis would be to worry that he had it!

This revelation not only allowed my client to stay with the Inner Child's impossible dilemma, but it did even more. It revealed why my client obsessed about "the worst" happening in many other situations. He was doing that because the Inner Child thought that it needed to obsess about "the worst" happening to prevent "the worst" from happening. In order to protect itself, the Inner Child had developed the "protective" thought, "No matter what I do, I will be hit." This translated into his not only feeling helpless in the world, but into his regarding of the world as a place that would never give him what he wanted and would always hurt him. Time and again this thought would reflect in events as well as in his body.

In many ways, sitting with the sensations instead of jumping to the hypochondria helped him understand and be with patterns that he had used his whole life in a futile attempt to escape from pain. Knowing this allowed him to EXPERIENCE the history rather than having to constantly act it out, think he was sick, not use his considerable talents, and not go for things he desired because he was sure "the worst" would happen.

As he allowed himself more and more to go through the process of looking right at the places in his body that he was afraid to look at (instead of shrinking from them or trying to change or get rid of them because he thought they contained disease) he found that he began to reclaim "disowned" areas of his body. What had previously been experienced as a "disease" that was attacking him and had to be gotten rid of gradually transformed into a deep connection with and empathy for the underlying experience of the Inner Child.

It was a great healing.

So hypochondria, when seen for what it actually is, can, like Dieting, like Tithing, like Relationship, be used as a vehicle to reconnect to and reclaim our Inner Child. When we can be with the sensations instead of going to the thoughts of illness, the sensations are gradually experienced as just sensations with no meaning, and the hypochondria disappears. We may still notice that our mind goes to the thought that we are ill, but we can immediately move to the underlying sensations and use each thought of illness to get closer to our Inner Child's early trauma.

USING ILLNESS TO HEAL OUR INNER CHILD

Sometimes, when the Inner Child creates "uncomfortable" sensations that we keep choosing to ignore or try to get rid of, the Inner Child has to resort to illness to try to get our attention.

I think this story, which occurred in a Thought Exchange seminar, illustrates the point clearly.

Joe (not his real name) came in to Thought Exchange and announced that he had just come from the doctor, and the doctor had told him he had an esophageal ulcer. Now, an esophageal ulcer can be a serious condition, not only because it often comes with pain and, in some cases, extreme acid reflux, but because it can turn into something called Barrett's syndrome, which is a pre-cancerous condition. Scary stuff.

I asked Joe what the doctor thought had caused the esophageal ulcer to be there. Joe said the problem was that he tended to eat pizza and ice cream late at night before going to bed, and the result was that when he spent the hours directly after eating lying down, he developed a case of acid reflux which ultimately began burning a hole in his esophagus.

Now, the typical medical solution to this is to prescribe an acid-killing drug to reduce stomach acid so the patient will stop burning a hole in his esophagus. As one might expect, Joe's doctor did prescribe such a drug, and told Joe to take it every day in order to heal the ulcer, or at least try and keep the ulcer at bay.

I was more interested in getting to the REAL source of the "problem."

The condition was ostensibly being caused by Joe eating rich foods before going to bed. So the first question I asked was, "What sensation do you get that tells you that you have to eat pizza and ice cream late at night?"

He thought about it and said, "I get an empty feeling around my heart and in my stomach."

So, Joe was having sensations of emptiness. These sensations were being generated by Joe's Inner Child, who needed Joe to feel and be with how empty the Inner Child felt.

Joe was afraid of these sensations because they reminded him of childhood pain that had never been faced. So he chose to push them under by eating late at night.

The Inner Child's attempts to be seen by Joe by creating uncomfortable sensations had failed. Now the Inner Child was forced to resort to a more forceful tactic. So the Inner Child created a "condition." An esophageal ulcer.

And what did Joe and the doctors do with that? The same thing Joe had done with the original sensations.

Suppress it, this time with medication.

Now Joe was twice removed from experiencing and being with his Inner Child, once by pizza and ice cream, and now by medication.

If Joe had continued on this path, I wouldn't have been surprised if the Inner Child had to resort to generating one of the "side effects" of the medication, which can be as serious as cancer, blood clots, liver damage, etc.

If he chose to do that, then the doctors might try to get rid of that by chemotherapy or more medication. And the unseen Inner Child would have to find bigger and bigger ways to fight to be seen.

So, the Inner Child had unseen trauma. It created uncomfortable sensations to try to get Joe to be with it so it could heal. Joe chose to eat to cover those sensations. The Inner Child created an esophageal ulcer to try to get Joe's attention. Joe was ready to cover the condition the Inner Child had created by taking medication. The Inner Child might then have to create the "side effects" of the medication by generating a more serious disease. If Joe still didn't want to notice the Inner Child, he would go on stronger medications which would further suppress the Inner Child, the result being that the Inner Child would have to try harder to get Joe's attention by creating more disease, side effects, etc.

Fortunately, Joe chose to go to the source. I told him that when he felt that emptiness in the evening, to simply be with it, experience it, notice the thoughts that came up around it. When he did this, he was able to connect with and be with a deep sadness from his childhood. This Inner Child was finally being seen by Joe's Inner Adult and became a recognized part of Joe's history. The result was that Joe didn't have to eat at night. This resulted not only in a healing of the esophageal ulcer, but in Joe's losing some weight he needed to lose. But the big bonus was that Joe was reunited with a piece of his disowned Inner Child, and this allowed him to experience, in deeper ways, thoughts that he had not allowed himself to think.

I want to be clear here that I'm not saying, "Never take medicine." Once we have created conditions, medicine or psychotropic drugs are often tools available to us to curtail and deal with these conditions. But I'm suggesting that we always look for the underlying cause, the sensations and thoughts we're trying to protect ourselves from by having these conditions, and try to be with these sensations and thoughts as much as possible. Even when we're being treated for serious diseases.

I believe that there are two basic interior responses we can have to illness. We can regard it as real, as something to be fought off, overcome, gotten rid of. Or we can regard it as a signal that there are sensations and thoughts from the past that are showing up in the present so that we can be with them.

As you might imagine, I recommend the latter, even while we're being treated medically.

PART X
OBSERVATIONS, ANECDOTES AND THINGS TO THINK ABOUT

In the course of teaching Thought Exchange and during the process of writing this book, many revelations, anecdotes, tips and observations have come to mind. I offer you the ones that seemed most helpful to me and most relevant to the subject of this book.

THE PAST DOES NOT PREDICT THE FUTURE

I know I used this example at the beginning of this book, but it's been such a powerful one that I think it bears repeating.

I often ask people I work with the following question:

If you tossed a coin 5,000 times and it came up tails EVERY time, what are the odds that it will come up heads on the next toss.

It's amazing how many people say 1 in 5,000.

The odds, ANY TIME you toss a coin are 50/50! No matter what has happened before.

But how it would feel and the thoughts you would have would be very different if you had just tossed 5,000 tails.

You would almost certainly have the thought that you never toss heads. That you're a tail-tosser. If you had been trying to toss heads and had failed 5,000 times, it's unlikely you would even attempt to toss the coin again.

So, in order to take advantage of the odds, which are always the same no matter what has happened in the past, or the unlimited possibilities, which are never diminished by what happened in the past, you must be willing to experience your "uncomfortable" sensations and think whatever thoughts you're thinking, while holding in mind what you want and knowing that the past has not diminished or changed the future in any way.

I love to collect stories of people who were very, very successful after being rejected over and over. I'm sure they felt the rejections. Rejections are painful and frustrating to everyone. But they were able to be with that pain and frustration rather than shrinking from it or trying to get away from it, and they kept going.

Depending on who you ask, Harry Potter was rejected by somewhere between nine and twelve publishers.

I heard that the song "You Needed Me," which, I believe, was the most played easy listening song of the 1980s, was rejected 202 times before Anne Murray recorded and had an enormous hit with it.

Colonel Sanders apparently had his idea for Kentucky Fried Chicken rejected something like 999 times. Fortunately, he asked for the thousandth time and got the "Yes."

There was one agent who apparently told the Beatles, at the very beginning of their career, that "groups are out!"

The point that I've been making throughout this book, and the point I want to make here, is that the manifestation, the success, is not the point. These people all held a Vision in mind, no matter what sensations and thoughts arose, and every time they saw something in the world that was not the Vision they wanted, they went back to their Vision. The reflection in the world is the result of, not the cause of, these people's awareness that they live in infinite possibility.

THE FACT THAT YOU HAVE A THOUGHT DOESN'T MEAN IT'S TRUE

When we understand that the ONLY place we live is in the invisible world of experience, we understand that thoughts are just thoughts. The fact that you have the thought that you have no value does not mean that you actually have no value. Conversely, the fact that you have the thought that you HAVE value doesn't mean that you actually have value. They're both just thoughts.

The fact that you have the thought that you want to kill someone doesn't mean that you're going to kill someone. "Negative" thoughts are nothing more than "protective" thoughts, designed to protect us from "uncomfortable" sensations. No matter what we're thinking, the Truth is that all possibilities ALWAYS exist, RIGHT NOW.

Every time I go to write a song, I think, "I can't write this." I notice that thought, and then I write the song. I don't fight with the thought. I don't have to prove it wrong or get rid of it. The fact that I have that thought does not in any way diminish or negate the possibility that I can write the song. Conversely, the fact that I have written hundreds of songs doesn't in any way prevent me from having the thought that I can't. It's just a thought. (An Inner Child's thought.) It's not the Truth. No thought is.

When you are not running away from or suppressing your thoughts and sensations, they have no power to make you do anything, to stop you from doing anything, to cause things to happen or not to happen. They're just thoughts.

THE TRUTH ABOUT AFFIRMATIONS

Affirmations, one of the most common and universal Spiritual tools, are also one of the most commonly misused and misunderstood Spiritual principles.

As I said earlier in this book, if we think that the physical world is where we live, NOTHING in Spirituality makes any sense. The challenge with Affirmations is that people keep trying to use them to "get" things, to "manifest" things, to "attract" things in the physical world, as though Affirmations either have magic powers, or, more frequently, as though they can be "heard" and "fulfilled" by whomever it is that gives out such things.

When people try to "use" Affirmations in this way, it seems that sometimes they work and sometimes they don't. The reason for this is that no matter WHAT you repeat to yourself, all you will see in the world is what you are ACTUALLY thinking. Not because your thoughts have changed the world, but because all you can see when you look at the world are your own thoughts.

Very often, when people try to use affirmations to get rich or "attract" the love of their life or find the perfect home or job, they're doing all this work because they think they don't have these things or that they're difficult or elusive to get. And since what we think is what we experience, the lack will keep being perceived in the mirror of the world. Even if the thing they're asking for appears, if they have the thought of lack, they will still experience lack. (See the next section for an example of this.)

When we understand that our whole life takes place in the invisible world of experience, Affirmations take on a whole different purpose and have a whole different usefulness.

In the invisible world, EVERYTHING is here, right now, because we can think and experience anything at any time. An Affirmation, as the name implies, is simply affirming that something is here, in the invisible world, in case you have forgotten this. It's not about getting anything, it's about KNOWING YOU HAVE IT.

So the Affirmation, "My perfect partner is here right now" is true. In the infinite world of possibilities, that is true RIGHT NOW. If you try to affirm, "My perfect partner is coming to me," you are trying to make something happen in the physical world. AFFIRMATIONS DON'T MAKE THINGS HAPPEN! Since infinite possibilities exist at all times, you may see the reflection of that Affirmation IF that is the thought you're actually holding. And if you're actually holding that thought, whether or not something manifests, you will experience living in that thought. But it is important to remember that even if you see the manifestation (reflection) of the Affirmation, if you are actually holding the thought of lack, you will experience lack, either in relation to the manifestation you see, or in another parallel area.

So Affirmations are useful in two ways. They remind us that something is always here when we may have forgotten. And when they "work" or "don't work" they help us to look in the mirror of the world to see what thought we are actually holding.

In short, it boils down to this.

Don't try to use Affirmations to get things, but rather to remind yourself that you already have them. In the ONLY place you could EVER have anything. INSIDE.

YOU WILL ALWAYS SEE WHAT YOU'RE THINKING

When you look at the world, what you're seeing is an exact mirror of your thoughts. No matter what mirror you look in, you will see what you think. Circumstances may change, but you'll always see your thought.

This story, taken from one of our Thought Exchange Workshops, beautifully illustrates this point.

A woman came in to Thought Exchange and shared, "I will never meet someone. I'm always going to be alone. I'll never find someone to be with."

We identified this as a thought, asked her to exchange that thought for the thought, "In 'The Great Unmanifested' it is, of course possible that I could meet someone," and asked her to feel any "uncomfortable" sensations that arose when she DARED to think that thought.

She exchanged the thought and we sent her off with the instruction that any time she noticed the "protective" thought that she'd never meet anyone, she was to exchange it for the thought "I can meet someone" and experience her discomfort.

We didn't see her for six months and then, one day, she came back to class. When it was her turn to share, she said, "I'm looking for a job and there are no jobs. I'll never get a job. I'll never find work. I was just saying to my husband..."

SHE HAD A HUSBAND!!!

And she hadn't even mentioned that! Her thought, which six months ago had seemed to be about a specific condition, obviously was about something deeper than that, because when one condition was "solved," the deeper thought simply transferred to another condition. The mirror of the world was still reflecting her more basic thought, just with different circumstances.

The undeniability of the fact that she had gotten something that she had been sure she'd never get, and had immediately switched to something else she was "sure" she'd never get, allowed us to uncover the deeper thought she held, which was something in the area of "I can't have what I want." This thought would come up whenever she wanted something. The reason it would come up was because, based on her childhood, the thought of wanting something produced "uncomfortable" sensations. To get away from these "uncomfortable" sensations, she would take on the "protective" thought that she couldn't have things, in order to try and stop the wanting that caused the "uncomfortable" sensations.

Once she knew about this, she gradually became able to want things, because she could tolerate the discomfort that went with the wanting, rather than going to the "protective" thought, "I can't have it."

There have been interesting studies that tell us that no matter what happens to people, they return to their "basic level of happiness or unhappiness" within 30 days. So when someone wins the lottery, they may be elated for 30 days but then they develop all sorts of "different" problems, perhaps related to having all this money, that mirror the problems they had before they won the lottery. This may explain why so many people who win the lottery end up losing all the money. Unless they can be with the DISCOMFORT that winning the lottery brings (and who would think of winning the lottery as "uncomfortable"?) they will reproduce the Inner Child's thoughts and sensations on the outside by creating conditions that seem to cause the discomfort.

WHAT YOU RESIST PERSISTS

One of the most familiar axioms of both physics and metaphysics is, "What you resist persists."

At face value, this means that if you push against something it will push back at you. If you resist a circumstance or a person or a condition, it will continue to be present, and the more you resist it, the more strongly it will remain in place.

The implied message in this is that if you resist something and it persists, then if you don't resist something it will not persist. It will disappear. This doesn't necessarily mean that the thing you're not resisting will actually not exist. It just means it will "disappear" as being a "problem" for you.

So, for example, if my heart pounds when I go on stage, the more I resist it and "need it to go away" the more it will seem to prevent me from going on stage. If I don't resist it, but just let it be, my heart will not necessarily stop pounding, but it won't stop me from going on stage. So for all intents and purposes, in my experience, it has "disappeared" and become nothing.

Now, I've known this principle for a long time and have often applied it when I would feel some area of resistance arise in my life. But recently, while teaching a class, I had one of those "a-ha" moments where I realized that there's a deeper application of this principle that might be counter-intuitive, but which explains a lot of the frustration and discomfort I've experienced over the years in my "quest for success."

When something upsetting happens, our first instinct is usually to resist it. And what happens when we do that? It persists, according to principle.

Then, something "good" happens, and what do we do? We welcome it! We DON'T resist it. So what happens, according to principle? IT DISAPPEARS!

So we've spent our lives resisting what we don't want and not resisting what we do want. And in doing so, time and again, we've persisted what we DON'T want (by resisting it) and disappeared what we DO want (by not resisting it!).

So according to this principle, we should resist (push back against) what we DO want, and offer no resistance to what we DON'T want.

There is a lot of precedence in spiritual teaching for this way of working with the "resist/persist" principle. In Kaballah, the ancient Jewish mysticism, they instruct you to RESTRICT what it is you want.

By pushing back against it, you experience it pushing toward you.

This explains why, for so many of us, success seems to

elude us. We have something good happen, we try to grab it, and then we watch it disappear.

I know, from my own experience, that this principle applies, but in thinking about it in terms of Thought Exchange principles, I think I know why.

Our lives are happening totally on the inside, where everything is infinite, where we already have everything and where there is nothing missing. When we think we "need" something, we are creating the erroneous thought of lack, and that thought must appear in the mirror of the world. There is really no lack, but we will see our thought of lack. So when we "want" something or "need" something or are reaching or grabbing for something (i.e. not resisting it) we are immediately in an internal state of not having that thing, so that thing MUST disappear from our consciousness. Only when we push against (resist) the notion that we need or want anything will it be restored to its true place of already existing inside of us. And when that happens, it will appear to be in the world ("mirror") before us.

When we have an awareness of our "negative" thoughts and "uncomfortable" sensations, and don't need to get rid of them by hoping to get something that will make them disappear, we have no need to create lack, and we will experience having it all at all times.

HAVING IT ALL MEANS HAVING IT ALL

When people say "I want to have it ALL," what they usually mean is, "I want to have the part of 'all' that feels good and that makes me comfortable." But, as we've learned in this book, you cannot have it all without having it ALL." "Negative" thoughts and "uncomfortable" sensations often come with the very things we want. So the only way to have it ALL is to have the capacity to experience things as they are. And this, of course, involves being able to experience "negative" thoughts and "uncomfortable" sensations when they arise as part of what it is we want. They don't mean anything, they don't have to be acted upon or gotten rid of. They just have to be experienced. When we can do that, we truly can experience "having it ALL."

SUCCESSFUL PEOPLE ARE NOT COMFORTABLE

So often, we envy "successful" people because we think that, with all their notoriety and position and money, they must be happy and comfortable. They may very well be happy, but there is no way they can be comfortable unless they can be comfortable with their discomfort.

Would you be "comfortable" having grown up extremely poor, having been physically abused, having to look good for television every day while the world is watching you, judging and criticizing your weight, having everyone in the world wanting something from you because they think you have everything? Oprah Winfrey probably isn't so comfortable with all that either.

Would you be comfortable having a voice that is considered to be one of the most perfect voices in the world and being judged on that level every time you open your mouth, being terrified to perform live but doing it anyway, being unable to go out in public because you will be mobbed, and feeling that you're a woman having to fight for the right to do work that men do all the time without question? Barbra Streisand probably isn't so comfortable with all that either.

Would you be comfortable having to make a public case every few years for why you should have your job, having your every move affect the entire world, having to deal with popularity ratings and partisan politics, being criticized by everyone and having to have constant around-the-clock protection because there is always the danger that you will be shot? The President of the United States probably isn't so comfortable with that either.

When I was a teenager, Dionne Warwick was my idol. I thought she was the most amazing singer and I envied her career, going around the world with that beautiful voice being lauded by audiences everywhere. One day, I opened the *New York Times* and there was a full page ad for Dionne Warwick's World Tour. In the ad, it listed her schedule. I don't remember it all, but it was something like:

> June 4th – Avery Fisher Hall, New York City
>
> June 6th – The Los Angeles Coliseum
>
> June 9th – TOKYO!
>
> And on and on for months!

I suddenly thought, "My God! This woman has to fly to each of these places and with very little rest get on the stage, look beautiful and be in excellent voice, after being on cross-country or intercontinental flights! I realized, in that instant, that although of course I'm sure Dionne loved to sing and enjoyed her career, it certainly wasn't easy, and was probably often exhausting and lonely.

ARE YOU WILLING TO BE UNCOMFORTABLE ENOUGH TO HAVE YOUR DREAMS COME TRUE?

Now I'm not saying that it's not good to have dreams, or that when our dreams come true we have to be unhappy. On the contrary, I'm saying that if you want to have your dreams come true, you have to be willing to be with the "negative" thoughts and "uncomfortable" sensations that may come with those dreams. Dreams often come with the experience of great fatigue, great pressure, great thoughts of doubt and uncertainty, fear, criticism and a thousand other pressures. So many of us turn away from living our dreams because we feel "uncomfortable" and we think we're not supposed to feel that way.

One of the most poignantly "amusing" comments I've ever heard came from one of my Thought Exchange Circle members. She is a single woman, and she was having a little pity party about being alone. At one point she turned to me and said, "Well, I'm all alone and you have a partner." My response was, "So?" And she said, "Well, when you're married or you have a partner, at least you know for sure that any time you come home with an upset or a problem there is someone there who will ALWAYS support you and ALWAYS agree with you!"

As you might imagine, every married person in the room nearly fell off their chair. I have NEVER known a relationship in which that is ALWAYS so.

(My partner, Shawn, commented, "She says that to you, and she KNOWS me!")

Whenever someone tells me that they long to be in a relationship, I ask them, "Are you sure? Are you willing to work that hard? Are you willing to sometimes be that bored? Are you willing to have one sexual partner and go through the hills and valleys of sexual interest and sexual differences with them? Are you willing to be that exposed to someone on a constant basis?"

Now, for me, the answer is YES. I find being in a relationship extremely gratifying, but it is because I am willing to experience the challenges. I'm not expecting to be ecstatic at all times. I'm working at something.

So when you find yourself wanting something, whether it be a career or a relationship or a house or an amount of money or a position in the world, ask yourself if you're willing to experience the discomforts that will also surely come with it. Achievement is not a way to get away from discomfort, as so many people think it is. Achievement is a way to express a part of the infinite power that we possess, but it does not take us away from our "problems." In fact, we have to be able to be with our "problems," with our "negative" thoughts and "uncomfortable" sensations, if we're to be able to not only achieve the successes we desire, but reap the benefits those successes have to offer.

BRAVE PEOPLE ARE NOT UNAFRAID

We often have the misconception that brave people are not afraid. Nothing could be further from the truth. Brave people may experience as much or more fear than the average person. They're just willing to experience it while doing what they want to do.

Since brave people are just people, they are potentially subjected to the same nerves in stepping out in front of tens of thousands of people, fighting in a war, even picking up the phone to make a difficult call, as we all are.

The way we cultivate bravery is to be able to hold a vision of what we want, allow ourselves to experience whatever "uncomfortable" sensations and "negative" thoughts we experience while holding that vision, and stay with the vision while having those "uncomfortable" sensations and thoughts.

Then we can think and act bravely because we're with what is, as invisible experience, and we can hold whatever thought and take whatever action we wish.

WHY WORRY?

When we worry, we are concerned that if something happens we will have a sensation that we think we are unable to tolerate. (Remember, the ONLY thing that really happens when something upsetting "happens" is that we have "uncomfortable" sensations. In fact, the only thing that ever happens when ANYTHING "happens" is that we have sensations of one sort or another and, based on our past, we make up thoughts about what these sensations mean.)

When we worry, we are thinking about the thing we're worried about, and thus experiencing the sensations that come with the thing we are worried about. So, in essence, worrying is keeping us in the perpetual state of which we are afraid. Were the thing we're worried about to actually happen, we would experience the same thoughts and sensations we're experiencing now, when we're worrying about it. So the WORST outcome would be that we would experience what we're already experiencing.

Essentially, if we're worried about something, it's because it already happened (and we already lived through it). Otherwise we wouldn't know to worry about it. The very act of worrying says, "I've experienced something earlier in life (that I got through). I'm experiencing that thing right now, and should what I'm worried about come to pass I will experience the same thing I'm experiencing now."

In the midst of worrying, if we can stop and experience the sensations we're experiencing and just be with them, there's nothing to worry about. That's it! We're experiencing the worst right now and nothing is happening except we're having sensations and noticing thoughts we're making up about them. Should the thing we're worried about actually come to pass in the future, we will experience exactly what we're experiencing now. By stopping now and just experiencing it now, we can get in touch with the fact that the sensations are meaningless, cannot harm us, and thus become nothing, whether they continue or not. We are no longer resisting the sensations, so we have no need to take on "protective" thoughts about them. When we are in this state, we are free to take on any thought we wish, and the only result of taking on those thoughts is that we may experience the "uncomfortable" sensations we're experiencing now.

As we know, what we're thinking determines what we're experiencing (it doesn't cause things to happen, it just determines how we experience those same things). So when we're holding the thoughts we want to hold (thoughts like, "Everything works out" or "I'm safe") we will experience hope and safety NO MATTER WHAT OUR SENSATIONS ARE.

So, the next time you're worried about the future, come to the present, simply experience it, and there's nothing to worry about. It means nothing. It can't get worse. It's just what it is. Painful, uncomfortable, scary? Yes. Dangerous, portending the future, meaningful? No.

DARE TO THINK THE THOUGHTS YOU WANT TO THINK

As I'm sure you've gathered by now, this book is about things that we know are true, but that somehow we don't seem to be able to do.

My suggestion, in the last section, that we simply not worry, and when we do that, feel our "uncomfortable" sensations and think our "negative" thoughts, is definitely one of those things that's easier said than done.

The reason for this is that our worrying is a big "protective" thought to keep us from "uncomfortable" sensations that we experienced in the past, that we thought could hurt us. So when we take our worrying away, we are left with "uncomfortable" sensations and "negative" thoughts that we have been afraid to feel and think, sometimes since early childhood.

Recently, after spending a lot of time working on this book and applying its principles to my own life, (something even I, "Mr. Thought Exchange," forget to do) I began to "break through" in a number of areas in my career and in my financial life.

I was selling some real estate and was starting to think that we might have a buyer. I had some good interviews with potential producers of my shows. A stubborn skin condition I was wrestling with for months was starting to show improvement. I was coming close to reaching my weight loss goal. Some financial issues began to straighten themselves out. An issue I was having with my singing voice was clearing up. And I was getting ready to sign a deal for my next book.

What I noticed was, that as these "good" things began happening, as soon as I DARED to think that they might actually be working out, my "protective" thoughts around each of them began to escalate.

The thought, "We might have a real estate buyer" came with the "protective" thought, "The buyer will fall through. I need this money to pay off some bills and it won't come through because I'm not allowed to have what I want."

The thought, "I've been having some good interviews with potential producers of my shows" came with the "protective" thought, "The producers, even though they really seem to like me and my shows, are going to drop them because I'm a person who doesn't get produced."

The thought, "A stubborn skin condition I've been wrestling with is starting to show improvement" came with the "protective" thought, "I'm really deathly ill and am going to find out that my skin condition means I have a serious underlying condition. Or at best, my skin condition will never go away and I'll itch for the rest of my life."

The thought, "I'm coming close to reaching my weight goal" came with the "protective" thought, "I'm getting thin too fast so I must be sick."

The thought, "Some financial issues are beginning to straighten themselves out" came with the "protective" thought, "As soon as I straighten out my financial issues, other ones will appear or I'll get sick."

The thought, "The issue I'm having with my singing voice is clearing up and I will be able to sing freely again," came with, "You'll never sing. You're too old. Your voice is too damaged. All of this stuff that seems to work will not work."

And the thought, "I'm getting ready to sign a deal for my next book, and it could be a best seller," came with the "protective" thought, "They're going to pull the deal. And even if they don't the book will never sell."

One morning, I woke up with all these fears and "protective" thoughts in my mind and thought, "What happens if I actually take on the thought that everything is going to work out, that all these things will either happen the way I'm planning, or that I'll be just as happy and taken care of if other things happen instead? What happens if I DARE to take on the thought that I'm fine, that I'm healthy, that I'm going to enjoy this day? That I'm going to hold the thought that all the things I'm working on are going to work themselves out one way or another, and that I'll know what to do and when to do it?"

What I realized was that when I did this, I was, in my mind, taking the risk that all the upsetting things (from my past) against which I was holding "protective" thoughts would happen.

I decided to take that risk.

Throughout the day, every time I took on a "positive" thought, I noticed the "uncomfortable" sensations and "protective" thoughts come up.

So when I DARED to KNOW that I am well, aches and pains and the thought that I'm sick came right up. I said, "So be it. Maybe I am sick. Maybe something terrible will happen. But RIGHT NOW I'm holding the thought of health anyway."

When I DARED to take on the thought that all my financial issues were resolved, I noticed that I began to feel "uncomfortable" sensations and think, "Either that won't happen because shocking, terrible things I haven't even thought of will happen, or I'll get sick and die or lose my career the minute the issues are resolved."

When I began to take on the thought that projects would actually happen," I immediately felt a sinking sensation and noticed that my "positive" thoughts in this area were immediately followed by, "All my pending projects are going to fall through."

As I DARED to take on the thoughts I wanted to take on, tolerating the escalating "uncomfortable" and "negative" thoughts that came with them, I came in closer and closer touch with the fact that my Inner Child actually thought that taking on those "positive" thoughts was the REASON things wouldn't work out. I was now experiencing why my Inner Child had taken on the "protective" thoughts in the first place, and why my Inner Child was so quick to jump to them now, and whenever I DARED to think a "positive" thought.

With all this going on, I decided to take the "RISK" of taking on the thoughts I wanted to take on anyway, regardless of what "uncomfortable" sensations and "protective" thoughts came up. In other words, I was saying, "Fine. Drop dead. Lose everything. I'm taking on the thoughts anyway!"

The amazing thing was that once I did this, several things started to shift in my perception of the world. When I could hold to the "positive" thoughts no matter what "uncomfortable" sensations and "negative" thoughts I experienced, several noticeable changes occurred.

I began to experience EVERYTHING that happened as "on the way" to my dreams rather than "in the way" of my dreams.

I began to instinctively take different actions in regard to my issues.

Different things appeared to be happening in the outside world. Different calls began coming in. Different opportunities began presenting themselves. And different outcomes began appearing.

And within all this, I began to notice I was not focusing on the "outcome" of my dreams because I knew, in this exact present moment, no matter what was "going to" happen, I was fine right now. And each exact present moment was just that. A present moment in which I'm fine because I'm holding the thought that I'm fine. (Even while experiencing "uncomfortable" sensations and "protective" thoughts.)

This, of course, is what all the New Thought books and courses tell us to do. "Hold positive thoughts no matter what." But I had been unable to do it until I could recognize that, to my Inner Child, this was perceived as an enormous risk, and that if I wanted to hold these thoughts I had to INCLUDE, not cancel or push away or overcome or release my Inner Child's "uncomfortable" sensations and "negative" thoughts.

So today, right now, see if you can DARE to hold the thoughts you want to hold. It will not only change the way you experience your life, but it will be an important vehicle for your Inner Child to show you what is going on in its world, and give you a chance to experience it with your Inner Child while living the life you want to live.

Hold the thoughts you want to hold and experience the "uncomfortable" sensations and "negative" thoughts that come with them.

I DARE you!!!

WHEN THE WORK GETS REALLY HARD, IT OFTEN MEANS YOU'RE GETTING CLOSER

Often people begin this work and are thrilled to notice that when they can simply be with the child's sensations and be aware of the child's thoughts, they feel better and things seem to work out better.

But we must remember that our Inner Child is usually very carefully protecting the deepest hurts and the most painful, impossible double binds, because it feels they are intolerable.

Since the object of the work is to completely feel what the Inner Child felt (feels–because remember, the Inner Child is living in the past, but the past ONLY exists in the present) at some point we're going to have to feel as in pain as the Inner Child felt, and as hopeless and stuck as the Inner Child felt.

So, at various points in this work, often when we're really letting go or allowing ourselves to be successful, we may suddenly find that we are in agonizing pain and our thoughts are of hopelessness, futility, no-way-out, etc. We must remember that these are the thoughts of the Inner Child, although that can be very difficult, because we are ACTUALLY thinking them.

When you are feeling EXTREMELY painful sensations, and thinking EXTREMELY hopeless thoughts, I recommend doing these steps.

1. First, do your best to remember that who you are is an invisible, located-nowhere Observer, Noticer, Experiencer, and try and plant yourself in the position of being the observer of these sensations and thoughts.

2. Now see how accurately you can observe the sensations you're experiencing as pure sensations. Your mind will, of course, go to thoughts, but see if you can keep coming back to the sensations. In almost every case, the sensations you're experiencing are not really intolerable, it's just that you have thoughts associated with them that seem intolerable. So truly see if you can just experience a tightness in your stomach, a lump in your throat, a sinking feeling throughout your torso, or whatever sensation you happen to be having.

3. When you can be with those sensations, turn your attention to your thoughts and see if you can observe them as pure, meaningless thoughts. Simply notice that you feel hopeless. Notice that whatever old thoughts used to stop you, thoughts like, "What's the use of going for this? What's the use of trying? Everyone else gets everything; I will never succeed," etc. are just the thoughts you're thinking now. Really see if you can be with them by Observing yourself thinking them.

4. Now look at your actual life, at what you're actually doing, and even if you're not doing well, at the possibilities it contains. Money isn't here? It could arrive. You may have an idea from where, but you may also not have to know. You're in a certain kind of trouble? Notice that you've probably been in that kind of trouble before and have found ways to get out of it.

You're going for something that has always failed to materialize in the past? See if you can remind yourself that the world always looks like your unconscious thoughts, so the reason you've experienced failure is that you've always held the unconscious thought that it would fail.

Notice that those thoughts are now conscious, and that no matter how many times you've failed, it's possible to succeed.

5. Don't expect to feel better. Be with the thoughts and sensations for as long as they last.

6. Keep going, doing what you want to do, moving forward on those "futile" tasks WHILE HAVING THE SENSATIONS YOU'RE HAVING AND THE THOUGHTS YOU'RE HAVING. This helps you differentiate between the Adult and the Inner Child, and it also lets the Inner Child know that its thoughts and sensations are not unhandleable and will not hurt you. As you do this, you will become less afraid of the thoughts and sensations, because you will know that they can't stop you from doing what you want to do. Gradually, they will simply become a part of doing what you want to do, rather than an impediment.

Become willing to do these steps and you will, over time, achieve not only deeper healing but Mastery over your life. The sensations and thoughts may never go away, but your relationship with them will completely change in that you will be able to accept them, move forward with them, and most importantly, not attribute meaning to them. Rather than getting rid of them (which even if you did get rid of them you might always live in fear that they would return) you are becoming accustomed to simply handling them WHENEVER they come up.

When you can do this, every time they come up (and they may come up, from time to time, forever) they will provide another opportunity for healing and moving forward.

For example, just this week, I hit a pocket of deep, empty sensations coupled with thoughts that my life is going nowhere, that it's all hopeless and that all the projects I'm working on are going nowhere.

So I did the steps.

1. I moved into the awareness that I am the Observer, and "looked at" what was going on.

2. I stayed with the sensations as sensations, no matter how painful. One thing that helps us to do this is the thought that I'm just going to do it for a little while. As I looked at the sensations I was having, I began to notice that they were not really painful or unbearable, I had just been interpreting them as that.

3. I looked at my thoughts and recognized them as thoughts I've had, on and off, but fairly consistently, all my life. Thoughts like, "What's the use of trying to do a publicity campaign on my next CD, of trying to raise money on Indiegogo for the next Nancy LaMott CD, of negotiating for my next Broadway show, of working with my financial planner to improve my finances? Why am I trying to write another book? I'll never get it right, never finish it and it will never sell. None of it will work." I sat with those thoughts, and whenever my mind jumped back to sensations, I continued to experience my sensations.

4. In looking at my actual life, I saw the following; I was in the middle of sending out an enormous and cost-free marketing message for my just-released CD's. I had written the copy for an Indiegogo campaign, had all the material for the CD lined up, and had an Indiegogo expert and a videographer I love and trust lined up. I was in the home stretch of negotiating my next Broadway show with a great producer. I had just had a meeting with my financial planner in which he told me that he thought I could cut several expenses easily. Also, some stocks I'd been holding for years had suddenly started to rise significantly in value.

5. Now mind you, and this is important, THIS DIDN'T MAKE ME FEEL ANY BETTER. I still felt the sensations

and had the thoughts. But it helped me to clarify that there is something going on in the present simultaneously with thoughts going on from the past , and the two are not necessarily the same. But I had become more willing and able to simply experience the sensations and think the thoughts.

6. Over the days I was feeling this, I was able to keep going. I recorded a tape that I needed to have for my publicity campaign. I read through the copy on my Indiegogo video to see if some ideas for how to actually make the video would rise to the surface. I called my attorney to check on the Broadway negotiation. I called my financial planner and told him I was anxious to speak with his insurance guy, and asked him to look into the stocks that were moving and come up with a strategy. And just this morning (a Saturday) when I woke up and realized I have nothing to do today and felt the emptiness and noticed the futile thoughts, I sat down and wrote this section of the book. And suddenly I'm thinking, "Great. I'm going to do a lot of writing on the book, maybe I'll even finish it next week, I have stuff I wanted to do in the yard which I'll have time to do, Shawn and I could go to the movies, we can call friends who have a great pool and spend the afternoon with them (it's 90 degrees out today) and I'm going to sit with these thoughts and sensations because perhaps the MOST IMPORTANT thing that's happening today is that I'm being with thoughts and sensations that have stopped me for my whole life. "

Same thoughts. Same sensations. Still there. Different possibilities. Because the position of Observer is the ONLY place from which you can see EVERYTHING. All the pain, all the possibilities.

HOPELESSNESS IS THE HEALING

Recently, in a Thought Exchange workshop, one member (we'll call her Kay, not her real name) spoke up and told us in a very distressed tone that she'd had it, she's through, life is hopeless, nothing is ever going to change, and she might as well kill herself now.

This woman is a very talented performer who, for the past few years, has been working in a large, upscale department store as a customer guide.

She related a long story about how everywhere she turns she is met with inexplicably rude and dismissive behavior by her coworkers, people falsely accuse her of things she didn't do, crazy-making coworkers and supervisors portray her as a manipulative, difficult person when she is just trying to be helpful, and on top of that, she feels totally stuck and stopped whenever she tries to do what she really wants to do, which is sing.

In this story, (which was told in the tone of voice and with the frustration and tears of a three year old) one crazy supervisor wouldn't let her work on the Fourth of July (which is a double pay day) for extremely arbitrary reasons, which were unfair, considering her seniority.

She then asked a sales clerk to please remove a metal tag for a customer on a machine which the sales clerk had behind her counter, and the sales clerk nastily told her to do it herself. When Kay told her that she'd been asked by her supervisor not to go behind the counter, the woman got nastier. Kay demanded to speak to this woman's supervisor, the woman said she would call her herself, she called the supervisor and told Kay that the supervisor would talk to her later. Kay walked over to another counter and asked the woman behind that counter to remove the tag. The woman smiled and said, "Sure," and removed the tag. Kay then felt compelled to go to the first woman to let her know that the other woman had simply done this for her. The woman behind the counter got even angrier, and demanded to know the name of Kay's supervisor. When Kay didn't answer and walked away, the woman followed her across the store screaming at her, asking her, "Who's your supervisor?"

Kay then went and told the crazy manager (the one who inexplicably wouldn't let her work on the Fourth of July) what had happened and he said something to the effect of, "Well, you know how difficult you can be. You must have done something!" Kay asked him if she needed to go to the union. He said, "Why would you threaten that?" He then threatened to take her to the HR director.

At this point in the story I stopped her with the observation, "This sounds EXACTLY like your childhood." It did, in fact, sound exactly like the kinds of things that routinely happened to her with her mother and father. Out-of-the-blue severe punishments for things she didn't do, erratic behavior toward her, conflicting information, characterizing her as difficult. The works.

When I pointed this out to her, she responded as many people in this situation do, saying, "Yes, but it's still happening now. The same stuff continues to happen and will never stop!"

I then suggested to her that yes, these things WERE happening NOW, but her Inner Child, living in the past, was reacting to them and functioning as though these things had the meaning and consequence in the present that they had had when she was a child. The tone in which she told the story and the direness and hopelessness she attributed to the occurrences were a child speaking, not an adult.

She then gave the next standard response, which was, "Are you telling me I'm making these things happen?"

My answer was, "Well, yes and no. These things are just happening, but your response to them is within the Inner Child's thought, so the reflection you're seeing in the mirror of the world is that Inner Child's thought." There are many ways in which an adult, whose life didn't depend on the results, would have acted differently and had a different interior experience.

We went through the incidents.

The supervisor wouldn't let her work on the day she wanted to work. That is disappointing but not completely devastating, unless the supervisor is viewed as a father from whom you're desperate to get something and who won't, no matter what, give it to you.

The woman behind the counter was having a bad day, and behaving as her Inner Child. Our member could have immediately walked away, not had to explain to her that she had been told not to go behind the counter, not had to call her supervisor, and just gone to the other counter and gotten what she needed done. But her Inner Child had needed to get this erratic, punishing person (just like her mother) to understand something that this person was obviously not going to understand.

After this happened, who did she go to to try and get the solace and support she needed? The crazy manager who was about as likely to give it to her as her father would have been years ago.

Now, in order to be able to take all these adult actions, her Inner Child would have had to be heard by someone. I had the very strong image in my head of a three year old running around a store filled with crazy adults trying to get them to understand her and feeling that she was in a life and death situation (which, for a three year old, this would have been.).

This three year old needed SOMEONE to understand her, to be with her, and the only person who could do that was her own Inner Adult, who was feeling, in her own body and mind, EXACTLY what her Inner Child was feeling.

At this point, another member of The Thought Exchange piped up and said that the problem was that if a person had never had experiences where he or she was treated with love and understanding, there was no capable Inner Adult within them who could take care of their own Inner Child.

This is a defense that is often used by the Inner Child to try to try find a way to get the adults in the present to heal its trauma from the past. It is also a way for the Inner Child to reproduce its past, by creating, in thought, the same situation it was in in the past, namely that one in which there is no competent adult around.

In fact, when we can simply stop and experience the sensations we're having as sensations and the thoughts we're having as thoughts, without acting on them, knowing that our EXPERIENCE of what's happening on the outside is simply a reflection of the thoughts we're holding, the very act of doing this means that these thoughts and sensations are being observed and experienced, and this is the Inner Adult observing the Inner Child.

Of course, we can't underestimate how difficult this is to do because, to the Inner Child, these circumstances feel truly dangerous. But if we can, even by rote, stop, feel the sensations as sensations and think the thoughts as thoughts, the Inner Child is observed, and we are safe, and free to act in the present world as the present adults that we are.

When our other member suggested that perhaps there wasn't an adult there, within Kay, to take care of Kay's Inner Child, I was concerned that we were being thrown off the track, giving Kay an excuse to stay in the experience of thinking she was still an adult-less child. This would encourage her to keep fighting, in the present, for things that could not be gotten from other people.

But Kay's response was quite surprising and amazingly powerful.

She said, "NO! There is no-one outside of me who can help me! My whole adult life, EVERYTHING I've done, EVERY interaction I've had, EVERYTHING I've aspired to, even when it seemed like I was functioning as an adult, has been for the futile and hopeless purpose of trying to get something from other people that my mother and father didn't give me. AND I CAN'T GET IT! I NEVER WILL! IT WILL NEVER HAPPEN! The ONLY place I can ever get that understanding is from my Inner Adult. And the understanding is that it's hopeless, that I'm in an impossible double bind, and that my Inner Child didn't get what she wanted and never will get it!"

Although this revelation, that her Inner Child's life happened to her and can never be fixed, and that it is 100% hopeless to try to get what the Inner Child needed from the present world, might seem like the end of the world, this in fact is the place to which all of this work is leading us, and this very hopelessness is the moment of true healing.

At last, the Inner Child's utter hopelessness, the FACT that at the time there was NOTHING that could be done, the FACT that the Inner Child is eternally sitting in this world of no hope, is recognized and felt by the Inner Adult. Until this time, our present self has been constantly trying to find a way out, to find a way for the past to have not been true, and in doing this, has essentially been staying away from and not truly recognizing what the Inner Child truly felt. At last, the Inner Child has gotten through what its experience truly was, and has someone who "gets it."

This does not change what happened, it doesn't make it go away, but the Inner Child is cared for. And when the Inner Child is cared for (and this care will go on for the rest of our lives – the Inner Child will ALWAYS remember what happened, ALWAYS feel the sensations and ALWAYS have the thoughts...although that being said, we may experience them differently as time goes on, because we will not be afraid of them and they will not mean to us, as adults, what they meant to the Inner Child); but when the Inner Child is cared for, we are then free to function as adults, to see the options that exist in the present that didn't exist in the past, to experience disappointment not as devastation, to accept losses and enjoy gains, and to use EVERY incident to either move what we want as adults forward, or get closer to our Inner Child, and by doing so, give our Adult more possibilities.

The challenge is that in order to heal, we must truly experience, in the present, the full magnitude of the hopelessness and frustration the Inner Child experienced in the past. I call this the eye of the needle, because at the moment we experience it, we are truly as frustrated and as hopeless as the Inner Child was. We cannot fix what happened, but we can be with it and by being with it, the Inner Child is getting what it needs.

It reminds me of a song that came to me when I was getting to the point of understanding the hopelessness that my own Inner Child had experienced.

The song is called "I Can Hold You," and I wrote it for me to sing to my own Inner Child.

There's a lyric in it that goes:

> I CAN HOLD YOU
> I CAN TAKE YOU IN MY ARMS
> LET YOU KNOW I UNDERSTAND
> AND THAT I ALWAYS WILL BE THERE
> AND WHEN I HOLD YOU
> THOUGH I CAN'T KEEP YOU FROM HARM
> I CAN LOVE YOU
> I CAN LISTEN
> I CAN CARE
> I CAN HOLD YOU
> THROUGH THE DARKNESS AND DESPAIR

For me, the most important understanding in this lyric is that I can't keep the child from harm, I can't keep what happened from happening, but I can be with the child and recognize its plight.

So when you find yourself in that true state of hopelessness, where everything around you seems to be conspiring to frustrate and hurt you, feel it, think it, but rather than fighting it, turn inward, to your Inner Child, and recognize that that's what it went through. And when you do that, you will automatically become aware that this is about the past, not the present, and your present adult and all the opportunities possible will kick in.

When I looked at Kay's situation at work, it amazed me how a whole department store worth of people seemed to conspire to recreate her childhood situation so she could experience it in the present and thus connect with her Inner Child's past experience. When she did this, her Inner Child was safe and her Adult self was free to live life the way she wanted to.

WHEN IN DOUBT, GO TO YOUR SENSATIONS

Throughout this book I've been talking about being with your "uncomfortable" sensations and "negative" thoughts. As you do this, it's important to remember "what causes what."

"Uncomfortable" sensations are usually generated by certain "positive" thoughts. Although this may seem counter-intuitive, if we remember that the reason for this is that those "positive" thoughts were, at one time, precursors to disappointment or pain for our Inner Child, it makes sense. We dare to think a thought that got us hurt (like "I'll ask that person out" or "I will get that job") and our Inner Child reacts with a tight throat, stomach ache, pounding heart, etc.

A chart of it would look like this.

In order to "get away from" the "uncomfortable" sensations, the Inner Child grabs for a "protective" thought that will not generate the "uncomfortable" sensations that the "positive" thought generated. It stands to reason that the protective thought will be the opposite of the "positive" thought. So, if the thought that generated the discomfort was "I can" then the "protective" thought will be "I can't."

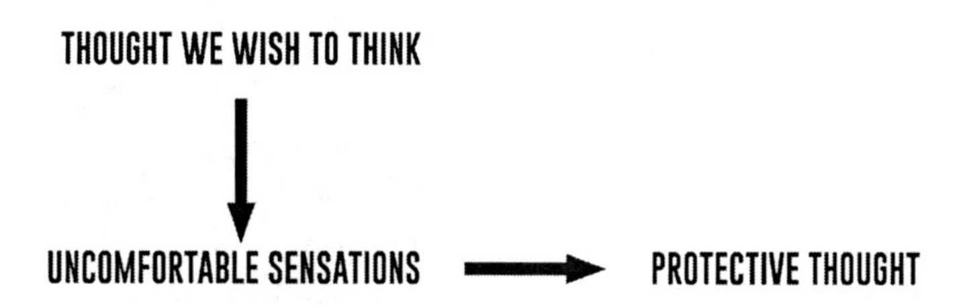

As I've been saying throughout this book, if you want to be able to stay with the thought you wish to hold, you have to be able to experience the sensations it generates AND notice the "protective" thoughts and identify them as "protective" thoughts.

It's important to identify "protective" thoughts as "protective" thoughts because this helps you to not take them on as thoughts you're holding. What we don't want to do is exchange the thought we wish to hold for the "protective" thought. If we do that, we will be enacting the "protective" thought in our experience.

We just want to notice the "protective" thought as something that comes with the thought we want to hold.

Once you've done that, it's important to realize that the ONLY reason we take on "protective" thoughts is to get away from the "uncomfortable" sensations generated by the thought we wish to hold. When we realize this, it follows that the more we can be with the "uncomfortable" sensations generated by the thought we wish to hold, the less we will take on "protective" thoughts (or at least, the less disturbing and attention-drawing we will find them).

So, when you are holding a thought you want to hold, experiencing the "uncomfortable" sensations that come with that thought, and noticing the "protective" thoughts that come with it, try to move yourself from the protective thoughts back to the uncomfortable sensations. The more you can do this, the more you will be able to stay with the thought you wish to hold.

So the chart ends up looking like this:

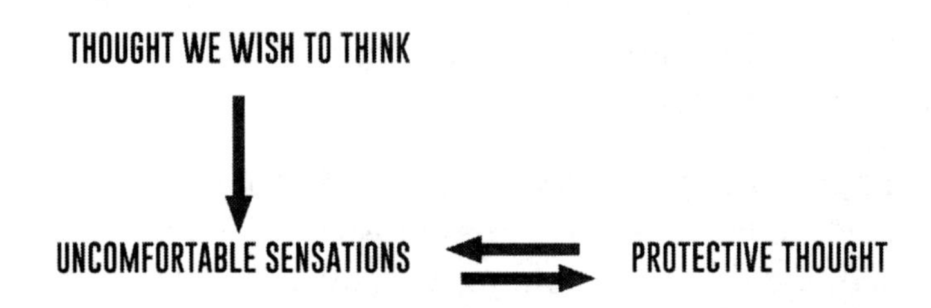

To sum it up;

When you take on a thought you wish to take on, notice and be with your sensations.

If you find yourself jumping to a "protective" thought, go back to your sensations.

You can also, of course, exchange the "protective" thought for the thought you wish to hold,

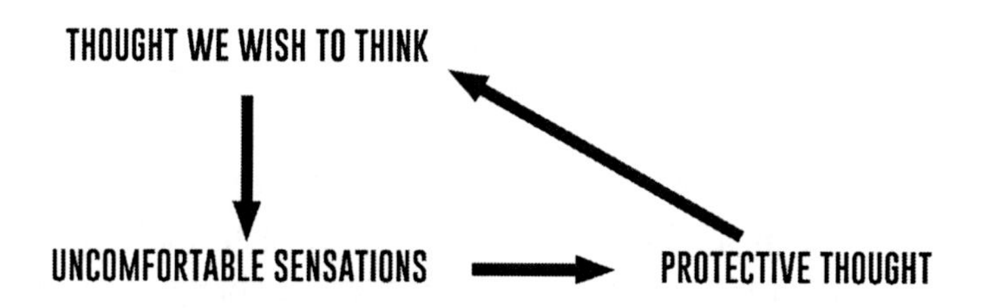

and guess what!

Yup! You'll be right back to the "uncomfortable" sensations.

Strangely enough, although many of us have spent our lives trying to get away from "uncomfortable" sensations, the key to freedom, to the experience of unlimitedness and the ability to hold any thought lies in our ability to experience our sensations.

So, when in doubt, go to your sensations.

> "When in doubt,
> go to your sensations."

IF I DO THIS WORK, WILL THE PAIN EVENTUALLY LESSEN AND GO AWAY?

In just about every Thought Exchange seminar I've ever taught, within an hour of my explaining that the pain of the Inner Child will ALWAYS be there (because what happened to the Inner Child will always have happened) somebody raises their hand and asks, "If we do this work, does the pain eventually lessen and go away? Or are you saying that we will have to suffer like this forever?"

This is a very important question, the answer to which is filled with complexity and subtlety. Let me walk you through it.

My first answer is usually, "Yes, it will always be there, but your relationship to it may change, so you may experience it quite differently."

In Truth, it may not ALWAYS be there, but the possibility of it showing up at any moment will always be there, because this pain is about a memory, and something in the present could always trigger the Inner Child. So unless you have the BASIC SKILL of being able to be with the Inner Child's thoughts and sensations, should they show up at any time, you have not mastered the pain. In fact, the pain has GOT you!

Here's the paradox. Whether the pain is going to be there or not, whether it's going to change or not, we are dealing, in the present, with an Inner Child from the past who is coming to us, via shared sensations and thoughts, with a problem. If a child came to you with a problem, would you let it know that you needed that problem to go away? Would you say, "You have a limited amount of time and then this problem has to be over?" Would you say, "I can't stand your problem, it's ruining my life, so I'm releasing you?" Of course not.

The way in which the Inner Child is accepted, embraced and listened to IS the healing. So even though, of course, we wish we weren't in this kind of pain, we wish it had never happened and we wish it would go away, the position we MUST take with the Inner Child is, "I am here for as long as you need me to be. I can feel this with you forever. I will never walk away from you, judge you or have the need to get rid of you." Only then does the Inner Child experience healing, not because the pain is gone, but because The Inner Child knows that its pain will always be felt and held by an adult who understands it 100% (since the Inner Adult experiences EXACTLY what the Inner Child experiences).

Once we've done this, sometimes the pain remains, sometimes it disappears and comes back from time to time, and sometimes we never have it again. (Although, of course, we can never say we will never have it again, because even if we haven't had it for years, it could still always come back.)

The point is, by being willing to be with it "forever" we no longer live in fear of its being there, but rather, even though we might have a preference for it not being there (who wouldn't?), should it be there, we know what to do. We have The BASIC SKILL. We can be with the Inner Child and continue to live in the present as an adult.

A wonderful example of this happened to me recently.

For the past seven years, I have appeared live on *The Today Show,* performing a new original song with a different Broadway star every month. It's live, national television, with millions of people watching.

Now, as I described earlier in this book, when I was 20 years old I was hospitalized for "Panic Disorder." The thing about panic is, once you've had it, even if you haven't had it in a while, you always know that you could have it. And the nature of panic is that it can come at any moment, without warning, and without any seeming relationship to what you're doing, how well you do it, or what's happening in the present. You're just suddenly feeling extremely "uncomfortable" sensations and thinking you're going to drop dead, be humiliated, have to run out of the room or off the stage, whatever.

As I described in an earlier chapter, for years I would perform with the feeling of full-blown panic. It's not that it lessened. I just learned to be with it and do what I was doing.

When I started doing *The Today Show,* I noticed, to my great surprise, that I wasn't scared. I wasn't feeling panicked. I wasn't nervous. I wasn't worried. This AMAZED me, but I took it as a piece of grace.

As time went on, I began to examine how I actually felt before a performance. I noticed that even though my perception was that I wasn't scared or worried, I was actually having many of the "nervous" symptoms that I'd always had. My heart was racing, my breath was a little short, I'd sometimes have the thought that I was going to screw up. The difference was, when these "uncomfortable" sensations and "negative" thoughts would come up, I would just notice them, have them, and go about my business. So my experience was that I wasn't scared. Not because I wasn't feeling or thinking anything, but because I was able to be with what I was feeling and thinking.

One morning I was REALLY tired. I had gotten to bed at 3AM and had been picked up in Connecticut for a 6AM rehearsal. I was warming up, going through my music, when suddenly I had the terrifying thought, "How do I know how to play the piano? Why, when I look at those dots on a page, do my hands know where to go?" I was about three minutes from going on, and I felt this hot wave of panic shoot up my belly into my head.

But fortunately, I had Thought Exchange and I had The BASIC SKILL. So I simply sat with that sensation and experienced it, and noticed that I was having the thought I was having.

The next thought that came to me was, "Hmm. Actually, I don't know how I know how to play the piano. In fact I never have known. But I do seem to know how to play the piano, even though I don't know why. So I'll play the piano, and if I forget how to play the piano on National Television, that'll be interesting!"

And with that I didn't think about it again and I played piano beautifully on TV.

So, the point is, there may be times when you feel "uncomfortable," there may be times when you don't, but as long as you have the ability to be with whatever sensations you're having and whatever "protective" thoughts you're having, should a time come when the old "uncomfortable" sensations and "negative" thoughts arise, you will know how to handle them by simply being with them.

WHAT ABOUT HEALING MODALITIES THAT PROMISE RELIEF OR RELEASE FROM TRAUMA? (And How Do We Use Thought Exchange in Conjunction With Those?)

Another thing that usually comes up when I talk about the idea that the Inner Child's trauma will always be there is, "What about healing methods that say that you can release the memory, that the memory can be erased from our brain, that we can be reprogrammed to not remember the past in the same way?"

Well, I actually have done most of those healing methods, and when I first did them, I went in with great hopes, only to find that they didn't work for me.

But, since many of them, such as EMDR, tapping, Brainspotting, Buddhism and others are based on excellent philosophy and science and created and practiced by brilliant, powerful healers, rather than trying to discredit them, I asked myself why I personally had been unable to reap the benefits they had to offer.

This question has actually been the source of all my research and development of The Thought Exchange. What is the missing piece for me? Why am I not able to apply and hold principles that seem to me to be sound?

What I found is this.

When I first did EMDR and tapping, for example, I did them with the hopes that I would somehow "magically" and "without pain" get away from things that were bothering me. I treated them sort of like a "miracle diet." You're never hungry, you eat all you want, you feel great and you lose all this weight without any physiological or psychological challenges. In other words, I did them with the idea that I could release, overcome or erase my Inner Child without feeling it or coming to terms with it. When I did this, rather than letting my Inner Child simply come up, reveal itself and be experienced by the adult me, (with all the pain and challenges doing this entails) I tried to push past the Inner Child and get away from it. And the Inner Child can NEVER let you do that. So my Inner Child would keep rebelling and trying to get my attention by creating more symptoms, more "uncomfortable" sensations and more "protective" thoughts like, "This can't work; I'll never get this; My damage is too great," no matter how much healing work I did.

After doing Thought Exchange work, and developing The BASIC SKILL of being able to be with my sensations and thoughts, I've gone back to some of those other modalities, and found them much more effective for me. The reason is that I was able to sit with what was coming up and simply go through the process rather than trying to control it or get away from discomfort.

So for me, the ability to be with whatever came up and to allow myself to experience it without manipulating it or trying to get around it was a prerequisite for being able to allow these other kinds of work to effect changes in me.

I think it all boils down to the idea that the goal is not to get rid of some part of ourselves, but to incorporate, come to terms with, allow, become less frightened of, shift our relationship with traumatized parts of ourselves, and ultimately embrace our whole selves. There's no "magic bullet" to doing that. I believe that any work that truly effects deep restructuring and healing does not "magically" step outside of our issues and erase them, but rather engages us in a process in which we actively restructure our relationship with those issues. And that almost always takes work and perseverance and time.

I'm always suspicious of work that is advertised as, "This is so amazing and effortless and your problems just disappear." I sometimes like to joke with my students by telling them, "Come to a Thought Exchange Workshop. You'll pay me. Nothing will happen. And you'll leave feeling worse than when you came in!" People who've done this work for a while get the joke. This work, and in my opinion, any work worth its salt, requires us to look at and experience things we've been afraid to look at and experience. This work is WORK!

So, if you have been doing other kinds of work and not having the success you've desired, try going into whatever modality you're working with without any agenda other than being with whatever sensations and thoughts come up. Apply the BASIC SKILL, let go to the process and let it work.

For me, in my personal experience, it's never a matter of letting go of or getting rid of anything. It's a matter of, more and more, being with what is, with less and less resistance. Sometimes, less pain. Sometimes, not. But more and more acceptance.

Thought Exchange and Inner Child work can help you do that with other modalities. And of course, other modalities that work for you can help you do that with Thought Exchange and Inner Child work. When it comes to doing our inner work, I love the motto "Never instead. Always in addition."*

When all is said and done, what are we really going for? Wholeness. Forgiveness. Peace. Love. Whatever helps us get there, I say, "Go for it!" And if Thought Exchange can help, I say, "Add it to the mix."

FORGIVENESS, LOVE AND PEACE (ARE ALL THE SAME THING)

Forgiveness, Love and Peace are perhaps considered the cornerstones, or the goals of spiritual practice. Interestingly enough, to me they are all the same thing.

Forgiveness, Love and Peace are all allowing things to be exactly as they are.

Forgiveness is not condoning or forgetting. Forgiveness is allowing that something happened, that the other person said or did this, and that I had the thoughts and sensations I had. Period. No right and wrong. Nothing happened that "shouldn't have happened." Just allowing what is to be. Then I don't have to fend anything off, don't have to get anyone else to "see" or "understand" or say anything, no apologies. Just, "I get it. This is the way it was, this is the way I felt and thought when it happened,and these are the sensations and thoughts I'm having about it now."

*Attributed to Rabbi Joseph Gelberman , Founder of The New Seminary For Interfaith Studies

Peace is not comfort. Peace is being with what is. And a big part of being with what is, is allowing myself to be with what I feel and think when what is, is. So I might have an accident. In order to be at peace with that accident, I must be willing to allow myself to accept that I had the accident and was injured in exactly the way I was injured.

But here's where people get stuck. They think that in order to be at peace and accept the accident, they have to be "fine" with it. NO. You have to be fine with however you are about the accident.

So I might notice that I'm in a lot of pain, that I don't like pain, that I think someone else is at fault and that I wish I'd never had the accident. Peace is accepting ALL OF THAT. "The way it is" includes the way I think and the sensations I have.

So don't try to be comfortable, just be with all that is, and you will experience Peace.

Love, as I understand it, is also nothing more than allowing everything to be just as it is. Love has nothing to do with being nice, with giving gifts, with talking in a certain tone of voice. Many people do all those things and are not experiencing love. Love is simply allowing everything to be as it is.

So, Forgiveness, Peace and Love have nothing to do with comfort. They have to do with being with everything you "see" and everything you "experience" inside, exactly as they are.

"PEACE AT ANY TIME" MEDITATION

Given that Peace is nothing more or less than being with everything exactly as it is, here's a meditation you can use to experience peace any time, anywhere, no matter what the circumstance.

Close your eyes.

With your eyes closed, notice how you know that you are here. Notice how you know that you exist. That you are present. There's a sense of consciousness, a sense of "I Am." This sense of consciousness is not located in any particular place, in fact it's invisible. It can't be seen. But it's definitely here, as an experience.

An invisible, non-physical, non-locatable experience.

So it could be said, that who you are is an invisible consciousness, located nowhere.

Now notice that you have sensations. Itching, tightness, shortness of breath, hotness, coldness, relaxation, calm, pounding, rushing. The experience of these sensations, like your consciousness, is invisible.

Notice the sensations you're having right now and just be with them. Nothing to change, nothing to release, just experience them as they are.

So it could be said that who you are is an invisible consciousness experiencing invisible sensations.

Now notice your thoughts. Notice that you can think of ANYTHING. Locate a baboon in your thoughts. Say, "Got it," when you've got it. "Got It." It shouldn't take you more than the time it takes to think of it for you to get it. And the time it takes to think of anything is infinitesimal. Now see yourself doing the twist on the rings of Saturn. Say, "Got it" when you've got it. "Got It." If you're having trouble seeing this, or are finding yourself saying, "Well, that's impossible, Saturn's rings are not solid and you can't breathe on Saturn," remember, I didn't ask you to take this into the physical universe, just to see it in the invisible world of unlimited possible thoughts.

Notice that all the things you "see" in this realm are invisible, not solid or physical. You have infinite choice of what you can see here, unlike in the physical world where it seems much harder to see things. And this infinite world is inside you and always available to you.

So it could be said that who you are is an invisible consciousness experiencing invisible sensations and containing unlimited, invisible thoughts.

In fact, what I have just described is YOUR ENTIRE WORLD OF EXPERIENCE, and is the ONLY PLACE IN WHICH YOU LIVE. All you truly are is an invisible consciousness experiencing invisible sensations and containing unlimited, invisible thoughts. PERIOD!

You are not the things that happen in the world. You are not even your body. You are an invisible consciousness experiencing these things as invisible thoughts and sensations.

Anything that happens in the physical world is only experienced as thoughts and sensations inside of you.

Sit for a moment and experience your whole self. Experience yourself as an invisible consciousness and simply have the thoughts and sensations you're having.

This is all you ever are. This is all that's ever happening. Nothing dangerous about it. No outcomes. No future. Nothing that has to happen. Nowhere you have to get. Nothing that can be lost, or gained for that matter. Just consciousness, thoughts and sensations, all the time, at every moment, no matter what's going on in the world.

WHAT YOU ARE EXPERIENCING RIGHT NOW IS PEACE. PEACE IS NOT NECESSARILY COMFORTABLE. PEACE DOES NOT FEEL ANY SPECIFIC WAY. PEACE IS SIMPLY BEING WITH WHAT IS. AND PEACE IS ALWAYS READILY AVAILABLE TO YOU. ALL YOU HAVE TO DO IS WHAT YOU JUST DID, CLOSE YOUR EYES, NOTICE YOUR SENSATIONS, NOTICE YOUR THOUGHTS AND SIMPLY BE WITH THEM. PEACE. ANY TIME. ANYWHERE.

So knowing this, knowing that you are really invisible and live only in the invisible world, open your eyes and look out at the visible world, which is not where you live. You're just looking out at it and experiencing it as YOUR thoughts and sensations.

I FINALLY LET GO

Years ago, a 15-year relationship I was in ended very suddenly, in one day, and not by my instigation. I was devastated, and began the long, slow process of healing, understanding the hand I had had in it, and looking down the road to see what healing would be and how it might occur.

As I am a songwriter by profession, and as I'm clear that my songs write me rather than me writing my songs, I sat down one day and "asked Spirit" how my healing was going to occur.

Over the next six months, piece by piece, this song came to me. It took me a long time to write, because I was writing about things that I myself didn't know about or understand, and not wanting to make the song platitudinous, I had to wait until the information was revealed to me.

When I look at this song now, it was, in fact, the path I took to healing. And in light of what I've been talking about in the last few sections of this book, it marked a shift in my life from attempted control to Faith.

I FINALLY LET GO

(Words and Music by David Friedman)

I FINALLY LET GO
OF WAITING AROUND FOR ONE DREAM TO COME TRUE
I FINALLY SAID NO
NO MORE LIVING AS THOUGH THERE WAS NOTHING TO DO
BUT SEARCH FOR ONE LOVE
AND IF THAT LOVE DIDN'T COME ALONG
WAS I NOTHING?
WAS LIFE NOTHING?

I FINALLY SAID "HEY,
GET OUT OF THE FUTURE, START LIVING TODAY"
I FINALLY SAID "WOW,
THERE'S SO MUCH TO BE THANKFUL FOR RIGHT HERE AND NOW
AND I'M MISSING IT
MISSING THE SMILES OF MY FRIENDS
MISSING THE BEAUTY THAT LIVES ALL AROUND ME
AND THE SUNSETS
AND THE MUSIC
THE MUSIC

I FINALLY SAID "WHY
KEEP RELIVING THE PAST 'TIL THE DAY THAT I DIE?"
I FINALLY SAID "GEE,
IF IT'S GONNA BE DIFFERENT IT'S GONNA BE ME WHO CHANGES IT.
ME WHO LET'S GO OF THE PAIN
ME WHO SURRENDERS TO THIS VERY MOMENT
TO THE HEARTBREAK
AND THE SADNESS
AND THE PASSION
AND THE LONGING
AND THE FEELING
THE FEELING

AND THEN I WENT DEEP INSIDE
AND THERE I FINALLY CRIED
FOR ALL OF THE WISHES THAT NEVER CAME TRUE
AND ALL OF THE GREAT THINGS I'D WANTED TO DO
AND ALL OF THE DREAMS THAT I NEVER WOULD KNOW
AND I LET 'EM GO
I LET 'EM GO

AND I FINALLY COULD SAY
"IF THERE'S NO MORE THAN THIS, I CAN STILL BE OK"
I FINALLY COULD SEE
IT WAS MORE THAN ENOUGH TO BE HERE, TO BE ME
LIVING EVERY DAY
AND WHEN I WAS FINALLY AWARE
THAT WHEN I'M ALONE THERE'S STILL SOMEONE THERE
AND THAT SOMEONE IS ME
THAT SOMEONE IS ME

THEN I FINALLY FOUND PEACE
'CAUSE THEN I FINALLY KNOW
THAT HAPPINESS COMES FROM INSIDE OF ME
AND THEN
ONLY THEN
I FOUND YOU

Recording available at MIDDERMusic.com
(A Different Light – David Friedman
sings his own songs)

There are several interesting things about this song in light of the subject of this book.

The first is, of course, that a big part of the process of healing was to allow myself to notice my wishes that hadn't come true, the achievements that hadn't happened, the dreams that had gone unfulfilled, in short, my "negative" thoughts, and "let 'em go."

Now the meaning of "let 'em go" is something that often confuses people involved in Spiritual work and New Thought. To me, "let 'em go" doesn't mean get rid of them or drop them. It means "allow them to be, let them keep going however they go, let them exist and stop trying to change them." In this context, "Let go" does not mean "get rid of." It means "allow things to be exactly as they are."

Another thing that might trip people up is the notion that, in the end, "I found YOU."

One of the biggest challenges in New Thought is that we do all this interior work, but underneath it, we still hold onto the notion that the purpose of doing this, the "goal," is a specific outcome or manifestation. As soon as we get into this kind of thinking, we are dead ducks, because manifestation, no matter what it is, can only reflect back to us what we're thinking inside, and if we're thinking we don't have enough, it doesn't matter what we see before us.

In Truth, although the end of the song would seem to suggest that what I found was a partner (and in fact that was what happened), we must remember that the partner is only a reflection of an inner shift. The "You" that I really found could more accurately be called The Observer within myself, God, Spirit, Acceptance. And as a result of that, what appeared before me was a partner, but that is not the point. One could be just as happy, just as at peace, just as forgiving, just as whole, just as filled with love without a partner.

At the bottom of all this, all our work is done simply to be able to include, accept and experience ALL THAT IS. And that definitely MUST include negativity, pain, doubt, "negative" thoughts and "uncomfortable" sensations. If we are trying to live lives where we only feel and think certain things and only have certain things happen, we are always in danger, because at any moment any of these things that are not what we think we want can occur. When we live in acceptance of and being with what is, our lives are working out at every moment and we experience whatever happens as Good.

PART XI

“NEGATIVE” THOUGHTS AND “UNCOMFORTABLE” SENSATIONS

CHAPTER 40

There IS Somewhere to GET (HERE!)

As I said in the Introduction to this book, so many of us spend so much time trying to get somewhere, trying to manifest things we think we don't have, while trying to release, let go of, change, transform or cancel things we have that we think we shouldn't have.

This NEVER works because all of those pursuits are trying to change something that IS, edit something that is part of what IS, and What IS is ALL there IS. What WAS can ONLY be experienced as part of what IS for us NOW. What WILL BE can also ONLY be experienced as part of what IS for us NOW.

The reason for this is that WHAT IS is what we're THINKING right now.

There's a wonderful Gertrude Stein quote that says (I paraphrase) "When you finally get there, you find that there's no 'there' there."

There's only HERE. NOW. The EXPERIENCE of this moment.

What we are striving for, what EVERY "problem" and "desire" and "dream" is for, is for us to be able to see, reflected in the mirror of the world, what we're thinking.

And what we're THINKING, when we're feeling limited or stuck or lacking, is that there is something in the present that we don't have.

That CAN'T be true. If we can just get to the PRESENT MOMENT, exactly as it is, we can be in the experience of Wholeness, Completeness, Unlimitedness, Peace, Forgiveness, Love, you name it!

So what keeps us from simply being in the present?

As you may have surmised by now, the premise of this book is that our fear of or unwillingness to experience keeps us from being in this moment, where all the happiness and contentment and peace are. And since "uncomfortable" sensations and "negative" thoughts are often an integral part of the present moment, we can't be in the present if we can't let ourselves experience them.

Being in the present, with what is, is ALL we want. And interestingly enough, if we can be with "uncomfortable" sensations and "negative" thoughts, we have all we want no matter WHAT is going on. Any time, anywhere, we are happy, whole and free.

CHAPTER 41

Healing Made Simple (Simple Doesn't Always Mean Easy)

Resetting Yourself to Infinite Possibility

So. You've read the book. You've absorbed the material. In this very short last chapter, I'm going to distill all that I have talked about into a few simple actions you can take that will allow EVERY experience to be one that heals and empowers you.

As the title of this chapter implies, it's not always easy to do this, but it is simple.

So here is all you need to know, and all you need to do in any uncomfortable or disturbing situation.

YOU ARE AN INVISIBLE CONSCIOUSNESS EXPERIENCING INVISIBLE THOUGHTS AND SENSATIONS

THESE THOUGHTS AND SENSATIONS ARE THE ONLY WAY IN WHICH YOU EXPERIENCE THE WORLD

WHEN WE THINK WE CAN'T TOLERATE A SENSATION, WE RUN FROM IT BY TAKING ON A "PROTECTIVE" THOUGHT. THAT THOUGHT IS USUALLY AN "I CAN'T" THOUGHT.

YOUR ABILITY TO EXPERIENCE YOUR SENSATIONS AND NOT RUN FROM THEM IS THE KEY TO BEING ABLE TO HOLD <u>ANY</u> THOUGHT.

So: Any time you meet a challenge, you feel bad, you see "failure" before you, do this simple process.

1. Go to the "Great Unmanifested" and see what it is you want. It's got to be there!

2. Experience any "negative" thoughts and "uncomfortable" sensations that come up when you are seeing what you want to see in the "Great Unmanifested."

3. Hold the Vision you wish to hold while experiencing these "uncomfortable" sensations and "negative" thoughts.

THAT'S IT! PERIOD! YOU'RE RE-SET.

You are using your "negative" thoughts and "uncomfortable" sensations to mirror your Inner Child, to heal your past by being with your Inner Child, and to restore your ability to think any thought and have any experience.

And that's what it's all about!

So, go forth and be "negative."

Go forth and be "uncomfortable."

Go forth and be WHOLE.

And live and enjoy your *SENSATIONAL* Life!

RECOMMENDED FURTHER RELATED READING

Pema Chodrun	*The Wisdom of No Escape* *When Things Fall Apart* *Any of her lectures on CD*
David Friedman	*The Thought Exchange - Overcoming Our Resistance to Living a Sensational Life*
David Grand	*Brainspotting*
Dennis Merritt Jones	*The Art of Uncertainty*
Nancy Napier	*Getting Through The Day* *The Child Within*
John Sarno	*Healing Back Pain*
Ekhart Tolle	*The Power of Now* *A New Earth*
Dr. Claire Weekes	*Hope and Help For Your Nerves*